THE LANGUAGE CONTINUUM
From Infancy to Literacy

Edited by James F. Kavanagh

Parkton, Maryland

YORK
PRESS

This book was manufactured in the United States of America. Typography by Brushwood Graphics, Inc., Baltimore, Maryland. Printing and binding by Maple-Vail Book Manufacturing Group, York, Pennsylvania. Cover design by Joseph Dieter, Jr.

Library of Congress Cataloging-In-Publication Data

The Language continuum : from infancy to literacy / edited by James F. Kavanagh.
    p.   cm. — (Communicating by language)
    Includes bibliographical references and index.
    ISBN 0-912752-29-7 : $25.00
    1. Children—Language.   2. Language acquisition.   3. Literacy.
I. Kavanagh, James F.   II. Series.
LB1139.L3L3238   1991
302.2'244—dc20   91-35642
                                                      CIP

Contents

Preface   vii
James F. Kavanagh

Chapter 1
The Acquisition and Development of Language: A Social Interactionist
   Account of Language and Literacy Development   1
David Dickinson and
Allyssa McCabe
Chapter 2
Getting Ready to Read: Learning How Print Maps to Speech   41
Benita A. Blachman
Chapter 3
Acquiring the Linguistic Code for Reading: A Model for Teaching and
   Learning   63
Ellis Richardson and
Barbara DiBenedetto
Chapter 4
Language Comprehension and Text Structure   115
Joanne F. Carlisle
Chapter 5
Written Language   147
Doris J. Johnson
Chapter 6
Teaching the Language-Handicapped Child   167
Regina Cicci

Index   195

Preface

A few years ago it would have been considered most unreasonable and illogical to bring together in the same book the work of authors who would in turn discuss how children acquire their first oral language, how they learn to read, how they learn to use written language, and how children with disabilities in these skills can be taught. Spoken language and written language were considered two separate and distinctly different skills or parallel processes in different modalities. The teaching of reading and remedial reading instruction were considered to be unrelated to a child's skill or lack of skill in acquiring oral language and in learning to create correctly spelled written prose.

But, authors* of the six chapters of this book, and the editor, believe that there is a *language continuum;* the skills of reading and writing (*literacy*) are built upon—are rational extensions of—the oral language acquired in *infancy* and the first years of life. Moreover, there is a symbiotic relationship between speech and reading. And, for a variety of reasons, early proficiency variations in oral language frequently affect the later acquisition of reading and writing.

The order of the presentations in this book, at least the first three chapters, is dictated by the chronological age of the child. Thus, the first chapter describes an activity that takes place when a child is younger than four years. The second chapter discusses linguistic skills of children at four years and beyond, and the third chapter examines skills of the five- to seven-year-old child.

This order reflects our agreement that there is a continuum of language skills for each particular child, and that that continuum corresponds roughly to the chronological ages of children. (Infants do not talk as well as five-year-olds; five-year-olds do not read as well as ten-year-olds.) However, we know that for a variety of biological and behavioral reasons there are significant individual cognitive and lin-

---

*Dr. Doris Johnson discussed the language continuum at an annual meeting of The Orton Dyslexia Society in 1968. Her paper appeared in the *Bulletin of the Orton Society* 18:1–11.

guistic differences among children that preclude an exclusive chronological presentation, especially in the years after infancy. (You may know some six-year-old children who talk, read, and write better than some ten-year-olds.)

Moreover, regardless of chronological or mental age, it seems that there are certain linguistic skills that must be acquired before more complicated skills can be achieved. (The nonreading five-year-old and the nonreading 25-year-old must learn to decode the orthographic symbols before they can read unfamiliar words.)

The production of this volume was precipitated by a language symposium conducted on March 21, 1991 during an annual conference of the New York Branch of The Orton Dyslexia Society. When the participants received invitations to take part in the symposium they also were asked to prepare chapters (larger than average chapters) for a book and then summarize those at the New York Orton Society meeting. Thus, unlike most published conference proceedings, which are edited versions of what was presented at a meeting, this book was under preparation before the conference, summarized for the audience, and then, with consideration for questions and discussions, finetuned immediately following the March conference.

Evolution of our knowledge about the relationships regarding listening and speaking, reading, and writing language parallels the research supported by the National Institute of Child Health and Human Development. At the Institute's first conference in a series called Communicating by Language held in April of 1964, and at all subsequent conferences in the series, the purpose was to determine what was currently known about language and then to identify directions for further research. At that first conference on the speech process the emphasis was on communicating with an organized code, but we confined our remarks pretty much to the production and reception of an audible signal; we did not discuss reading. In 1972, when *Language by Ear and by Eye* (MIT Press) was published, Communicating by Language definitely included reading, reflecting the strong interest of psychologists, linguistics, and speech scientists in the relationship between speech and learning to read.

The accumulated knowledge in our field of interest as reflected by each of the thirteen research conference publications in the Communicating by Language series are now revealed in this volume. As in the previous volumes, we want to explore what we know today about communicating with language, but here our purpose is not primarily to point toward future research. Rather, we are pleased to bring to the reader current information about the acquisition and development of language, the uses to which it is put, and the difficulties some experience with it. Our goal is to provide current information in a clear and concise manner that is meaningful to teachers, therapists, and parents. Scientists are, however, encouraged to use this material as a base for further exploration.

James F. Kavanagh, Ph.D.
April 1991

Chapter • 1

The Acquisition and Development of Language
A Social Interactionist Account of Language and Literacy Development

David Dickinson and Allyssa McCabe

OVERVIEW OF LANGUAGE
DEVELOPMENT FROM BIRTH TO FIVE YEARS

The process of language acquisition can be thought of as being like a French braid rather than as a sequential process. Like a braid, language consists of multiple strands—phonology, semantics, syntax, discourse, reading, and writing—that are picked up at various times and woven in with the other strands to create a beautiful whole. As we consider the development of this language braid, we first separately examine milestones of development in each of these strands. After this, we examine the way in which a typical five-year-old has integrated these various aspects of language acquisition. Having addressed the description of language acquisition, we can then turn to an

Authors are listed alphabetically. The original research reported in this chapter from the Home-School Study of Language and Literacy Development was supported by grants from the Ford Foundation and the Spencer Foundation to Catherine Snow and David Dickinson.

explanation for this complex process, followed by a discussion of the implications of the language acquisition process for emerging literacy.

Phonological Development

At birth, infants have been listening to their mothers' voices for over four months, and this results in a demonstrable preference not only for high-pitched voices relative to low-pitched voices (Kearsley 1973), but for their own mothers' voices in particular (DeCasper and Fifer 1980). At one month, infants will adjust the rate of their sucking, demonstrating that they are capable of discriminating even closely related speech sounds from each other (Eimas et al. 1971; Aslin, Pisoni, and Jusczyk 1983). For the first six months of life, infants can discriminate speech sounds of foreign languages that sound identical to their parents' speech sounds, but between the ages of six and twelve months, infants shift from phonetic to phonemic speech perception; they lose this capacity to discriminate sounds that are functionally equivalent in their native language (Werker and Tees 1984; Werker and Lalonde 1988).

Phonological perception lays the groundwork for and precedes phonological production (Edwards 1974; Kuczaj 1983). Normal phonological development requires both the ability to hear normally (Oller and Eilers 1988) and to produce babbling (Locke and Pearson 1990); abnormalities in either respect diminish the extent to which phonology develops. At birth, infants are capable of producing eight speech sounds (Irwin 1949), almost all of them vowels (Lieberman et al. 1971) and almost all of them in the context of crying. At about two months, infants start to vocalize more pleasantly; they begin to coo. At six months, infants engage in what is termed "reduplicated babbling" (e.g., "Bababa"), beginning work on what will be a lengthy project in mastering the consonants of their language (Stark 1986). By eight months, infants increasingly approximate the speech sounds of their native language when they babble, so that adults given sufficiently long passages of babbling are capable of identifying children's native language (Boysson-Bardies, Sagart, and Durand 1984). The developmental process of phonological production shows both some consistencies in terms of the order in which sounds are mastered and some individual differences (Ferguson and Farwell 1975). Between one and two years of age, however, all children engage in actively trying to solve the difficult problem of how to talk like people around them (Ferguson and Macken 1980).

Phonological production is largely complete by the age of four (Ingram 1986), although slight departures from standard pronunciation may continue until the age of eight and one-half years (Sanders 1972). It should be noted that whereas some elementary school children continue to display articulation problems such as lisps, many can discern the difference between sounds they cannot themselves produce distinctively. It is only when kindergarten and first-grade children can neither perceive nor produce various speech sounds that reading problems are likely to follow.

Semantic Development

By the end of the first year of life, infants' phonology is sufficiently sophisticated that they are capable of producing a few recognizable words. These words are acquired slowly at first, and most of a child's first fifty words are the general names of objects, particularly objects that readily engage a child's attention (e.g., "light") or that the child can manipulate ("sock") or both ("cat") (Nelson 1973). Children overgeneralize their early words either playfully or because they have such a modest vocabulary (Hudson and Nelson 1984). For example, children at times may request a slice of "salami" that they then proceed to refer to as "a moon" in the context of playing with it, but at other times they may call a cowcatcher in front of a train a "sweep-broom" because they do not know the correct word for it.

At eighteen months, many children go through a "vocabulary explosion" during which the process of acquiring vocabulary is considerably accelerated (Goldfield and Reznick 1990). Estimates of quantitative vocabulary growth during the preschool years vary widely, but some estimate the acquisition of two to four new words per day (Smith 1926), and estimates of total vocabulary acquired by the age of five vary between 8,000 and 15,000 words (Anderson and Freebody 1981; Carey 1978).

There are individual differences in both the rate of vocabulary acquisition and the type of vocabulary acquired (Bloom 1970; Nelson 1973; Bretherton et al. 1983). Some "referential" children tend to produce one word at a time between the ages of one and two years, are relatively easy to understand, and name objects considerably more than they name specific people or actions, or engage in ritualistic phrases such as "thank-you." Other, more "expressive," children tend to imitate relatively more than their referential counterparts, produce somewhat unintelligible phrases, and talk about personal and social issues relatively more than referential children. This contrast is perhaps more usefully thought of as a continuum with few children showing extremes of these styles of language acquisition and most children showing a combination of strategies (Goldfield and Snow 1989). Children's particular strategies may affect the kinds of input that will enhance their language acquisition (Hampson 1990).

In addition to quantitative expansion in semantic development, there are qualitative expansions. Preschool children deepen their understanding of the words they produce, culminating in the ability to define them formally (Snow et al. in press), an ability with strong links to prereading skills (Dickinson and Snow 1987).

Syntactic and Morphological Development

Toward the end of their second year, children begin to combine words in their utterances. At first this is largely a matter of linking two nouns ("mommy sock") or one noun and one verb "Eve read." At about two and one-half years children also add grammatical morphemes such as prepositions (especially *in* and *on*), plurals, possessives, and even an occasional inflection of a verb (Brown 1973). In acquiring grammatical morphemes, children demonstrate a capacity for rule-learning that goes beyond simple imitation. That is, children will overregularize verbs by saying, for example, "I goed to the store yesterday," something they do not hear adults saying. First-grade children will even apply such rules to novel words they could not possibly have heard anyone say (Berko 1958), readily coming up with "wugs" as the plural of "wug," for example. In general, however, children can imitate grammatical constructions before they can comprehend them, and comprehend them before they produce them (Fraser, Bellugi, and Brown 1963; Lovell and Dixon 1967; Golinkoff and Hirsh-Pasek 1987).

Preschool children are still in the process of oral mastery of the grammatical system of their language. They produce some form of negative and question constructions, but they do not understand all passive constructions and are just beginning to use and understand relative clauses (see Tager-Flusberg 1989, for a review). It is not until about seven years of age that children demonstrate a comprehension of some relatively complicated syntactic constructions such as "Is this doll easy to see or hard to see?" or an understanding of the difference between "The wolf is happy to bite." versus "The duck is fun to bite." (Chomsky 1969; Cromer 1970).

At about two and one-half years, children begin to combine sentences, at first usually by connecting them with "and" (Bloom et al. 1980). Initially, such connections do not add meaning to the individual propositions connected, but children come to use coordination to express temporal relationship (e.g., "It was so hot I kept on changing and changing my pillow *and then* next morning we had to go back"), then causal (e.g., "She wanted to hurt him, so she hit him"), and finally contrastive, or adversative, relationships such as, "My little sister's cute *but* my big sister is awful and ugly" (Bloom et al. 1980). By the time they are three, children also are using conjunctions such as "and then," "when," "because," "so," "then," and "but." Despite the fact that they are quite capable of using a variety of connectives (Bloom et al. 1980) and despite the fact that they use even causal connectives quite accurately from the age of four on (McCabe and Peterson 1985), children continue to use "and" frequently to encode temporal and causal relationships between clauses, relationships that would more explicitly be encoded by use of *then* or *so* (Peterson and McCabe 1987). This is because children use connectives not only to express meaningful relationships between sentences, but also to serve a variety of pragmatic, discourse-level functions (Peterson and McCabe in press). For example, children lace their personal narratives with "and" as a means of heralding an upcoming event in a sequence of such events (Peterson and McCabe 1991).

Discourse Development

The most fundamental feature of language acquisition after the age of five is the change of function of linguistic categories from the sentential level to the level of extended spans of discourse (Karmiloff-Smith 1986). Yet this is a process that begins much earlier. At about 22 months (Eisenberg 1985; Sachs 1982), children begin to refer to real past events, at first with much assistance from adults. At two years, they tend to talk about negative past events, especially injuries, and to evaluate these experiences (Miller and Sperry 1988). Even in their fictional productions, children aged two to five show a preoccupation with themes of aggression, death, hurt, or misfortune (Ames 1966; Pitcher and Prelinger 1963). Between three and five years of age, children tell each other many personal narratives, increasing the length and complexity of their narratives, as well as the chances of a response from their peers (Umiker-Sebeok 1979).

Although children tell each other many forms of narrative (personal anecdotes, parodies, film retellings, fantasies), over half of their conversational narratives concern real personal experiences (Preece 1987). While at the age of four, children tend to omit some events necessary for listeners to make sense of their personal narratives and to narrate events out of sequence, by the age of five they rarely have trouble sequencing events in oral narratives (Peterson and McCabe 1983). Five-year-olds do, however, tend to end their personal narratives prematurely, dwelling on a climactic event at the end of their narration. Six-year-olds tell a well-formed story that orients a listener to who, what, and where something happened, that narrates a sequence of events which build to some sort of climax or high point, and that then resolves the story by telling how things turned out (Peterson and McCabe 1983). Examples of typical personal narratives from preschool children are given in table I.

Preschool children are capable of structuring their oral personal narratives in a more sophisticated way than general scripts of personal experience or fictional stories (Hudson and Shapiro 1991). This comparative advantage of fact over fiction in terms of structural sophistication does not apply to the story-writing of older school-aged children (Freedman 1987), perhaps as a result of increased exposure to fictional stories from books. In spontaneously told fantasy stories, seven- to nine-year-old children's plots approximate those of fairy tales (Botvin and Sutton-Smith 1977; Hudson and Shapiro 1991).

Most of the aforementioned work has been done on white English-speaking children. It is critical to realize that there are substantial cultural differences in the way in which children structure their narratives. African American children tell what has been called a topic-associating kind of narrative (Michaels 1981). Hawaiian children tell talk-stories that weave teasing and fantasy into repetitive routines for a number of participants (Watson 1975). In a manner reminiscent of *haiku*, Japanese children tell extraordinarily succinct collections of experiences, often given in sets of three lines, rather than narrating the details of what happened on one occasion as do white English-speaking children (Minami and McCabe 1990).

When children from different cultures attend integrated classrooms, the stories they tell or write at school are often misunderstood (Michaels 1991). Teachers may mistake their culturally different style of narration for rambling or learning disabled speech. Children whose narrative productions are interrupted by teachers unaware that the children are producing different, rather than deficient, narratives report frustration at their unsuccessful communicative gestures (Michaels 1991).

But consequences of cultural mismatches between children's ways of telling a story and the structure of stories valued in classrooms probably are not confined to children's productions. Mismatches may well affect the extent to which children can understand stories read to them or by them. Unfortunately, evidence pertinent to this point largely comes from experiments with adults. An impressive number of stud-

Table I.   Examples of Typical Oral Personal Narratives from Young Children*

Three-year-old Two-Event Narrative:
ADULT: Did you like the puppy?
NED: He taste my knee.
ADULT: He tasted your knee?
NED: Yeth. An' puppy <u>chase</u> me.

Four-year-old Leapfrog Narrative:
At three and four years of age, children typically put together more than two events, but they often do so erratically or in violation of chronology. In the following example, the four-year-old narrator conveniently omits what she did that broke her sister's arm and led to being spanked:
BETH: My sister had, she's had, she broke a arm when she fell in those minibike. She had, she went to the doctor, so I, my dad gave me spanking, and I . . .
ADULT: Your dad gave you what?
BETH: A spanking to me. And she had to go to the doctor's to get a cast on. She had to go get it, get it off, and, and it didn't break again. She still got it off. She can't play anymore. She <u>can</u> play rest of us now.

Five-year-old's Stories End at the High Point:
At five years, children tell a well-ordered story, but they often end at the high point. The high point is the emotional climax of a narrative, and it is not always a positive one, as in the following narrative:
MARILYN: Know something? The other day I had to go to the doctor's. And I had to get a shot. In the arm. And my <u>Mommy</u>, she didn't <u>care</u> about me getting a <u>shot</u>. And my babysitter took me to get a <u>shot</u>. With my brother. And my <u>mother</u> didn't <u>care</u>. And so my mother didn't <u>care</u>. I cared, but my <u>mother</u> didn't. My <u>mother</u> cares now, but not much. <u>She</u> don't care a <u>lot</u>. She only cares a little bit. My mom don't care much about me. She <u>don't care</u> much about me. Just a little . . . <u>not</u> much.
Older children might well have gone on to provide a resolution of the climax.

Six-year-old Classic Narrative:
By six, children tell stories that meet our expectations of what a good story is: they begin by orienting their listener about who and what was involved and when things took place. They build up a series of events to a high point, and then go on to resolve the events. In the following narrative, for example, the six-year-old narrator tells what happened after the climactic event of getting poked:
MARK: There's, um, where I got poked. You know them pencil things that Eversharp thing that you sharpen that you open and you sort of go like that?
ADULT: That you open so they go like that?
MARK: Yeah, and one side's the sharp side and the other side's just a handle like? You know they have these little holes and the pencil goes right down there?
ADULT: Uh-huh?
MARK: And also they have a poker and stuff. But the poker went right through there and came right through here, and hit that (points to arm). And it got over there and came out. And it was all dirty cause there was pencil lead down there. And we had to get it out and we had to squeeze and squeeze and all the blood just <u>rolled</u> on the floor. Just like this (gestures). It just falled. Goed like this, and it <u>hit</u> the floor.

Adapted from Peterson and McCabe (1983).

*Underlined words indicate stress placed on these words by speaker.

ies, however, have found the same thing: adults recall significantly less from stories that conform to a cultural pattern quite different from their own than they do from stories from their own culture (Dube 1982; Kintsch and Greene 1978). Thus, children who do not already tell the standard kind of topic-centered story, which begins with orientation, builds to a climax, and then resolves the action, may not be able to use the stories they hear in school to develop the story-telling style valued in classrooms.

Emergent Literacy

Research during the past decade has led to the realization that, as they acquire language, preschool-aged children also construct considerable literacy-related knowledge. Children as young as two who are exposed to books begin to understand how books are used (Scollon and Scollon 1981; Snow and Ninio 1986), become sensitive to and begin to re-produce the language of books when they are pretending to read (e.g., "behind them were dark, dark eyes") (Purcell-Gates 1988; Pappas and Brown 1987), and become familiar with what print looks like (e.g., con-ventional shapes, typical word length) (Ferreiro and Teberosky 1982; Ganopole 1987; Morgan 1987). Additionally, a number of studies exam-ining the emergence of children's abilities to interpret the meaning of print found in the environment (e.g., road signs, fast food restaurant logos, names of familiar products) find that all children reared in so-cieties that include such print displays develop this ability. There are few social class differences in ability to interpret such print (Dickinson and Snow 1987; Harste, Woodward, and Burke 1984; Goodman 1984). However, it should be noted that the movement from making sense of contextualized print into decoding removed from such contexts re-quires children to focus only on print and to assume a more analytic orientation toward print and language (Ehri and Wilce 1985; Mason 1984). As we discuss later, this is a transition that is difficult for many children.

In everyday settings children provide evidence, in the way they pretend to read familiar books, of their construction of increasingly so-phisticated notions about how books convey meaning as they move through a sequence of stages. In their reproductions of stories they move from picture-governed attempts that include considerable inter-action with the adult observer to monologues that include minimal re-liance on pictures or adults and frequent use of verbatim chunks of story texts (Sulzby 1985). Details of how children progress through these stages appear to vary by linguistic and cultural group (Sulzby and Zecker 1991), but the general outlines of this development are interesting because it demonstrates the early emergence of literacy-related language skills and the links between oral and written language skills.

Part of children's emerging literacy is development of knowledge that supports early writing development. As they are exposed to and engage in literacy events, children become increasingly more adept at differentiating between pictures and print. When they are as young as three, children distinguish between pictures and writing, demonstrate through their representational play that they understand what the activity of writing entails (i.e., communicating intentions to an audience through conventional forms), and even begin to demonstrate the ability to produce graphic forms that reflect sensitivity to how their native language appears when printed (Harste, Woodward, and Burke 1984). During the preschool years, writing develops in ways that reflect individual differences more than age-related norms (Clay 1975), but some regularities in writing begin to emerge as children move from kindergarten through elementary school (Dickinson, Wolf, and Stotsky 1989; Calkins 1986).

Summary: Typical Five-year-olds

The typical five-year-old child enters kindergarten with phonology largely in place, a vocabulary estimated to be at least 10,000 words, basic syntactic competence, but with complicated passives, complement constructions, etc., yet to be fully mastered. The white English-speaking five-year-old's oral personal narratives are chronologically ordered, but end prematurely. All children exposed to literacy have begun constructing literacy-related knowledge, but individual differences in the richness of this exposure are pronounced. One five-year-old may be able to read stories and write sentences, while another five-year-old may be learning the alphabet.

Although we have discussed them separately, it is important to recognize that the strands of language acquisition influence each other reciprocally. This reciprocal process can be seen clearly in the case of the relationship between literacy-related knowledge and phonology. As we discuss later, phonological processing abilities enable the five-year-old to read, and reading increases awareness of phonological representations (Ehri 1979; Ellis 1990; Read et al. 1986; Wagner 1988). Furthermore, as five-year-olds learn to read, their familiarity with printed forms affects how they perceive language (Ehri 1984, 1985), as this knowledge can help correct the remaining nonstandard pronunciations they commit. For example, "Fanksgiving" will yield to "Thanksgiving" in the face of what they learn about phoneme/grapheme correspondences.

THEORETICAL ACCOUNTS OF LANGUAGE ACQUISITION

Regrettably, at the present time there is not a consensus as to how language develops. Few people now ascribe to the strict behavioral approach outlined by B.F. Skinner (1957), in which the child is said to learn language only as a result of environmental stimulation and reinforcement. At present there are at least two major competing theoretical accounts of language acquisition. The first account was inspired by the influential linguist, Noam Chomsky (1965), who argued that children are born with a language acquisition device that enables them to master syntactic constructions that are not directly represented in any physical way by the spoken language of adults. This approach attributes large innate capacity to children, though there is disagreement as to whether children are born with grammatical capacity that does not change over time (Gleitman and Wanner 1982), or whether, in fact, children's grammars become reorganized. Pinker (1984), for example, argues that children make use of correspondences between meaning and form in the parental language addressed to them to revise their innate grammatical structures. He points to such correspondences between syntax and semantics in adult input to very young children: all agents are subjects of verbs in such input, while 88% of actions are verbs, among other relationships.

Other theoreticians agree that there is bootstrapping into the grammar of a language, although they disagree that bootstrapping is a semantic process, as Pinker proposes. Some argue that children make use of correspondences between syntax and prosody (Cooper and Paccia-Cooper 1980) or between syntax and morphology (Maratsos and Chalkley 1980). Some theoreticians reverse the direction of influence among these strands of language and argue that syntax, such as is manifest by means of morphological inflections, enables children to understand something of the meaning of verbs, for example (Hirsch-Pasek et al. 1988).

Social Interactionism

Whereas behavioral and linguistic approaches to language acquisition are on opposite extremes of the empiricism-nativism pole, *social interactionism* is an approach that acknowledges biological contributions to the language acquisition process but emphasizes also the way that language is acquired socially. To begin with, the amount of time that adults talk directly to children is related to IQ between birth and three years (White 1978), and is related to academic achievement between the ages of three and five years (Wells 1981). These global measures of language are predictive of intellectual accomplishment for several reasons (Snow et al. 1984):

1. To begin with, such language is *semantically contingent* (i.e., what the parent says meaningfully relates to what the child says). For example, if a child says, "truck," an adult might respond, "A big, big, yellow truck, isn't it?" In such exchanges children hear language related to their own but providing a little more information on a topic of interest to them. Repeatedly, investigators find that semantically contingent speech facilitates children's language acquisition (Clarke-Stewart 1973; Cross 1976; Snow 1984; Wells 1980).

2. Children acquire *communicatively useful language* from all that they are exposed to; that is, children learn the words that apply to objects and experiences that interest them, ignoring words for objects and experiences that are not salient to them. For example, although young children undoubtedly hear the articles *a, and,* and *the* quite frequently—these are the most frequent words used in English—they never include these among their early vocabulary; the words refer to nothing of interest to them.

3. Children *imitate selectively* as a technique to keep conversation going, to practice unfamiliar forms of language, and to learn new forms (see Peters 1983 and Snow 1983 for review); they do not mechanically imitate upon request. Despite learning theory accounts that foreground child imitation as a key mechanism of the language acquisition process, adult imitation of children may be more important than child imitation of adults in the language acquisition process. Only when children find imitation communicatively useful will they engage in it.

4. Children *negotiate meaning* with their parents, with parents requesting clarification from them and vice versa. Communication allows for second, third, and fourth chances for success in optimal parent-child encounters.

Distinctive Features of Adult-Child Conversations

There are two important formal qualities of the exchange of language between adults and infants: (1) the use of a specialized speech register by the adults, and (2) infants' reliance upon routines.

Specialized Speech Registers. Adults simplify, frequently re-peat, and in other ways modify their speech when talking to young children (Snow 1972, 1977). Among the most salient of such modifica-tions is the adoption of a higher-pitched register with more exagge-rated and varied prosody to infants than to adults, a practice that is common to virtually all cultures studied and to both fathers and mothers (Fernald et al. 1989). Such prosody gains infants' attention, expresses positive affect, and facilitates speech perception and lan-guage comprehension (Fernald et al. 1989). At four months, infants pre-fer their mothers using babytalk versus other registers (Fernald 1985), although such a register is used even before this time (Snow 1977).

While talk between adults and children begins by being firmly rooted in the here-and-now, such talk shifts to description of past events (Sachs 1982). Often talk about the past concerns experiences shared between parent and child, and often the parent takes the lead (Eisenberg 1985; Sachs 1982). Adults adopt an identifiably different prosody when telling, as opposed to reading, stories to children (Levin, Schaffer, and Snow 1982). In short, distinctive prosody serves as a signalling device, captivating children's attention and providing a salient cue about the general communicative purpose of the particular language produced.

Interactional Routines. Caregivers establish routines in talk to preverbal infants. In the context of these routines, adults may treat in-fants' burps, coughs, and cooing as full-fledged responses to be re-sponded to as if they were actual speech (Snow 1977). Treating the in-fant as a full-fledged partner in turn-taking becomes a self-fulfilling prophecy as the infant does in fact take over more of the work of com-municating with age (Snow, Perlmann, and Nathan 1987). Routines scaffold and extend the complexity of children's verbal performances; in the second year of life, for example, child speech is more complex in the context of routines with familiar, in contrast with unfamiliar, books.

Routines between adults and children are characteristic of all cul-tures studied, although the nature of those routines varies consider-ably from one culture to another (McCabe 1987). For example, there are cultural differences in the extent to which adults talk to children about shared past experiences (Schieffelin and Eisenberg 1984). Even within a particular country, there may be differences among various socio-economic classes, for example, in the extent to which speech is re-quired to be explicit, elaborated, or decontextual versus implicit, restricted, or contextualized (Bernstein 1971; Heath 1983). In a middle-class community in America, adults typically engage children in discourse with fully explicit noun phrases, whereas in a working-class community such discourse is often elliptical with extensive anaphoric references (Heath 1983). Working-class speakers are concerned with collaborative message construction (Hemphill 1989), in which listeners are expected to interpret ambiguous pronouns, among other things.

In the academic realm, however, the production of explicit discourse is advantageous to children. Preschool children who produce decontextualized word definitions are characteristically middle-class, and these children fare better in a variety of preliteracy tasks (Dickinson and Snow 1987). As they move into elementary school, children's ability to produce such explicit "decontextualized" speech is related to reading progress (Snow 1983). Discourse style relates to literate productions as well as literate comprehension. That is to say, children who are accustomed to disambiguating pronouns in oral narratives by means of prosody, for example, are more likely to produce ambiguous oral and written compositions that are judged poor by many teachers (Michaels and Collins 1984), as in the following example from a fourth-grade boy telling the story of a film he has just seen:

> "This guy . . . this man was pickin' pears and so the this guy (a different character, said with prosody contrasting to previous mention of "this guy") he was riding around . . . he was riding on his bike."

That boy produced written compositions that were full of unspecified pronouns. In contrast, a boy who used words to disambiguate oral story retellings, as in the next example, produced written compositions that were not as frequently ambiguous:

> "Well there was this man and he was collecting some kind of fruit and then a boy came along on a bicycle. The man that was . . . that was collecting the fruits. . . ."

The second boy could rely on his oral language system for referencing characters in compositions, while the first boy needed to learn a different way of keeping participants straight when he began to write (Michaels and Collins 1984).

In sum, parents, consciously or not, employ a variety of means to make language predictable for very young children. Use of distinctive prosodic registers makes certain communicative purposes predictable (e.g., affectionate babytalk or story-reading registers). Use of routines establishes predictable responses expected from young participants. Use of certain language routines at home makes the routines of language in classrooms predictable and relatively easy for children (e.g, making yourself clear, and your meaning explicit), while other children must learn a different set of rules for language use as well as a different means of expressing language, namely print.

Specific Mechanisms that Improve Language Acquisition

Parental Imitation. Although many have emphasized child imitation of adults as a key factor in language acquisition, it seems that imitation in the other direction is actually more influential. In a study of 50 adoptive and 50 biological children and parents, parental imitation of infant vocalizations was documented to be one of the most important and most clearly nongenetic forms of direct environmental influence to foreshadow communicative development (Hardy-Brown and Plomin 1985).

Parental imitation of child speech takes many forms. One of the most important of these is the phenomenon called "expansions" or "recasts." Expansions such as "Truck go? That truck is going away." use a child's words in the same order but add new words to make an expanded, grammatically correct sentence (Brown, Cazden, and Bellugi-Klima 1969). Recasts include expansion, but also adult utterances that relate semantically to what a child has said, but also delete or reorder information the child presented (Nelson 1973). Adult recasts in home, school, or laboratory have facilitated many aspects of language acquisition, including the acquisition of verbs, overall syntax, comprehension, mean length of productive utterances, overall semantic complexity, and complexity of noun phrases (see Nelson 1989, for review).

Parental Questions. In addition to parental imitation, parental questions of children are a key factor in language acquisition. Infants attend more to rising versus falling contours of naturally produced questions in English (Sullivan and Horowitz 1983). A few months later, children respond vocally to many adult questions, but this responsiveness depends on the type of question mothers ask them. One-year-olds respond to questions in the following descending order: Permission requests ("May I sit in this chair?"), repairs ("Doggie did what?"), verbal reflectives (Child: "The doggie's driving." Mother: "He is?"), real questions ("Do you have to go potty?"), test questions ("Is this red or green?"), reflections on action ("You're putting the dollies to bed, aren't you?"), and reports ("That's too many people in there, isn't it?"). Parents differ in the extent to which they wait for their questions to be answered, with waiting a necessary prerequisite for young children's responsiveness (Olsen-Fulero and Conforti 1983). Young children also have a tendency to repeat their utterances verbatim in response to neutral queries (e.g., "What?"), whereas they respond to specific queries (e.g., Child: "Put it in there." Mother: "Put it where?" Child: "In the bucket") with requested information (Anselmi, Tomasello, and Acunzo 1986). This child responsiveness to questions is fortunate given that adult input to children typically contains many questions (Snow 1977).

Parental Corrections. In child language research, parents first were characterized as not correcting the syntax of their children's language so much as the content of what was said (Brown and Hanlon 1970). Parents were observed to approve such syntactically flawed, but semantically apt, utterances as "He a girl." but to reject such semantically flawed, but syntactically impeccable, utterances as "There's the animal farmhouse." when that house is in fact a lighthouse instead. Even if parents attempted to correct the syntax of their children, it was argued, that correction would either be ignored (McNeill 1966) or outright detrimental to a child's language acquisition, especially if frequent enough (Nelson 1973). Because children never received direct negative feedback about their early syntactic mistakes, some theorists concluded that syntax must be largely biologically hard-wired in children (Pinker 1984).

However, closer scrutiny of adult-child interchanges revealed a difference between how parents respond to well-formed versus ill-formed child utterances. Parents either repeat verbatim or extend the topic of conversation following children's well-formed utterances (Bohannon and Stanowicz 1988; Demetras et al. 1986; Penner 1987). But their responses to ill-formed utterances tend to be different. Frank corrections of children's mistaken labels, for example, *do* happen and while children may temporarily avoid using the label in question, that avoidance is fleeting; such corrections are ultimately beneficial (Ninio and Bruner 1978). More importantly, *implicit* feedback (e.g., Child: "Do something different now." Mother: "Do something different now? What are we gonna *look at now*?") to children's mistakes is more common than the kind of explicit feedback ("No, that's not right") examined by Brown et al. (Demetras, Post, and Snow 1986). Implicit feedback, particularly in the form of clarifying questions, frequently follows children's ill-formed utterances (Bohannon and Stanowicz 1988; Demetras, Post, and Snow 1986). Parents also have been found to expand ungrammatical utterances more frequently than grammatical ones (Penner 1987).

Thus, parents often use many of the aforementioned mechanisms—imitation, expansions, and questions—to provide feedback to children about grammatical mistakes. In fact, children may assimilate their own errors unless those errors are corrected (Platt and MacWhinney 1983). Simply accepting a child's mistaken label is not effective in providing children with the opportunity for self-correction (Chapman, Leonard, and Mervis 1986); most effective is correction of a mistaken label along with explanation and demonstration of the basis for that correction ("That's not a ball, it's a yo-yo. See, it goes up").

Implicit feedback about errors is probably more effective than explicit feedback because it *is* indirect, polite, and in the service of communication rather than didacticism.

Commands?   Some adults rely upon commands as a way of communicating with their children. Such a communicative means has not been associated with optimal language acquisition (Nelson 1973; Jones and Adamson 1987; Yodor and Kaiser 1989; see Bretherton et al. 1983, for review). A command usually refers to a desirable state of affairs not present at the time of the utterance, so that it is difficult for very young children to map language on to experience (Nelson 1973).

Contextual Factors in Facilitative Language

Adult Conversational Partners.   Even within a particular culture, adults differ from each other in the kind of language they speak to children. To begin with, mothers differ from other mothers. Depressed mothers of infants fail to use the exaggerated intonation contours characteristic of babytalk, and are slower to respond to infant vocalizations than are nondepressed mothers (Bettes 1988). Mothers also differ in the extent to which they ask questions versus give commands, as well as in the extent to which they discuss objects of interest to their one-year-olds versus talking about personal matters (Nelson 1973). Mothers display discernable differences in their speech to children even when they are not addressing their own child (Smolak and Weinraub 1983), so it is not simply the case that some children elicit different kinds of input from adults.

Compared to mothers, fathers more frequently use rare vocabulary to their children (Ratner 1988) and ignore or request clarification, especially in a nonspecific way (e.g., "What?"), in response to child verbalizations (Tomasello, Conti-Ramsden, and Ewert 1990). Fathers are said to present children with communicative challenges in preparation for exchanges with unfamiliar adults (Gleason 1975).

Children and Family Structure.   Children themselves play an unwitting role in the kind of language they receive, as their role in conversations contributes to the creation of language environments that, in turn, differentially affect subsequent language development (Hampson 1990; Yoder and Kaiser 1989). Furthermore, the structure of the family into which a child is born affects the kind of language they receive, surprisingly enough. Twins, for example, receive less speech directed specifically to them and participate in fewer and shorter conversations with their mothers, compared to singletons; mothers use more commands when speaking to twins than to singletons (Tomasello, Mannle, and Kruger 1986). Younger children receive more directive language than older children both from their parents (Nelson 1973; Jones and Adamson 1987) and from their older siblings, with such input negatively correlated with measures of child language acquisition (Jones and Adamson 1987). At the same time, later-born infants receive less metalingual talk (e.g., "What is this called?") than their older, firstborn siblings, and such talk positively correlates with child language acquisition (Jones and Adamson 1987). Such differential input to children occupying different positions in birth order and different family constellations could account for the well-known decrement in IQ as a function both of birth order and family size (Zajonc and Markus 1975).

Interactions with Objects. The contexts in which conversations occur also affect the quality of language addressed to children. The least amount of misinterpretation occurs when infants and mothers manipulate toys together, while the most amount of misinterpretation occurs when mothers and infants are gazing directly at each other (D'Odorico and Franco 1985). While mothers use basic vocabulary in free play with children (e.g., juice), they use more specific vocabulary both in very routine settings such as lunch (e.g., orange versus apple juice) or in very novel settings such as when new toys are introduced to children (Lucariello and Nelson 1986). Both mothers and fathers talking both to sons and daughters vary their speech as a result of the kinds of toys they are playing with; specifically, dolls elicit considerable talk, including lots of questions and labels, while vehicles elicit little talk and shape-sorters provoke lots of attention-getting comments, directives, and little overall variation in the kind of language used (O'Brien and Nagel 1987).

Meal Times and Car Talk. Events that may be especially conducive to extended talk about nonpresent events are occasions when conversation provides the prime source of entertainment. Two such settings are times when children ride in cars with parents and mealtimes. Analysis of recordings of parents' conversations with children has revealed that these settings include considerable talk about past events—especially in middle class families (Heath 1986).

Mealtimes are occasions during which considerable narrative and explanatory talk may occur. For example, Diane Beals' analysis of tapes of dinner table conversations collected as part of the Home-School Study of Language, an on-going study of factors supporting development of low-income children directed by Dickinson and Snow, has revealed that about 15% of the dinner table conversation time includes personal narratives and about 17% includes different kinds of explanations (e.g., motivation, physical-causal). She found significant correlations between three kindergarten literacy measures and the amount of explanatory talk during dinner table conversations when children were three years old and the amount of dinner time narrative talk when they were four years old: print-related knowledge—$r = .50$, $p = .02$; spoken vocabulary (PPVT)—$r = .56$, $p = .01$; story comprehension—$r = .48$, $p = .03$. Furthermore, an examination of nonschool factors related to reading success showed a relationship between reading progress and amount of time spent eating dinner (Anderson, Wilson, and Fielding 1988).

Book Reading. Preschool children differ considerably in the amount of early experiences they have with books at home and in preschool (Dickinson et al. in press; Teale 1984), differences that are related to later reading and academic achievement (Goldfield and Snow 1984; Heath 1982; Teale 1984). They also differ in the kinds of experiences they have, as some parents and teachers extend the text and draw children into the story with discussions about the story while others read the story and encourage minimal discussion (Dickinson et al. in press; Dickinson and Keebler 1989; Dickinson and Smith 1991; Heath 1982). Some evidence indicates that such discussions are important because they result in better story understanding and subsequent recall (Mason and Allen 1986; Morrow and Smith 1990). This variability in experience with books is important because children who have *listened* to many stories are at a decided advantage when they enter school; the most distinguishing characteristic of children judged to be competent in oral language in classrooms is the experience of listening to stories (Wells 1985a).

While it is scanty, available evidence indicates that the key to providing children book reading experiences that foster language growth and prepare them for school, is to pose open-ended questions and move beyond labeling pictures to discuss more cognitively challenging matters such as issues of motivation and causality. Such discussions have been shown to result in increased vocabulary acquisition among two and one-half-year-olds (Whitehurst et al. 1987), and increased recall of stories (Flood 1977). Adult discussion of the meaning of the story helps children learn to construct elaborated interpretations of pictures (Snow and Goldfield 1982), a focus that dovetails well with children's natural inclination to ask questions about the pictures in books.

An intriguing early (and therefore somewhat tentative) result from the Home-School Study of Language and Literacy lends support to the possible causal link between the kind of talk that occurs as books are read and subsequent literacy. Jeanne DeTemple has found a relationship between the total amount of nonimmediate talk about the books by mothers (e.g., discussing language, motivations) when children were three and one-half and literacy when children were five.

Extensive opportunities to read and discuss books also changes children's orientation toward language, enabling them to take the metalinguistic stance of focusing more on the grammatical form of sentences and less on the general meaning intended (Reeder, Wakefield, and Shapiro 1988). A related finding of a shift in oral language functioning resulting from book reading is the finding that opportunities to hear and discuss books affects the organization of children's lexicons. Children whose parents use high levels of superordinate labels when reading books to them when they were two and one-half have been found to be more likely to use and understand superordinates one year later (Watson 1989). These varied benefits for language acquisition that result from exposure to books will, of course, continue after the preschool years as children continue to learn words from listening to stories (Elley 1989; Dickinson 1985) and as they begin reading independently (Nagy, Herman, and Anderson 1985).

Among all kinds of books, those that tell a story may be the most important kind to read to preschool-aged children. Books that tell a story are decontextualized, "sustained, symbolic representations of possible worlds," and as such provide the opportunity to learn some of the essential characteristics of written language (Wells 1985b, p. 253). If this is true, it may be unfortunate that there is evidence that the frequency with which such books are read to three- and four-year-olds declines with age. It seems that teachers shift from books with a strong narrative line to books with predictable rhyming text as they strive to foster children's attention to print (Dickinson et al. in press).

Television. A recent study has reviewed all research prior to mid-1987 in the United States and Europe that examined the relationship of television viewing to reading skills (Beentjes and Van der Voort 1988). Those authors concluded that although there was evidence both for no effect of television viewing and for a negative relationship between television viewing and reading achievement, the latter was more often found to be the case. The amount of time spent viewing television occurs at the expense of leisure reading and other cognitively stimulating activities. The better the alternative activities available to children, the more vulnerable they are to the disadvantages of television viewing; that is, television viewing seems to depress the reading achievement of socially advantaged children and intelligent children more than that of their disadvantaged or less intelligent peers. Regardless of IQ or social class, however, a number of studies find that children who report watching over four to six hours of television per day pay a price in terms of delayed reading achievement (Beentjes and Van der Voort 1988).

Under certain circumstances, however, television viewing can be found to have a positive relationship to language, if not necessarily literacy, development. That is, when parents watch programs such as *Sesame Street* with children under the age of three, they engage in the kind of stimulating talk that has been associated with language acquisition, almost as if they were treating television as a "talking picture book" (Lemish and Rice 1986). Between the ages of three and five, children have been found to acquire considerable vocabulary while viewing *Sesame Street*, although this advantage of viewing decreases for older children (Rice et al. 1990). Preschoolers find it easier to learn words for objects and attributes from television programs than for other kind of things such as actions, and five-year-olds are particularly adept at acquiring such vocabulary, doing substantially better than three-year-olds given comparable viewing time (Rice and Woodsmall 1988).

Summary. To summarize, optimal language acquisition is accomplished as parents question and imitate children, expanding, recasting, clarifying, and otherwise subtly correcting and extending children's comments in a semantically contingent, communicative way. Provision of comments closely related to what children have just said gives them the opportunity to analyze their utterances and extract information about socially more acceptable ways of saying what it was they were trying to say. Optimal input is more likely under some circumstances than others; parents who prefer to question and comment about toys to their infants and who have infants who are interested in toys are likely to accomplish language acquisition in an optimal way (Goldfield 1987). Less optimal language acquisition results from too little adult input, from too many commands and not enough questions, comments, and implicit corrections, and from interactions that focus on certain kinds of toys (e.g., vehicles) at the expense of other kinds of toys or no toys at all.

Settings that enhance language acquisition are those such as meal times and book reading in which language plays a major role in maintenance of the activity or is the only activity of interest. Parent-child routines that evolve in such settings provide opportunities for children and parents to construct explanations and to move through space and time making connections among events that are likely to facilitate development of literacy-related discourse skills.

New Strains on the Strands: Learning to Read

As young children move through their days at home and in preschools talking and playing with parents and siblings, they slowly construct multiple strands of linguistic competence without much conscious awareness or anxiety. However, as we are all too aware, this situation changes dramatically once children begin to encounter the demands that are associated with early reading instruction. New levels of conscious analysis of language are required and taxing performance demands are placed on the language system. Therefore, a weakness in any of the strands of early language skills or in language analysis skill may manifest itself in the form of a reading problem.

Language-literacy Relationships. We have described language as being composed of multiple strands. One implication of this insight is that breakdowns in any of the language strands may have detrimental effects on reading. Consistent with this speculation, studies of language-disabled children have found impairments in each strand we have described that are linked to reading problems. Furthermore, long-term prognosis for language and literacy functioning is related to the particular language function affected, with articulatory problems being the ones most likely to fade in importance with age (Hall and Tomblin 1978). It now appears that it may be possible to identify children at risk for language-based reading problems in the early phase of language acquisition. A longitudinal study by Scarborough and Dobrich (1990) traced the development of four language delayed children from the time they were two and one-half through second grade. They found that, despite what appeared to be a recovery from initial language problems around the age of five, three of these children later had trouble learning to read.

In this section we briefly mention some of the work linking reading to particular strands of language functioning. However, because subsequent chapters also deal with some of these issues, we deal with it briefly, emphasizing links at the discourse level that receive less attention later.

The Phonological Strand. Massive evidence now demonstrates the critical importance of phonemic awareness to early reading (for reviews see Adams 1990; Elbro 1990; Stanovich 1986; Valtin 1984). Of special interest is the fact that longitudinal work done by Bradley and Bryant has traced the roots of phonemic awareness back into the third year of life. They found that, after controlling for maternal education, IQ, and child's vocabulary, knowledge of nursery rhymes among three-year-olds is related to reading success among six-year-olds (Bryant et al. 1989). Nursery rhyme knowledge appears important because of its relationship to later skill detecting phonemes, and not because it simply reflects general language ability (Bryant, Maclean, and Bradley 1990).

Considerable evidence now suggests that dyslexic children often have problems with the phonological strand of language functioning. Difficulties in repeating words, distinguishing words with similar sounds (Elbro 1990), and interpreting speech degraded by noise (Brady, Shankweiler, and Mann 1983) are suggestive of incomplete phonological representations that may account for some of the reading problems of dyslexic children. In addition, considerable evidence indicates that these children have weak phonemic awareness abilities (reviewed by Elbro 1990).

The Discourse Strand. Several studies also suggest that dyslexic readers may have discourse-level deficits. Problems among disabled readers have been identified in tasks that tap oral skills such as ability to recall scripts, which are highly familiar sequences of events (Feagans and Short 1984), directions (Feagans and Short 1986), narratives (Graybeal 1981; Weaver and Dickinson 1982), and narrative construction tasks (Roth and Spekman 1986). Dyslexic children seem to have problems at the intersentential level; when asked to recall stories, they tend to omit causal and temporal links (Liles 1985; Roth and Spekman 1986; Weaver and Dickinson 1982) and to provide fewer of the important details of the story that are likely to be tested for in schools (Hansen 1978; Graybeal 1981; Johnston 1982; Weaver and Dickinson 1982; Levi et al. 1984; Griffith, Ripich, and Dastoli 1986; Roth and Spekman 1986). In general, oral narrative performance tends to be an indicator of future literacy achievement (Michaels 1981; Feagans 1982).

The roots of discourse-level difficulties associated with reading problems can be traced at least to kindergarten. Children's ability to tell a complete version of the Three Bears has been found to be associated with later reading success (de Hirsch, Janksy, and Langford 1966). Cross-sectional work also reveals a strong relationship between discourse comprehension among kindergartners and other measures of

early literacy such as ability to define words, phonemic awareness, and early print skills (Dickinson and Snow 1987). It is likely that deficiencies in discourse skills linked to reading will be found even earlier; a longitudinal study that followed 87 language-impaired and normally developing children from ages four to five and one-half found that the ability to recall a short story was the best overall predictor of language development (Bishop and Edmundson 1987).

Language or Processing Deficiencies

The core assumption of this chapter is that linguistic representations are critical for reading success (see also Snow and Dickinson 1991). Although this assumption is not disputed, accounts of the causes of reading breakdowns vary. We have mentioned two types of language-based explanations for reading problems: (1) incomplete linguistic representations at the phonological and discourse levels at least, and (2) poorly analyzed linguistic knowledge. An additional emerging explanation for reading problems emphasizes a third explanation, the importance of *efficient cognitive processing*. Reading disabled children are slow to retrieve information from memory and these problems can be identified as early as kindergarten (Wolf, Bally, and Morris 1986). These children also display slower processing across a range of other language strands (Shankweiler and Crain 1986), as well as in motoric processing (reviewed by Wolf in press). This line of evidence raises the possibility that neurologically based inefficiencies in a temporal processing mechanism may account for some of the relationships between language abilities and reading problems (Wolf in press). However, it should be noted that relationships between processing speed and reading are strongest for decoding and weakest for comprehension (Wolf, Bally, and Morris 1986; Spring and Davis 1988).

This type of processing-based explanation for reading problems shifts the focus away from questions of whether or not reading disabled children lack particular linguistic structures to consideration of the efficiency with which they use them. One way of explaining why some skills are used without conscious awareness is to posit that the information they contain has been well "encapsulated." This notion of *information encapsulation* (reviewed by Stanovich 1990) places a high value on knowledge representations that are well developed and easily accessed. This approach suggests that opportunities for practice using language and print skills in varied contexts is vital because it is through such experiences that children become adept at efficiently accessing the necessary knowledge.

The notion of encapsulation suggests that frequently used representations such as the phonological distinctions used in one's native language, are likely to be well encapsulated because they are highly practiced, whereas discourse level operations (e.g., marking a transition point in an argument, keeping references to multiple characters clear) that are used less frequently, are likely to be less routine. Thus, reading problems associated with highly practiced skills such as phonological processing and word retrieval probably tend to have a biological base whereas discourse level difficulties probably include more examples of environmentally based problems. The converse of this conclusion is that, especially during the preschool years, intervention efforts aimed at providing children with richer discourse skills may be of special importance because such efforts provide opportunities for use of linguistic processes that children otherwise might experience only rarely. Such experiences may help a broad range of children who are at risk for encountering problems with reading, not because of biologically based problems, but because of limited opportunities to acquire some of the critical strands of language skill.

Supporting Language Growth through Standard Preschool Programs

As we have outlined, the preschool years are a time of enormous growth of the language and print-related abilities that provide the foundations for later literacy skills. While reviewing the social interactionist perspective on language development we described how these abilities may be nurtured in homes. We now turn to research linking early language development to experiences in preschool. This work is of special importance to those of us interested in finding ways of bolstering the language skills of children at risk for later reading problems before they experience reading failure.

As we noted above, early language development is optimized when children engage in frequent interactions that provide them interpretable language data and when they are helped to analyze those data to abstract underlying regularities. We noted that, in western industrialized societies, it is adults who are most able to engage children in interactions with the following beneficial characteristics: (1) conversational topics are extended for several turns, (2) topics dealt with include nonpresent events, and (3) adults respond to children's current interests and level of comprehension. In addition to having opportunities for actively participating in such events, children also may benefit from being spectators to or minor participants in speech events that include uses of language that surpass their current level of productive language skill. For example, as discussed earlier, dinner table conversations and book reading provide occasions for both types of beneficial language experiences.

Typical Preschool Language-learning Opportunities. If we assume that experiences supportive of language development in preschool settings are similar to those in the home, descriptions of preschools present a rather discouraging picture. Middle and working class girls in preschools in England are provided language experiences more likely to support language growth in the home than in preschool. In the homes, compared with preschool, four to five times more utterances by adults and children include language that is used for cognitively complex purposes (Tizard et al. 1983b), there are more total requests of children for labels, recall of events and explanations, and relatively few failures by children to respond to adult questions (Tizard et al. 1982). Also, there are nearly 10 times more questions asked of mothers than teachers, with questions reflecting child curiosity being nearly nonexistent in the speech of working class girls in school but not at home, and many more adequate responses to child queries in the home (Tizard et al. 1983a; see Tizard and Hughes 1984 for an overview).

Another study done in a British nursery school found low levels of talk about nonimmediate events and dramatic variations in children's language experiences in the same classroom (Michell 1982). For example, one child (Gemma) spent 82% of her time interacting with adults while another (Katherine) spent only 2% of her time with adults. The importance of this difference can be seen in the fact that conversational topics varied by conversational partner, with "personal descriptions," the category that included personal narratives, and explanations being found in 29.3% of the children's conversations with adults but in only 10.3% of their conversations with children. Not surprisingly, Gemma told many more personal narratives and gave more explanations than Katherine.

As part of the Home-School Study of Language and Literacy Development we have audiotaped children in preschool classrooms throughout a routine morning in order to determine the amount of time children spend engaged in different kinds of talk. We find that teachers spend relatively little time engaging children in cognitively challenging talk. On average 47% of the recorded time was coded as "nonlanguage" (i.e., comments or topics of conversation lasting less than five seconds). Talk with features likely to support language devel-

opment is relatively rare, with only 18% of the time including cognitively challenging talk: reading and discussing books (5%), talk
about past or future events (6%), talk expanding children's knowledge
about the social and physical world (1%), and pretending (6%).

As we noted earlier, conversations among peers tend to be qualitatively different from conversations between children and adults. An
indication of how these differences are seen in preschools comes from
correlations between the content of our children's talk and the identity
of their conversational partner. Amount of time spent talking with
other children is strongly related to talk during pretending episodes, a
type of interaction that might signal rich language (Nelson and Seidman 1984) and may support development of literacy-related skills
(Williamson and Silvern 1988). Amount of time spent interacting with
adults was related to less "nonlanguage" time, to procedural and explanatory talk (i.e., how to do things, "what we will do next"), to skill
routines (e.g., counting, alphabet recital), and to talk dealing with behavior management. Aside from the reduced nonlanguage time, this
cluster of correlations suggests that, in general, teachers are focusing
on discrete skills rather than striving to extend children's language and
thinking. This finding echoes the results of Tizard and Hughes (1984).

Book Reading.   Book reading is an activity that occurs in nearly
all preschools, and as we noted, in homes it has been shown to provide
wonderful opportunities for fostering language and literacy skills. Programs that include increased exposure to books have been found to
have beneficial effects in a Head Start setting (Dickinson 1989), in kin-
dergartens (Brown, Cromer, and Weinberg 1986) and in first grades
(Feitelson, Kita, and Goldstein 1986); therefore careful attention should
be given to book reading in preschools. The work discussed earlier on
book reading in the home suggests that more discussion about books
as they are read is generally better. In preschools researchers have
found that increasing the amount and kind of discussion with groups
increases story recall (Mason and Allen 1980). Analysis of how teachers
read to children reveals different styles of book reading (Dickinson and
Keebler 1989; Dickinson and Smith 1991), with only one style (found in
only 8 of 25 preschool classrooms) including significant amounts of discussion of cognitively challenging topics.

Improving Language-learning Opportunities in Preschool

Research from preschool settings suggests that they currently tend not
to be organized to optimize language learning opportunities, but they

do hold unrealized potential. Concerted efforts to help teachers realize the importance of social interaction for language development and to provide strategies for creating activity settings that are conducive to supporting children's language, might well increase the extent to which preschools foster language development and, therefore, help reduce some children's long-term risks of reading failure.

Given its clear importance in the home, book reading is an activity worthy of special consideration. Although most teachers read books to the entire group at one time, experimental research has shown that small group discussions are likely to be more lively and rich (Morrow and Smith 1990). Furthermore, tentative early results from the Home-School Study suggest that teachers' reports of reading to small groups and individuals when children are three may be related to literacy growth when children are five. Thus, efforts to increase the amount of active interaction around books might be enhanced by finding ways to work with small groups.

Of course, the bulk of a preschool teacher's time is spent engaging in informal conversations, not in structured group activities. Can this time be put to better uses? Examinations of how teachers engage children in conversation during lunch time and free play (Dickinson 1991; Smith and McCabe 1991) make clear that teachers' talk changes as they cope with the shifting demands of classroom life. However, it appears that teachers who place a high value on engaging children in extended and rich conversations are able to encourage relatively high levels of such talk, given conducive settings (Dickinson 1991). Especially conducive settings are times when teachers are stationary and children approach them (Dickinson 1991; Tizard and Hughes 1984).

Specific Recommendations for Educational Practice

On the basis of the prior research we have reviewed, we would urge teachers to adopt the following guidelines:

1. *Set language development of all children as an important overriding instructional goal.*
   Not only do children who are delayed or whose family does not speak English at home need work in language facilitation, all children do. Language development is very much an unfinished process at the age of five years for all children, and it is by means of work on language development that literacy skills will be improved.

2. *Plan ahead: strive to engage children in extended one-on-one conversations.*

   Plan to have times when one teacher is stationary and children are encouraged to approach him or her and engage in conversation. Equally important, to the extent possible, respond to children's interests and extend their language.

3. *Be flexible: be prepared to set aside prepared agendas in order to extend topics of immediate concern to children.*

   Often the best language learning opportunities are those that arise by chance. For example, children who are interested in seating arrangements for circle time are in a state of preparedness for acquiring vocabulary such as "next to" or "beside" and supplying this kind of vocabulary at this time may well be more effective than talk about the planned topic.

4. *Encourage talking among children.*

   A silent classroom is a classroom where language acquisition is not taking place because children acquire language in the context of social interaction. Fantasy play is an especially potent context for such talk; provide time, props, and encouragement for children's sociodramatic play.

5. *Read aloud often, repeating favorite books of each child.*

   As children have repeated experiences with books the vocabulary becomes familiar and the stories become resources for children's pretend play.

6. *Discuss books as you read them.*

   Prepare children for new books before you start reading them, draw them into the books with questions that require prediction and analysis, and follow up the books with discussions that link to children's lives. Be aware that discussions should change and become deeper as books are re-read.

7. *Don't confine the importance of books to reading time.*

   Encourage children to act out the stories they read. Quote books. Discuss them at relevant times throughout the day (e.g., "I bet you feel just like the girl in *Angel Child, Dragon Child* who gets mad and hits the bully who threw a snowball at her? But remember what happened to her when she did fight back?").

8. *Value and encourage even very young children's interest in print.*

   Encourage writing as a means of communicating among even very young children and encourage children's "pretend" writing. When appropriate, embed explicit information about print and how it works in ongoing activities (e.g., say names of letters as you

write children's names, point to large print as you read Big Books, verbalize the reason you are writing notes).

Summary: Connecting the Strands

We have traced the remarkable progression of language growth as children move from expressing needs and emotions through cries and babbling sounds, to the wonderful explosion of language as parents and children engage in talk about toys and ongoing activities, and finally, to when parents and children share experiences through purely verbal means as they tell personal narratives. As children are acquiring these skills through supportive interchanges with others they also are building knowledge about print and are becoming familiar with how books convey meaning. Children whose development proceeds well in all these areas will move through elementary school weaving together these multiple strands, creating both a beautiful and sturdy braid of literacy competencies. However, for the many children who, because of biological or environmental reasons, are at risk for failing to learn to read, it is vital that we seriously examine the kind of social interaction that fosters language acquisition and strive to ensure that educational settings incorporate as much of this interaction as possible. Many dedicated and gifted teachers already are attempting to do this, but there is a pressing need to provide the training and resources that will make all classrooms conversationally rich, communicatively powerful, and intellectually engaging.

Conclusion

In sum, young children acquire language primarily in contexts that provide them with adult talk that responds to what the children themselves say about topics of interest to them. Children negotiate meaning with adults in these contexts; adults imitate children at least as much as children do adults. Topics of conversation change with age, from the here-and-now to past experiences, fantasy play, and stories read from books.

Mechanisms for facilitating language and literacy instruction change less dramatically than do topics over time. Just as interactive routines and special intonation supported children's early efforts at language acquisition, so will similar interchanges support their acquisition of literacy. The prosody of adults' reading is distinct from talking, just as the prosody of their earlier talk to children was distinct from talk to adults. Routines too, support the acquisition of literacy as well as language. *Any book read often enough becomes predictable.* Conversations that enable children to comprehend texts of interest to them can provide a *social predictability* above and beyond whatever predictability is or is not in the text itself. Social predictability, emerging as it does from repeated readings of children's favorite books, will ultimately enable a child to extract a story that is literate in overall form and close in wording to the particular text. Under these conditions children can readily and successfully mesh specific print with their own oral language version. Thus, we see that the oral competencies children have acquired as they learn to speak work in concert with their emerging awareness of language and understanding of how print functions, which enables them to weave in smoothly the new strand of decoding abilities.

REFERENCES

Adams, M.J. 1990. *Beginning To Read.* Cambridge, MA: MIT Press.

Ames, L.B. 1966. Children's stories. *Genetic Psychology Monographs* 73:337–96.

Anderson, R.C., and Freebody, P. 1981. Vocabulary knowledge. In *Comprehension and Teaching: Research Reviews*, ed. J. Guthrie. Newark, DE: International Reading Association.

Anderson, R.C., Wilson, P.T., and Fielding, L.G. 1988. Growth in reading and how children spend their time outside of school. *Reading Research Quarterly* XXIII:285–303.

Anselmi, D., Tomasello, M., and Acunzo, M. 1986. Young children's responses to neutral and specific contingent queries. *Journal of Child Language* 13:135–44.

Aslin, R.N., Pisoni, D.B., and Jusczyk, P.W. 1983. Auditory development and speech perception in infancy. In *Handbook of Child Psychology: Vol. 2. Infancy and Developmental Psychobiology*, eds. M.M. Haith and J.J. Campos. New York: Wiley.

Beentjes, J.W.J., and Van der Voort, T.H.A. 1988. Television's impact on children's reading skills: A review of research. *Reading Research Quarterly* 23(4): 389–413.

Bettes, B.A. 1988. Maternal depression and motherese: Temporal and intonational features. *Child Development* 59:1089–1096.

Berko, J. 1958. The child's learning of English morphology. *Word* 14:150–77.

Bernstein, B. 1971. *Class, Codes and Control, Vol. 1: Theoretical Studies Towards a Sociology of Language.* London: Rutledge and Kegan Paul.

Bishop, D.V.M., and Edmundson, A. 1987. Language-impaired 4-year-olds: Distinguishing transient from persistent impairment. *Journal of Speech and Hearing Disorders* 52:156–73.

Bloom, L. 1970. *Language Development: Form and Function in Emerging Grammars.* Cambridge, MA: MIT Press.

Bloom, L., Lahey, J., Hood, L., Lifter, K., and Fiess, K. 1980. Complex sentences: Acquisition of syntactic connectives and the semantic relations they encode. *Journal of Child Language* 7:235–61.

Bohannon, J., and Stanowicz, L. 1988. Adult responses to children's language errors: The issue of negative evidence. *Developmental Psychology* 24:684–89.

Botvin, G.N., and Sutton-Smith, B. 1977. The development of structural complexity in children's fantasy narratives. *Developmental Psychology* 13:337–88.

Boysson-Bardies, B., de, Sagart, L., and Durand, C. 1984. Discernible differences in the babbling of infants according to target language. *Journal of Child Language* 11:1–15.

Brady, S., Shankweiler, D., and Mann, V. 1983. Speech perception and memory coding in relation to reading ability. *Journal of Experimental Child Psychology* 35:345–67.

Bretherton, I., McNew, S., Snyder, L., and Bates, E. 1983. Individual differences at 20 months: Analytic and holistic strategies in language acquisition. *Journal of Child Language* 10:293–320.

Brown, M.H., Cromer, P.S., and Weinberg, S.H. 1986. Shared book experiences in kindergarten. *Early Childhood Research Quarterly* 4:397–406.

Brown, R. 1973. *A First Language: The Early Stages.* Cambridge, MA: Harvard University Press.

Brown, R., and Hanlon, C. 1970. Derivational complexity and the order of acquisition in child speech. In *Cognition and the Development of Language,* ed. J.R. Hayes. New York: Wiley.

Brown, R., Cazden, C., and Bellugi-Klima, U. 1969. The child's grammar from I to III. In *Minnesota Symposium on Child Psychology,* Vol. 2, ed. J.P. Hill. Minneapolis: University of Minnesota Press.

Bryant, P.E., Bradley, L., MacLean, M, and Crossland, J. 1989. Nursery rhymes, phonological skills and reading. *Journal of Child Language* 16:407–28.

Bryant, P.E., MacLean, M., Bradley, L.L., and Crossland, J. 1990. Rhyme and alliteration, phoneme detection, and learning to read. *Developmental Psychology* 26:429–538.

Bryant, P., MacLean, M., and Bradley, L. 1990. Rhyme, language, and children's reading. *Applied Psycholinguistics* 11:237–52.

Calkins, L.M. 1986. *The Art of Teaching Writing.* Portsmouth, NH: Heinemann.

Carey, S. 1978. The child as word learner. In *Linguistic Theory and Psychological Reality,* eds. M. Halle, J. Bresnan, and G.A. Miller. New York: Cambridge University.

Chapman, K.L., Leonard, L.B., and Mervis, C.B. 1986. The effect of feedback on young children's inappropriate word usage. *Journal of Child Language* 13:101–17.

Chomsky, C. 1969. *The Acquisition of Syntax in Children from Five to Ten.* Cambridge, MA: MIT Press.

Chomsky, N. 1965. *Aspects of the Theory of Syntax.* Cambridge, MA: The MIT Press.

Clarke-Stewart, K.A. 1973. Interactions between mothers and their young children: Characteristics and consequences. *Monographs of the Society for Research in Child Development* 38 (Serial No. 153).

Clay, M. 1975. *What Did I Write?* Portsmouth, NH: Heinemann.

Cooper, W.E., and Paccia-Cooper, J. 1980. *Syntax and Speech.* Cambridge, MA: Harvard University Press.

Cromer, R.F. 1970. Children are nice to understand: Surface structure clues for the recovery of a deep structure. *British Journal of Psychology* 61:397–408.

Cross, T. G. 1976. Motherese: Its association with rate of syntactic acquisition in young children. In *The Development of Communication: Social and Pragmatic Factors in Language Acquisition*, eds. N. Waterson and C. Snow. New York: Wiley.

DeCasper, A.J., and Fifer, W.P. 1980. Of human bonding: Newborns prefer their mothers' voices. *Science* 208:1174–1176.

De Hirsch, K., Jansky, J.J., and Langford, W.S. 1966. *Predicting Reading Failure.* New York: Harper and Row.

Demetras, M., Post, K., and Snow, C. 1986. Feedback to first language learners: The role of repetitions and clarification questions. *Journal of Child Language* 13:275–92.

Dickinson, D.K. 1985. First impressions: Children's knowledge of words gained from a single exposure. *Applied Psycholinguistics* 5:359–73.

Dickinson, D.K. 1989. Effects of a shared reading program on Head Start language and literacy environment. In *Riskers, Makers, Risk Takers, Risk Breakers,* eds. J. Allen and J. Mason. Portsmouth, NH: Heinemann.

Dickinson, D.K. 1991. Teacher stance and setting: Constraints on conversation in preschools In *Developing Narrative Structure*, eds. A. McCabe and C. Peterson. Hillsdale, NJ: Lawrence Erlbaum Associates.

Dickinson, D.K., and Keebler, R. 1989. Variation in preschool teachers' styles of reading books. *Discourse Processes* 12:353–75.

Dickinson, D.K., and Smith, M.W. 1991. Styles of reading books in preschool. Annual conference of the American Educational Research Association, April, Chicago, IL.

Dickinson, D.K., and Snow, C.E. 1987. Interrelationships among prereading and oral language skills in kindergartners from two social classes. *Early Childhood Research Quarterly* 2:1–25.

Dickinson, D.K., De Temple, J.M., Hirschler, J.A., and Smith, M.W. In press. Book reading with preschoolers: Co-construction of text at home and at school. *Early Childhood Research Quarterly.*

Dickinson, D.K., Wolf, M.A., and Stotsky, S. 1989. "Words move": The interwoven development of oral and written language in the school years. In *Language Development* 2nd ed., ed. J. Berko-Gleason. Columbus, OH: Merrill.

D'Odorico, L., and Franco, F. 1985. The determinants of baby talk: Relationship to context. *Journal of Child Language* 12:567–86.

Dube, E.F. 1988. Literacy, cultural familiarity, and "intelligence" as determinants of story recall. In *Memory Observed*, ed. U. Neisser. San Francisco: W.H. Freeman and Company.

Edwards, M.L. 1974. Perception and production in child phonology: The testing of four hypotheses. *Journal of Speech and Hearing Research* 20:766–80.

Ehri, L. 1979. Linguistic insight: Threshold of reading acquisition. In *Reading Research: Advances in Theory and Practice*, Vol. 1, eds. T.G. Waller and G.E. MacKinnon. New York: Academic.

Ehri, L. 1984. How orthography alters spoken language competencies in children learning to read and spell. In *Language Awareness and Learning to Read*, eds. J. Downing and R. Valtin. New York: Springer-Verlag.

Ehri, L.C. 1985. Effects of printed language acquisition on speech. In *Literacy,*

Language and Learning: The Nature and Consequences of Reading and Writing, ed. D. Olsen. New York: Cambridge University Press.

Ehri, L.C., and Wilce, L.S. 1985. Movement into reading: Is the first stage of printed word learning visual or phonetic? *Reading Research Quarterly* 20: 163–79.

Eimas, P.D., Siqueland, E.R., Jusczyk, P., and Vigorito, J. 1971. Speech perception in infants. *Science* 171:303–06.

Eisenberg, A.R. 1985. Learning to describe past experiences in conversation. *Discourse Processes* 8:177–204.

Elbro, C. 1990. *Differences in Dyslexia.* Copenhagen: Munksgaard.

Elley, W. 1989. Vocabulary acquisition from listening to stories. *Reading Research Quarterly* XXIV:174–87.

Ellis, N. 1990. Reading, phonological skills and short-term memory: Interactive tributaries of development. *Journal of Research in Reading* 13:107–22.

Feagans, L. 1982. The development and importance of narrative for school adaptation. In *The Language of Children Reared in Poverty,* eds. L. Feagans and D. Farran. New York: Academic Press.

Feagans, L., and Short, E.J. 1984. Developmental differences in the comprehension and production of narratives by reading disabled and normally achieving children. *Child Development* 55:1727–1736.

Feagans, L., and Short, E.J. 1986. Referential communication and reading performance in learning disabled children over a three year period. *Developmental Psychology* 22:177–83.

Feitelson, D., Kita, B., and Goldstein, Z. 1986. Effects of listening to series stories on first graders' comprehension and use of language. *Research in the Teaching of English* 20:339–56.

Ferguson, C.A., and Farwell, C.B. 1975. Words and sounds in early language acquisition. *Language* 51:439–91.

Ferguson, C.A., and Macken, M.A. 1980. Phonological development in children's play and cognition. In *Children's Language* (Vol. 4.), ed. K.E. Nelson. New York: Gardner Press.

Fernald, A. 1985. Four-month-old infants prefer to listen to motherese. *Infant Behavior and Development* 8:181–95.

Fernald, A., Taeschner, T. Dunn, J., Papousek, M., De Boysson-Bardies, B., and Fukui, I. 1989. A cross-language study of prosodic modifications in mothers' and fathers' speech to preverbal infants. *Journal of Child Language* 16(3):477–502.

Ferreiro, E., and Teberosky, A. 1982. *Literacy Before Schooling.* Portsmouth, NH: Heinemann.

Flood, J.E. 1977. Parental reading styles in reading episodes with young children. *The Reading Teacher* May:864–67.

Fraser, C., Bellugi, U., and Brown, R. 1963. Control of grammar in imitation, comprehension and production. *Journal of Verbal Learning and Verbal Behavior* 2:121–35.

Freedman, A. 1987. Development in story writing. *Applied Psycholinguistics* 8:153–70.

Ganopole, S.J. 1987. The development of word consciousness prior to first grade. *Journal of Reading Behavior* XIX:415–36.

Gleason, J, 1975. Fathers and other strangers: Men's speech to young children.

In *Developmental Psycholinguistics: Theory and Application,* ed. D. Dato. Washington, DC: Georgetown University Press.

Gleitman, L.R., and Wanner, E. 1982. Language acquisition: The state of the art. In *Language Acquisition: The state of the Art,* eds. E. Wanner and L.R. Gleitman. Cambridge, MA: Harvard University Press.

Goldfield, B.A. 1987. The contributions of child and caregiver to referential and expressive language. *Applied Psycholinguistics* 8(3):267–80.

Goldfield, B.A., and Reznick, J.S. 1990. Early lexical acquisition: Rate, content, and the vocabulary spurt. *Journal of Child Language* 17:171–83.

Goldfield, B.A., and Snow, C.E. 1984. Reading books with children: The mechanics of parental influence on children's reading achievement. In *Understanding Reading Comprehension,* ed. J. Flood. Newark, DE: International Reading Association.

Goldfield, B.A., and Snow, C.E. 1989. Individual differences in language acquisition. In *The Development of Language,* ed. J. Berko-Gleason. Columbus, Ohio: Merrill Publishing Co.

Golinkoff, R., and Hirsh-Pasek, K. 1987. A new picture of language development: Evidence from comprehension. Paper presented at the Twelfth Annual Boston University Conference on Language Development, October, Boston, MA.

Goodman, Y. 1984. The development of initial literacy. In *Awakening to Literacy,* ed. H. Goelman, A. Oberg, and F. Smith. Exeter, NH: Heinemann.

Graybeal, C.M. 1981. Memory for stories in language-impaired children. *Applied Psycholinguistics* 2:269–83.

Griffith, P.L., Ripich, D.N., and Dastoli, S.L. 1986. Story structure, cohesion, and propositions in story recalls by learning-disabled and nondisabled children. *Journal of Psycholinguistic Research* 15(6):539–50.

Hall, P.K., and Tomblin, J.B. 1978. A follow-up study of children with articulation and language disorders. *Journal of Speech and Hearing Disorders* XLIII: 220–26.

Hampson, J.E. 1990. Do mothers facilitate rapid language acquisition for expressive children? Paper presented at the Fifth International Congress for the Study of Child Language, July, Budapest, Hungary.

Hansen, C.L. 1978. Story retelling used with average and learning disabled readers as a measure of reading comprehension. *Learning Disability Quarterly* 1:62–69.

Hardy-Brown, K., and Plomin, R. 1985. Infant communicative development: Evidence from adoptive and biological families for genetic and environmental influences on rate differences. *Developmental Psychology* 21:378–85.

Harste, J., Woodward, V., and Burke, C. 1984. *Language Stories and Literacy Lessons.* Portsmouth, NH: Heinemann.

Heath, S.B. 1982. What no bedtime story means: Narrative skills at home and school. *Language in Society* 11:49–76.

Heath, S.B. 1983. *Ways with Words: Language, Life and Work in Communities and Classrooms.* Cambridge, MA: Cambridge University Press.

Heath, S. 1986. Separating "things of imagination" from life: Learning to read and write. In *Emergent Literacy: Writing and Reading,* eds. W. Teale, and E. Sulzby. Norwood, NJ: Ablex.

Hemphill, L. 1989. Topic development, syntax, and social class. *Discourse Processes* 12(3):267–86.

Hirsch-Pasek, K., Naigles, L., Golinkoff, R.M., Gleitman, L.R., and Gleitman, H. 1988. Syntactic bootstrapping: Evidence from comprehension. Paper presented at the Boston University Conference on Language Development, October, Boston, MA.

Hudson, J.A., and Shapiro, L. 1991. From knowing to telling: The development of children's scripts, stories, and personal narratives. In *Developing Narrative Structure*, eds. A. McCabe and C. Peterson. Hillsdale, NJ: Lawrence Erlbaum Associates.

Hudson, J., and Nelson, K. 1984. Play with language: Overextensions as analogies. *Journal of Child Language* 11:337–46.

Ingram, D. 1986. Phonological development: Production. In *Language Acquisition*, 2nd ed., eds. P. Fletcher and M. Garman. Cambridge: Cambridge University Press.

Irwin, O.C. 1949. Infant speech. *Scientific American* 181(3):22–24.

Johnston, J.R. 1982. Narratives: A new look at communication problems in older language-disordered children. *Language, Speech, and Hearing Services in Schools* 13:144–55.

Jones, C.P., and Adamson, L.B. 1987. Language use in mother-child and mother-child-sibling interactions. *Child Development* 58:356–66.

Karmiloff-Smith, A. 1986. Some fundamental aspects of language development after age 5. In *Language Acquisition*, 2nd ed., eds. P. Fletcher and M. Garman. Cambridge: Cambridge University Press.

Kearsley, R. 1973. The newborn's response to auditory stimulation: A demonstration of orienting and defensive behavior. *Child Development* 44:582–90.

Kintsch, W., and Greene, E. 1978. The role of culture-specific schemata in the comprehension and recall of stories. *Discourse Processes* 1:1–13.

Kuczaj, S.A. 1983. "I mell a kunk"—Evidence that children have more complex representations of word pronunciations which they simplify. *Journal of Psycholinguistic Research* 12(1):69–73.

Lemish, D., and Rice, M.L. 1986. Television as a talking picture book: A prop for language acquisition. *Journal of Child Language* 13:251–74.

Levi, G., Musatti, L., Piredda, L., and Sechi, E. 1984. Cognitive and linguistic strategies in children with reading disabilities in an oral storytelling test. *Journal of Learning Disabilities* 17(7):406–10.

Levin, H., Schaffer, C.A., and Snow, C. 1982. The prosodic and paralinguistic features of reading and telling stories. *Language and Speech* 25:43–54.

Lieberman, P., Harris, K.S., Wolff, P., and Russell, L.H. 1971. Newborn infant cry and nonhuman primate vocalization. *Journal of Speech and Hearing Research* 14:718–27.

Liles, B.Z. 1985. Cohesion in the narratives of normal and language-disordered children. *Journal of Speech and Hearing Research* 28:123–33.

Locke, J.L., and Pearson, D.M. 1990. Linguistic significance of babbling: Evidence from a tracheostomized infant. *Journal of Child Language* 17:1–16.

Lovell, K., and Dixon, E.M. 1967. The growth of the control of grammar in imitation, comprehension, and production. *Journal of Child Psychology and Psychiatry* 8:31–39.

Lucariello, J., and Nelson, K. 1986. Context effects on lexical specificity in maternal and child discourse. *Journal of Child Language* 13:507–22.

Maratsos, M., and Chalkley, M.A. 1980. The internal language of children's syntax: The ontogenesis and representation of syntactic categories. In *Children's Language* Vol. 2, ed. K. Nelson. New York: Gardner Press.

Mason, J.M. 1984. *Acquisition of Knowledge about Reading in the Preschool Period: An Update and Extension* (Tech. Rep. No. 318). University of Illinois at Urbana: Center for the Study of Reading.

Mason, J.M., and Allen, J. 1986. A review of emergent literacy with implications for research and practice in reading. In *Review of Research in Education*, ed. C.Z. Rothkopf. Washington, DC: American Educational Research Association.

Mattingly, I.G. 1972. Reading, the linguistic process, and linguistic awareness. In *Language by Eye and Ear*, eds. J.F. Kavanagh and I.G. Mattingly. Cambridge, MA: MIT press.

McCabe, A. 1987. *Language Games to Play with Your Child*. New York: Fawcett Columbine.

McCabe, A., and Peterson, C. 1985. A naturalistic study of the production of causal connectives by children. *Journal of Child Language* 12:145–59.

McNeill, D. 1966. A study of word association. *Journal of Verbal Learning and Verbal Behavior* 5:548–57.

Michaels, S. 1981. "Sharing Time": Children's narrative styles and differential access to literacy. *Language in Society* 10:423–42.

Michaels, S. 1991. The dismantling of narrative. In *Developing Narrative Structure*, eds. A. McCabe and C. Peterson. NJ: Lawrence Erlbaum Associates.

Michaels, S., and Collins, J. 1984. Oral discourse styles: Classroom interaction and the acquisition of literacy. In *Coherence in Spoken and Written Discourse*, ed. D. Tannen. Norwood, NJ: Ablex.

Miller, P.J., and Sperry, L.L. 1988. Early talk about the past: The origins of conversational stories of personal experience. *Journal of Child Language* 15:293–315.

Michell, L. 1982. Language styles of 10 nursery school children. *First Language* 3:3–28.

Minami, M., and McCabe, A. 1990. *Haiku* as a discourse regulation mechanism: A stanza analysis of Japanese children's personal narratives. Paper presented at the Boston University Conference on Language Development, October, Boston, MA.

Morgan, A.L. 1987. The development of written language awareness in black preschool children. *Journal of Reading Behavior* XIX:49–67.

Morrow, L.M., and Smith, J.K. 1990. The effects of group setting on interactive storybook reading. *Reading Research Quarterly* XXV:213–31.

Nagy, W., Herman, P.A., and Anderson, R.C. 1985. Learning words from context. *Reading Research Quarterly* 20:233–53.

Nelson, K. 1973. Structure and strategy in learning to talk. *Monographs of the Society for Research in Child Development* 38.

Nelson, K.E. 1989. Strategies for first language teaching. In *The Teachability of Language*, eds. M.L. Rice and R.L. Schiefelbusch. Baltimore: Brookes Publishing Co.

Nelson, K., and Seidman, S. 1984. Playing with scripts. In *Event Knowledge: Structure and Function in Development*, eds. K. Nelson et al. Hillsdale, NJ: Lawrence Erlbaum Associates.

Ninio, A., and Bruner, J. 1978. The achievement and antecedents of labelling. *Journal of Child Language* 5:1–14.

O'Brien, M., and Nagel, K.S. 1987. Parents' speech to toddlers: The effect of play context. *Journal of Child Language* 14:269–79.

Oller, D.K., and Eilers, R.E. 1988. The role of audition in infant babbling. *Child Development* 59:441–49.

Olsen-Fulero, L., and Conforti, J. 1983. Child responsiveness to mother questions of varying type and presentation. *Journal of Child Language* 10:495–520.

Pappas, C., and Brown, E. 1987. Learning to read by reading: Learning how to extend the functional potential of language. *Research in the Teaching of English* 21:160–84.

Penner, S. 1987. Parental responses to grammatical and ungrammatical child utterances. *Child Development* 58:376–84.

Peters, A. 1983. *The Units of Language Acquisition.* Cambridge: Cambridge University Press.

Peterson, C., and McCabe, A. 1983. *Developmental Psycholinguistics: Three Ways of Looking at a Child's Narrative.* NY: Plenum.

Peterson, C., and McCabe, A. 1987. The connective 'and': Do older children use it less as they learn other connectives? *Journal of Child Language* 14(2):375–82.

Peterson, C., and McCabe, A. 1991. Linking children's connectives use and narrative macrostructure. In *Developing Narrative Structure*, eds. A. McCabe and C. Peterson. NJ: Lawrence Erlbaum Associates.

Peterson, C., and McCabe, A. In press. On the threshold of the storyrealm: Semantic versus pragmatic use of connectives in narratives. *Merrill-Palmer Quarterly.*

Pinker, S. 1984. *Language Learnability and Language Development.* Cambridge, MA: Harvard University Press.

Pitcher, E.G., and Prelinger, E. 1963. *Children Tell Stories.* New York: International Universities Press, Inc.

Platt, C.B., and MacWhinney, B. 1983. Error assimilation as a mechanism in language learning. *Journal of Child Language* 10:401–14.

Preece, A. 1987. The range of narrative forms conversationally produced by young children. *Journal of Child Language* 14:353–73.

Purcell-Gates, V. 1988. Lexical and syntactic knowledge of written narrative held by well-read-to kindergartners and second graders. *Research in the Teaching of English* 22:128–60.

Ratner, N.B. 1988. Patterns of parental vocabulary selection in speech to very young children. *Journal of Child Language* 15:481–92.

Read, C., Yun-Fei, Z., Hong-Yin, N., and Bao-Qing, D. 1986. The ability to manipulate speech sounds depends on knowing alphabetic writing. *Cognition* 24:31–44.

Reeder, K., Wakefield, J., and Shapiro, J. 1988. Children's speech act comprehension strategies and early literacy experiences. *First Language* 8:29–48.

Rice, M.L., and Woodsmall, L. 1988. Lessons from television: Children's word learning when viewing. *Child Development* 59:420–29.

Rice, M. L., Huston, A.C., Truglio, R., and Wright, J. 1990. Words from "Sesame Street": Learning vocabulary while viewing. *Developmental Psychology* 26(3):421–28.

Roth, F., and Spekman, N. 1986. Narrative discourse: Spontaneously generated stories of learning-disabled and normally achieving students. *Journal of Speech and Hearing Disorders* 51:8–23.

Sachs, J. 1982. Talking about the there and then: The emergence of displaced reference in parent-child discourse. In *Children's Language*, ed. K.E. Nelson. Hillsdale, NJ: Lawrence Erlbaum Associates.

Sanders, E.K. 1972. When are speech sounds learned. *Journal of Speech and Hearing Disorders* 37:55–63.

Scarborough, H.S., and Dobrich, W. 1990. Development of children with early language delay. *Journal of Speech and Hearing Research* 33:70–83.

Schieffelin, B.B., and Eisenberg, A.R. 1984. Cultural variation in children's conversations. In *The Acquisition of Communicative Competence*, eds. R.L. Schiefelbusch and J. Pickar. Baltimore, MD: University Park Press.

Scollon, R., and Scollon, S. 1981. *Narrative, Literacy and Face in Interethnic Communication*. Norwood: Ablex.

Shankweiler, D., and Crain, S. 1986. Language mechanisms and reading disorder: A modular approach. *Cognition* 24:139–68.

Skinner, B.F. 1957. *Verbal Behavior*. Englewood Cliffs, NJ: Prentice-Hall.

Smith, M.E. 1926. An investigation of the development of the sentence and the extent of vocabulary in young children. (*Studies in Child Welfare*, Vol. 3, No. 5). Iowa City: University of Iowa.

Smith, M.W., and McCabe, A. 1990. Socrates versus the drill sergeant: Dimensions of variation in preschool teachers' discourse. Paper presented at the annual meeting of the American Educational Research Association, April, Boston, MA.

Smolak, L., and Weinraub, M. 1983. Maternal speech: Strategy or response? *Journal of Child Language* 10:369–80.

Snow, C.E. 1972. Mothers' speech to children learning language. *Child Development* 43:549–65.

Snow, C.E. 1977. The development of conversation between mothers and babies. *Journal of Child Language* 4:1–22.

Snow, C.E. 1983. Literacy and language: Relationships during the preschool years. *Harvard Educational Review* 53:165–89.

Snow, C.E. 1984. Parent-child interaction and the development of communicative ability. In *The Acquisition of Communicative Competence*, eds. I.R.L. Schiefelbusch and J. Pickar. Baltimore, MD: University Park Press.

Snow, C.E., and Dickinson, D.K. 1991. Skills that aren't basic in a new conception of literacy. In *Literate Systems and Individual Lives: Perspectives on Literacy and Schooling*, eds. A. Purves and E. Jennings. Albany, NY: SUNY Press.

Snow, C.E., and Goldfield, B. 1982. Building stories: The emergence of information structures from conversation. In *Analyzing Discourse: Talk and Text*, ed. D. Tannen. Washington, DC: Georgetown University Press.

Snow, C.E., Cancino, H., Gonzalez, P., and Shriberg, E. In press. Giving formal definitions: An oral language correlate of school literacy. In *Literacy in Functional Settings*, ed. D. Bloome. Norwood, NJ: Ablex.

Snow, C.E., and Ninio, A. 1986. The contracts of literacy: What children learn from learning to read books. In *Emergent Literacy: Writing and Reading*, eds. W.H. Teale and E. Sulzby. Norwood, NJ: Ablex.

Snow, C., Midkiff-Borunda, S., Small, A., and Proctor, A. 1984. Therapy as social interaction: Analyzing the contexts for language remediation. *Topics in Language Disorders* 4(4):72–85.

Snow, C.E., Perlmann, R., and Nathan, D. 1987. Why routines are different:

Toward a multiple-factors model of the relation between input and language acquisition. In *Children's Language*, Vol. 6, eds. K. Nelson and A. Van Kleeck. Hillsdale, NJ: Lawrence Erlbaum Associates.

Spring, C., and Davis, J.M. 1988. Relations of digit naming speech with three components of reading. *Applied Psycholinguistics* 9:315–34.

Stanovich, K. 1986. Matthew effects in reading: Some consequences of individual differences in acquisition of literacy. *Reading Research Quarterly* 21:360–406.

Stanovich, K. 1990. Concepts in developmental theories of reading skill: Cognitive resources, automaticity, and modularity. *Developmental Review* 10:72–100.

Stark, R.E. 1986. Prespeech segmental feature development. In *Language Acquisition* (2nd ed.), eds. P. Fletcher and M. Garman. Cambridge: University Press.

Sullivan, J.W., and Horowitz, F.D. 1983. The effects of intonation on infant attention: The role of the rising intonation contour. *Journal of Child Language* 10:521–34.

Sulzby, E. 1985. Children's emergent reading of favorite storybooks: A developmental study. *Reading Research Quarterly* 20:458–81.

Sulzby, E., and Zecker, L.B. 1991. The oral monologue as a form of emergent reading. In *New Directions in Developing Narrative Structure*, eds. A. McCabe and C. Peterson. Hillsdale, NJ: Lawrence Erlbaum Associates.

Tager-Flusberg, H. 1989. Putting words together: Morphology and syntax in the preschool years. In *The Development of Language*, ed. J. Berko-Gleason. Columbus, OH: Merrill Publishing Co.

Teale, W.H. 1984. Reading to young children: Its significance for literacy development. In *Awakening to Literacy*, eds. H. Goelman, A. Oberg, and F. Smith. Exeter, NH: Heineman.

Tizard, B., and Hughes, M. 1984. *Young Children Learning*. Cambridge, MA: Harvard University Press.

Tizard, B., Hughes, M., Pinkerton, G., and Carmichael, H. 1982. Adults' cognitive demands at home and at nursery school. *Journal of Child Psychology and Psychiatry* 23:105–16.

Tizard, B., Hughes, M., Carmichael, H., and Pinkerton, H. 1983a. Children's questions and adults' answers. *Journal of Child Psychology and Psychiatry* 24:269–81.

Tizard, B., Hughes, M., Carmichael, H., and Pinkerton, H. 1983b. Language and social class: Is verbal deprivation a myth? *Journal of Child Psychology and Psychiatry* 24:533–42.

Tomasello, M., Conti-Ramsden, G., and Ewert, B. 1990. Young children's conversations with their mothers and fathers: Differences in breakdown and repair. *Journal of Child Language* 17:115–30.

Tomasello, M., Mannle, S., and Kruger, A.C. 1986. Linguistic environment of 1- to 2-year-old-twins. *Developmental Psychology* 22(2):169–76.

Umiker-Sebeok, D.J. 1979. Preschool children's intraconversational narratives. *Journal of Child Language* 6:91–109.

Valtin, R. 1984. Awareness of features and functions of language. In *Language Awareness and Learning to Read*, eds. J. Downing and R. Valtin. NY: Springer-Verlag.

Valtin, R. 1984. The development of metalinguistic abilities in children learning to read and write. In *Language Awareness and Learning to Read*, eds. J. Downing and R. Valtin. NY: Springer-Verlag.

Watson, K.A. 1975. Transferable communicative routines: Strategies in group identity in two speech events. *Language in Society* 4:53–72.

Watson, R. 1989. Literate discourse and cognitive organization: Some relationships between parent's talk and 3-year-olds' thought. *Applied Psycholinguistics* 10:221–36.

Weaver, P.A., and Dickinson, D.K. 1982. Scratching below the surface structure: Exploring the usefulness of story grammars. *Discourse Processes* 5:225–43.

Wells, C.G. 1980. Adjustments in adult-child conversation: Some effects of interaction. In *Language: Social Psychological Perspectives*, eds. H. Giles, W.P. Robinson, and R.M. Smith. Oxford: Pergammon Press.

Wells, G. 1981. Some antecedents of early educational attainment. *British Journal of Sociology of Education* 2:181–200.

Wells, G. 1985. *Language Development in the Pre-school Years*. New York: Cambridge University Press.

Wells, G. 1985. Pre-school literacy-related activities and success in school. In *Literacy, Language, and Learning*, eds. D.R. Olson, N. Torrance, and A. Hildyard. Cambridge, England: Cambridge University Press.

Werker, J.F., and Lalonde, C.E. 1988. Cross-language speech perception: Initial capabilities and developmental change. *Developmental Psychology* 24:672–83.

Werker, J.F., and Tees, R.C. 1984. Cross-language speech perception: Evidence for perceptual reorganization during the first year of life. *Infant Behavior and Development* 7:49–64.

White, B.L. 1978. *Experience and Environment*. NJ: Prentice-Hall, Inc.

Whitehurst, G.J., Falco, F.L., Lonigan, C.J., Fischel, J.E., De Baryshe, B.D., Valdez-Menchacha, M.C., and Caulfield, M. 1987. Accelerating language development through picture book reading. *Developmental Psychology* 24:552–59.

Williamson, P.A., and Silvern, S.C. 1988. The contribution of play, metaplay, and narrative competence to story comprehension. Paper presented at the annual meeting of the American Educational Research Association, April, New Orleans.

Wolf, M. In press. Letter-naming, naming speed, reading, and the contribution of the cognitive neurosciences. *Reading Research Quarterly*.

Wolf, M., Bally, T., Morris, R. 1986. Automaticity, retrieval processes, and reading: A longitudinal study in average and impaired readers. *Child Development* 57:988–1000.

Yoder, P.J., and Kaiser, A.P. 1989. Alternative explanations for the relationship between maternal verbal interaction style and child language development. *Journal of Child Language* 16:141–60.

Zajonc, R.B., and Markus, G.B. 1975. Birth order and intellectual development. *Psychological Review* 82:74–88.

Chapter • 2

Getting Ready to Read
Learning How Print Maps to Speech

Benita A. Blachman

"The Reading Wars" was the title of a recent article in a special edition of *Newsweek* magazine (Kantrowitz 1990). Regrettably, it is an apt title to describe the dissension in the reading community over how reading is to be taught to young children. If we agree that "the ability to read well is basic to our national survival" (Chall 1989, p. 521), then perhaps the passion that fuels the reading controversy will be easier to understand. Unfortunately, the losers in this "reading war" are too often the children who are not getting the best that we have to offer. As educators and researchers debate the value of phonic versus meaning-based approaches to reading (the most popular, at the moment, being whole language) or, as they are more generically referred to, skills-based approaches versus literature-based approaches, a significant number of children continue to fail to learn to read. Even as adults, it is estimated that 20% of the population continue to have severe problems with the most common reading activities (Stedman and Kaestle 1987).

AN EMPHASIS ON LANGUAGE

Instead of focusing on theoretical divisions in the field, it might be more constructive to ask if there is anything related to reading about which we all agree. It is safe to say that there is now a consensus that reading is a language-based activity. Although today we tend to take this simple observation for granted, in the '60s and well into the '70s a different point of view prevailed. The alternative viewpoint was perhaps best summarized by George Spache (1961), a noted authority in the reading field, who wrote: "It seems fairly obvious that reading, like most school work, is primarily a visual act" (p. 3). As a consequence of the emphasis on vision, the focus at that time in explaining reading problems was on identifying and remediating deficits in visual perception. Eventually the visual perceptual deficit explanation of reading difficulties was questioned, and numerous researchers presented evidence that directly contradicted it (Benton 1975; Larsen and Hammill 1975; Vellutino 1977, 1979). In the last two decades, we have seen a renewed interest in a language-based view of reading and its disabilities (Kamhi and Catts 1989; Kavanagh and Mattingly 1972; Liberman 1971, 1983; Shankweiler and Liberman 1989; Vellutino 1979, 1987). In the context of that perspective, we have made great strides in our understanding of literacy acquisition.

As a consequence of the emphasis on language that pervades the reading community, a number of promising practices are appearing in preschool, kindergarten, and first grade classrooms that emphasize the creation of a rich environment of oral and written language (Anderson et al. 1985; Durkin 1989). In *Becoming A Nation of Readers: The Report of the Commission on Reading* (Anderson et al. 1985), written under the auspices of the National Academy of Education and sponsored by the National Institute of Education, the Commission reports that:

> Reading must be seen as part of a child's general language development and not as a discrete skill isolated from listening, speaking, and writing. Reading instruction builds especially on oral language. If this foundation is weak, progress in reading will be slow and uncertain (p. 30).

The Commission, charged with the task of synthesizing the best research in reading and translating that research into guidelines for practice, proceeded to describe the elements needed to foster the emerging literacy of the preschool and kindergarten child. The essential elements included, for example, extended conversations at home with parents and experiences with written language. Specific emphasis was placed on conversations that require reflection and that will help children "exercise their memories . . . and . . . learn to give complete descriptions and tell complete stories" (p. 23). At the same time, it was suggested that experiences with written language, especially reading aloud to children, should be a priority. To stress its importance, reading aloud to children was described as "the single most important activity for building the knowledge required for eventual success in reading" (p. 23).

The Commission advised continued opportunities in kindergarten to stimulate oral language development and listening comprehension through thoughtful discussions—for example, discussions about the storybooks that have been read to the children. The Commission also pointed out that this emphasis on oral language development, although necessary, is not sufficient to guarantee success in reading. Children need to acquire knowledge about written language related to both form (e.g., we hold the book right side up and turn the pages from front to back) and function (e.g., it can entertain, instruct, or direct). They also need to acquire knowledge of letter names and knowledge about the relationships between letters and sounds. Learning to write (whether it is with paper and pencil, with plastic letters, or in front of a computer screen) and encouraging writing, for example, through accepting and encouraging invented spellings (e.g., such as *t* for tame, followed by *tm, tam,* and eventually *tame*), is a way to facilitate the acquisition of letter-sound correspondences. It is also a way to encourage a child to use his or her knowledge of written language to communicate with others (Anderson et al. 1985, p. 34).

Although I have taken some liberties in my summary of the Commission's recommendations for preschool and kindergarten children (most notably in deleting some ideas and emphasizing others), it is hard to see how educators from either the phonics/skills-based orientation or the meaning/literature-based orientation to beginning reading could disagree with the recommendations made by this panel. Indeed, if these recommendations were actually in place in all of our preschool and kindergarten classrooms (along with recommendations for later years, such as the suggestion that children should spend more time in independent reading and writing and less time on workbooks), we would be much further along toward our goal of "becoming a nation of readers."

DIFFERENCES IN PRESCHOOL LITERACY EXPERIENCES

It is important to remember, of course, that children come to school with differing levels of awareness about the conventions of written language and about the connections between oral and written language. A vivid description of these differences and their influence on literacy acquisition is described by Adams (1990) in her book *Beginning to Read: Thinking and Learning about Print*. For example, Adams describes her own child's experiences with print, especially having been read to on a regular basis, and calculates that somewhere between 1,000 and 1,700 hours will have been spent reading to John "one-on-one, with his face in the books" (p. 85) before he enters first grade. Others also have found that this frequency of reading to children is commonplace in culturally mainstream homes (Heath 1983). In addition, Adams also estimates that her son spent 1,000 hours watching "Sesame Street," and another 1,000 hours in written language activities, such as playing with magnetic letters on the refrigerator, playing word games in the car and on the computer, and participating in oral and written language activities at preschool. As Adams so aptly puts it, "Any way we work it, it seems a safe bet that John and the majority of his culturally mainstream peers will have experienced thousands of hours' worth of pre-reading activities before entering first grade" (p. 86).

In striking contrast, according to Adams (see also, Feitelson and Goldstein 1986, Heath 1983, Teale 1986, cited in Adams 1990), are the children who have never, or only rarely, been read to, who are living in homes without books, without models of adults who value reading and who read for their own pleasure, without magnetic letters, paper, pencils, crayons, and certainly without a home computer with letter and word games. In addition, there are the children who, despite exposure to a rich oral and written language environment as pre-schoolers, fail to make the necessary connections between print and speech that facilitate literacy acquisition.

Ideally, these differences in preschool literacy experiences and in learning needs will be taken into account by knowledgeable kinder-garten and first grade teachers, who will modify their instruction to accommodate a wide range of individual differences. But, as we know, this ideal is not always reached. If nothing else, these vast differences in preschool experience and in the ability to take advantange of appro-priate literacy experiences when they are available, suggest that any single approach, regardless of its orientation, will not meet the needs of all children. For children who haven't learned to recognize the words on the page, an approach that relies only on continued exposure to literature (however "good" the literature) will leave them without the direct instruction they need to make the connections between print and speech. On the other hand, a model that relies too heavily on di-rect instruction in isolated skills (skills that many children will already have acquired) will leave children without the enrichment and oppor-tunites for rewarding literacy experiences that all children need and deserve.

LEARNING HOW PRINT MAPS TO SPEECH

If, as I suspect, most would accept the recommendations selected from *Becoming A Nation of Readers*, then where, you may wonder, does the great controversy over the teaching of beginning reading lie? One important point of disagreement concerns the way in which children come to understand how print maps to speech. Specifically, we now know that one of the fundamental tasks facing the beginning reader is to develop the realization that speech can be segmented and that these segmented units can be represented by printed forms (Liberman 1971). Although it is obvious to literate adults that the letters of the alphabet more or less represent phonological segments of speech, this awareness cannot be taken for granted in the young child. To appreciate the complexity of the task facing the beginning reader, one must first appreciate the complex relationship among the phonemes in the speech stream. Speech, unlike writing, "does not consist of separate phonemes" produced one after the other "in a row over time" (Gleitman and Rozin 1973, p. 460). Instead, as Liberman and Shankweiler (1991) explain, "in producing the syllable 'ba,' for example, the speaker assigned the consonant we know as 'B' to the lips, and the vowel we know as 'A' to a shaping of the tongue, and then produced the two elements at pretty much the same time" (p. 5). This merging or coarticulation of the phonological segments during speech production (the folding of the consonants into the vowels) (Liberman et al. 1967; Liberman 1971) has advantages for speech but, as we shall see, obscures the segmental nature of the speech stream and makes it difficult for the young child to access the phonological units that are represented by an alphabet. Liberman and Shankweiler (1991) help us understand this phenomenon:

> The advantageous result of such coarticulation of speech sounds is that speech can proceed at a satisfactory pace—at a pace indeed at which it can be understood (Liberman, Cooper, Shankweiler, and Studdert-Kennedy 1967). Can you imagine trying to understand speech if it were spelled out to you letter by painful letter? So coarticulation is certainly advantageous for the perception of speech. But a further result of coarticulation, and a much less advantageous one for the would-be reader, is that there is, inevitably, no neat correspondence between the underlying phonological structure and the sound that comes to the ears. Thus, though the word "bag," for example, has three phonological units, and correspondingly, three letters in print, it has only one pulse of sound: The three elements of the underlying phonological structure—the three phonemes—have been thoroughly overlapped and merged into that one sound—"bag". . . .

> [Beginning readers] can understand, and properly take advantage of, the fact that the printed word *bag* has three letters, only if they are aware that the spoken word *"bag,"* with which they are already quite familiar, is divisible into three segments. They will probably not know that spontaneously, because, as we have said, there is only one segment of sound, not three, and because the processes of speech perception that recover the phonological structure are automatic and quite unconscious (pp. 5–6).

As we now know from extensive research conducted during the last fifteen years, developing an awareness of the phonological segments in words is an important prerequisite to understanding how an alphabetic transcription represents speech. "That transcription will make sense to beginning readers only if they understand that the transcription has the same number and sequence of units as the spoken word" (Liberman and Shankweiler 1991, p. 6). An important insight in early reading acquisition is the recognition that, for some children, difficulty in learning to decode occurs precisely because they lack an awareness of the segmental nature of speech and, thus, never fully understand how an alphabet works (Freebody and Byrne 1988; Juel 1988; Stanovich 1986; Williams 1987). The research clearly indicates that children who can demonstrate their phonological awareness by, for example, categorizing words according to common initial, middle, or final sounds, or by counting, deleting, or reversing phonemes, are more likely to be among our better readers. Children who lack this awareness are likely to be among our poorest readers (Blachman 1984; Blachman and James 1986; Bradley and Bryant 1983; Juel 1988; Juel, Griffith, and Gough 1986; Lundberg, Olofsson, and Wall 1980; Mann 1984; Mann and Liberman 1984; Share et al. 1984; Stanovich, Cunningham, and Cramer 1984; Torneus 1984; Vellutino and Scanlon 1987).

In addition to the evidence that phonological awareness is a highly significant and consistent predictor of early reading achievement, there is now evidence from large-scale training studies here and abroad that phonological awareness can be heightened in kindergarten and first grade children (as well as older learning disabled children) through direct instructional activities (Ball and Blachman 1991; Blachman et al. 1991; Bradley and Bryant 1983; Cunningham 1990; Fox and Routh 1984; Lundberg, Frost, and Peterson 1988; Treiman and Baron 1983; Williams 1980). This instruction (taking a variety of forms, as we shall see in this chapter) has been shown to have a positive effect on the acquisition of both reading and spelling. It appears that once children are taught to recognize that speech can be segmented and that these segmented units are represented by letters, the systematic relationships between letters and sounds are easier to grasp and utilize in both reading and writing. To take full advantage of an alphabetic writing system, one must first understand the alphabetic principle. This necessitates learning about the segmental nature of speech and its relationship to print.

In contrast to this view regarding beginning reading, there are those who argue that the use of written language does not require a "high level of conscious awareness of the units . . ." (Goodman and Goodman 1979, p. 139). They suggest as a corollary—and, I might add, without any research to support their premise—that activities that require "breaking whole (natural) language into bite-size, abstract little pieces . . . words, syllables, and isolated sounds" (Goodman 1986, p. 7) make learning to read more difficult. The Goodmans believe that learning to read is as natural as learning to speak (Goodman 1986; Goodman and Goodman 1979). Indeed, it would be convenient if reading and writing were "biologically primary" (Liberman and Liberman 1990) in the same way that speech is biologically primary. Then, reading and writing, like speech, might require only exposure to language to trigger the underlying biological mechanism and get it started. Unfortunately, this is not the case. As noted recently, "although it is popular for authors to cite examples of children who have acquired reading on their own, . . . for the vast majority of children the initial stages of reading must be traversed with the aid of some type of guided instruction from a teacher" (Stanovich 1986, p. 396). We are beginning to realize that, for many children, direct instruction is required to help them understand how print maps to speech.

Teaching Phonological Awareness

Numerous researchers have suggested that phonological awareness activities should be incorporated into the kindergarten and first grade classroom, before children have had a chance to fail in reading and spelling (Adams 1990; Blachman 1989; Juel 1988). There is now a considerable body of research to provide direction for the practitioner who wants to heighten the phonological awareness of children before and during early reading instruction (see Blachman in press for a detailed description of these activities). Although there is no cookbook for the practitioner to follow, the following review of some of the large-scale phoneme awareness training studies reveals an array of activities that can be used by the classroom teacher or clinician. One of the important ways in which these studies differ is whether or not the phonological awareness instruction is combined with instruction linking the phonological segments to the letters of the alphabet. In the first two studies (Cunningham 1990; Lundberg, Frost, and Peterson 1988), activities to enhance phonological awareness are provided without making the connection to letters. In the next group of studies (Bradley and Bryant 1983, 1985; Ball and Blachman 1988, 1991; Blachman et al. 1991), the connections between the phonological segments in words and the alphabet letters that represent those segments are made explicit during training.

Phonological Awareness Instruction Without Making Explicit the Connections Between Sound Segments and Letters. In one of the largest studies to date, Lundberg, Frost, and Peterson (1988) provided eight months of metalinguistic training to 235 nonreading children in kindergarten classrooms in Denmark. Even though these children were a year older than their counterparts in kindergarten classrooms in the United States, they were not likely to have had much in the way of "informal literacy socialization" (p. 266). By electing to provide a program of instruction that did not include making connections between the sound segments in words and the letters that represent those segments, Lundberg and his colleagues were able to evaluate the impact of training in phoneme awareness, uncontaminated by letter/sound knowledge and prior to formal reading instruction.

In each classroom, the entire group of 15 to 20 children participated in a program that began with listening games, and was followed by rhyming games and segmentation of sentences into words. During the second month of the intervention, children learned to segment multisyllabic words into syllables through a variety of clapping and rhythmic activities. In the third month, phonemes were introduced. Children were first taught to identify initial phonemes, and in the fifth month they learned to segment two-phoneme words and then moved on to more complex items. The program emphasized games, but the authors stress that careful attention was paid to the sequencing, duration, and frequency of the activities. In a previous study, Olofsson and Lundberg (1983) had found that when the structure was varied across treatment conditions, only the most structured group showed improvement from pretest to posttest. The most structured group had participated in lessons three to four times per week for 15 to 30 minutes per lesson, while in the least structured group the teachers introduced the phoneme awareness activities more spontaneously during the normal play activities of the day.

In the more recent Lundberg study (Lundberg et al. 1988), the children who participated in the metalinguistic training demonstrated significantly greater metaphonological awareness than the control children. Although there were no differences between the two groups on measures of prereading after the kindergarten intervention, when the children were tested a year later at the end of first grade, the treatment children significantly outperformed the control children in spelling. At the end of second grade, the treatment children outperformed the control children in both reading and spelling. Thus, Lundberg and his colleagues were able to demonstrate that phonological awareness can be heightened in children who have not yet learned to read, and when formal literacy instruction begins in first grade, this heightened awareness appears to have a facilitating effect on the acquisition of reading and spelling skills.

In a more recent study, Cunningham (1990) also investigated the impact of a phoneme awareness training program that did not include instruction in the connections between sound segments and letters. (It should be noted, however, that although the connections between letters and sounds were not introduced during the treatment activities, the first grade children in this study were involved in formal reading instruction in their classrooms during this 10-week period. We are not told whether letter name and letter sound instruction was taking place in the kindergarten classrooms during this 10-week period.) Kindergarten and first grade children participated in 10 weeks of instruction, meeting twice a week, in groups of four or five for 15 to 20 minute lessons. In a program adapted from *The ABD's of Reading* (Williams 1979), children learned to represent the sounds in words by moving wooden chips. Both segmenting and blending activities were included in the program. At the end of the intervention, the trained kindergarten and first grade children significantly outperformed the control children on measures of phoneme awareness and on a general measure of reading ability.

These studies clearly demonstrate the facilitating effect on beginning reading development of training in phonological awareness, even when the connections between the sound segments and letters are not made explicit during the intervention. By not including instruction in the connections between sounds and letters, these researchers were able to isolate and evaluate the effect of training in phonological awareness. It should also be noted, however, that in the study by Lundberg et al. (1988), the effect of the phonological awareness training on literacy was not evident until the children had been exposed to formal reading and spelling instruction a year later in first grade. It appears that once letter-sound relationships were introduced in first grade, the phonological awareness training the children had had in kindergarten gave them an edge over the control children that was apparent in their superior reading and spelling scores at the end of grade two. By demonstrating that phonological awareness can be heightened outside the context of reading instruction, and that this awareness has an impact on the acquisition of reading and spelling once formal instruction begins, Lundberg and his colleagues have added support to a causal link between phonological awareness and reading acquisition—an important theoretical contribution. However, it does not necessarily follow that instruction in phonological awareness is *best* when provided outside the context of formal reading instruction, or that one should isolate these phonological awareness activities from activities that help children make connections between sound segments and letters. The next group of studies demonstrates the value of phonological awareness instruction that also incorporates letter-sound training.

Phonological Awareness Instruction that Makes Explicit the Connections Between Sound Segments and Letters. In a ground-breaking longitudinal and experimental training study in England, Bradley and Bryant (1983, 1985) not only established a causal relationship between phonological awareness and reading and spelling acquisition, but they also demonstrated the value of creating a link between the segmented sound units and and their corresponding printed symbols. In their longitudinal study, Bradley and Bryant found a significant relationship between the performance of 368 four- and five-year-olds on a sound categorization task and the reading and spelling of these same children three years later. An experimental training study was also conducted with 65 of these children who had low pretest scores on the sound categorization pretest. These children were randomly assigned to one of four groups matched on age, sex, IQ, and sound categorization ability. Children in the first group participated in 40, individually administered lessons spread over two years, during which they learned to categorize or group pictures on the basis of shared sounds. For example, the children were taught that *hen* could be grouped with *men* and *pen* because they rhymed, and also that *hen* could be grouped with *hat* and *hill* because they shared an initial sound. The children later worked on recognizing shared middle and final sounds. A mainstay of the program was a game called "the odd one out." Pictures of objects that rhymed or shared an initial, middle, or final sound were placed on the table, along with one picture that did not belong. The children were asked to identify the "odd one out" and to explain their choice. Children in the second experimental group also received the identical instruction in sound categorization that was provided to the first group, but this group also learned to represent the common sounds with plastic letters. For example, using the words *pen* and *hen*, the letters common to both words stayed on the table, while the children changed the *p* to an *h*. In the third group, established to control for the "special attention" provided to the children in the first two groups, the children also participated in 40 individually administered lessons spread over two years and practiced categorizing the same pictures used by the treatment groups. However, the children in this group were taught to categorize the pictures on the basis of semantic categories (e.g., *hen* and *dog* were grouped together because both are animals). The fourth group received no intervention.

The research of Bradley and Bryant has both theoretical and practical significance. Their results indicated that, although the children trained in sound categorization outperformed the children who did not receive this training, the most successful children were those who were trained in sound categorization and who also learned to represent the common sounds with plastic letters. These children had significantly higher reading and spelling scores than the children in the two control groups, and they also had significantly higher spelling scores than the children in the sound categorization only group. Recalling that the training consisted of only 40, 10-minute lessons spread over two years, it is even more impressive that in a follow-up study (Bradley 1988), conducted four years after the original study ended, children who learned to make the connections between sound categories and letter strings maintained their superior position in reading and spelling.

Although the Bradley and Bryant study answered some important questions by exploring the incremental benefit of connecting the sound segments to letters during the phoneme awareness instruction, their study also raised a new question. Because these researchers did not include a group that received only letter training, it was not possible to determine whether the *combination* of sound categorization plus letter training made the difference in reading and spelling achievement, or whether the letter training component itself was responsible for the superior performance on reading and spelling measures.

To answer this question, and also to explore the feasibility of working with groups of kindergarten children (rather than providing one-to-one instruction as in the Bradley and Bryant study), we (Ball and Blachman 1988, 1991) embarked on a phonological awareness training study in three, inner-city schools in a large urban district in upstate New York. Ninety kindergarten children were randomly assigned to one of three groups. The first group of children received instruction in phoneme segmentation and also in letter names and sounds. The second group of children (control group I) received instruction in a variety of language activities (such as having stories read to them and general vocabulary development) and also received instruction in letter names and sounds using the same letter stimuli that were used by our treatment group. The third group was a no intervention control group. The children in the phoneme segmentation group and the language activities control group met in groups of four or five, four times a week for seven weeks, for 15 to 20 minute lessons. The lessons were taught outside the regular classroom by specially trained teachers.

The children in the phoneme awareness group followed a scripted, three-part lesson plan. At the beginning of each lesson, the children engaged in an activity called *say-it-and-move-it* (adapted from Elkonin 1963, 1973). Using a variety of manipulatives, such as disks, tiles, or blocks, the children learned to move the appropriate number of disks to represent the number of sounds in a one-, two-, or three-phoneme word. Initially, children represented one sound with one disk. The teacher would say, "Show me /i/" (or, for example, /a/ or /s/). The children would repeat the sound slowly, and as they were repeating it they would use one finger to move one disk from the top half of an 8½" by 11" sheet to the left end of an arrow (drawn from left to right) on the bottom half of the page. When the children were successful at representing one sound with one disk, the teacher moved on to one sound repeated twice, such as /i/ /i/. Again, the children repeated the sounds and represented each sound with a disk. Next, two phoneme words (e.g., *it, up*) were introduced and segmented following the same procedure. After modeling by the teacher, the child repeated the word slowly, moving a disk to represent each sound. After success with two-phoneme items, three-phoneme items were introduced, being careful initially to select words that begin with continuous sound letters (letters that can be held with a minimum of distortion) (e.g., *sun, lip, fan*). After the third week of say-it-and-move-it activities, a limited number of letters that had previously been mastered by the children were added to the blank tiles. Each item to be segmented during that lesson contained only one of the letter tiles. Children now had the option of segmenting each word using all blank tiles, or using a combination of one letter tile and blank tiles to represent the sound segments in the word.

The second activity each day was selected from a variety of *segmentation-related activities*. For example, the teacher might select a sound categorization game adapted from Bradley and Bryant (1983, 1985). Using pictures of words that rhymed or that shared initial, final, or medial sounds, the teacher would display three pictures with shared sounds and one picture that did not belong. The children would select the one that did not belong and explain their choice. An alternative activity was what Elkonin, a Russian psychologist, called "sound analysis" (1963, 1973). The children were given a picture of a word to be segmented (e.g., *leg*) and were taught to move disks into boxes at the bottom of the page as the word was pronounced slowly. The number of boxes corresponded to the number of sound segments in the word. In another segmentation-related task, children learned to hold up a finger for each sound in a spoken word. The children also had an opportunity to practice blending activities by correcting "mistakes" made by a puppet who told stories and sometimes mispronounced key words by segmenting them.

The third activity in each lesson emphasized *letter names and sounds*. The nine letters that were introduced during the seven week training (*a, m, t, i, s, r, u, b, f*) were selected because they generate a substantial number of real words. These letters, as well as illustrations of key words and phrases, were presented on 8½" by 11" cards. For example, the *r* card depicted a red *rooster* in *red running* shoes. A variety of games that emphasized these sound-symbol associations were introduced, and the children played one game each day (e.g., a Bingo game was used that required the child to match the letter on the game board to a spoken sound or the initial sound of a pictured object).

As indicated earlier, the children in the language activities control group spent the same amount of time in their small groups as the phoneme awareness children. However, in the language activities group, the children worked on more general language activities, such as vocabulary development and listening to stories. In addition, the children in this group completed *letter name and letter sound* activities that were identical to those just described for the phoneme awareness children.

Prior to the intervention, the three groups of children did not differ on age, sex, race, SES level, phoneme segmentation, letter name knowledge, letter sound knowledge, or reading ability as measured by scores on the Word Identification Subtest of the Woodcock Reading Mastery Tests. After the intervention, the phoneme awareness group outperformed both control groups on phoneme segmentation, on reading (as measured by the word identification subtest of the Woodcock and a list of 21 phonetically regular words developed for this study), and on a developmental spelling test created for this study. It is important to note that, after the intervention, both the phoneme awareness group and the language activities group did not differ from each other on letter sound knowledge (both groups had received identical instruction in letter sounds), and both groups significantly outperformed the no intervention control group on letter sound knowledge. However, only the phoneme awareness group significantly outperformed the no intervention control group in phoneme segmentation, reading, and spelling. An increase in letter sound knowledge, by itself, did not appear to have an impact on phoneme segmentation, reading, or spelling. We conclude that it is the *combination* of phoneme awareness training and learning to connect the sound segments to letters that makes a difference.

Thus, we now had additional evidence to document the positive effect on reading and spelling of training groups of kindergarten children in phoneme awareness. However, in this study (Ball and Blachman 1988, 1991) and in several of the others reviewed (Bradley and Bryant 1983, 1985; Cunningham 1990), the children received their instruction outside the regular classroom from specially trained teachers who were brought to the schools by the researchers. If we believe that instruction in phoneme awareness is an important ingredient in the kindergarten classroom, as many have suggested (see, for example, Adams 1990; Blachman 1989; Juel 1988), then we need to demonstrate the effectiveness of these activities when they are provided by regular kindergarten teachers to small groups of children within their classrooms.

To investigate this model of instruction, I received a three-year grant from the National Center for Learning Disabilities (formerly the Foundation for Children with Learning Disabilities) and embarked on a project to train inner-city kindergarten teachers and teaching assistants to provide this instruction in their classrooms (Blachman et al. 1991). Eighty-four treatment children (drawn from all 10 of the kindergarten classrooms in two low-income, inner-city schools in upstate New York) and 75 control children (drawn from all 8 of the kindergarten classrooms in two demographically comparable schools) participated in the study. The kindergarten teachers and teaching assistants participated in a series of seven, two-hour inservice workshops to learn how to provide the phoneme awareness program. During the workshops, they had opportunities to practice activities to use in their classrooms and to share questions and concerns about the program and the needs of individual children.

The treatment children met in small groups of four or five in their regular classrooms, with either their kindergarten teacher or teaching assistant providing the intervention (adapted from Ball and Blachman 1988, 1991). Each small group met for 15 to 20 minutes a day, four days a week for 11 weeks, and each phoneme awareness lesson consisted of the three steps previously described: *say-it-and-move-it, a segmentation-*

related activity, and letter name and letter sound training. Because the intervention in this study was an expanded version of our earlier program (this intervention was eleven weeks instead of seven), we were able to extend the *say-it-and-move-it* activities by using more letter tiles during the last three weeks of the intervention. Whereas in the earlier study (Ball and Blachman 1988, 1991) children used, at most, one letter tile plus blank tiles to represent a three-phoneme word, some children in this study progressed to using letter tiles to represent each sound in a three-phoneme real word (e.g., *sat*). Children without mastery of letter sounds continued to use blank tiles throughout the intervention.

To have a better appreciation of the children involved in this study, it is important to remember that both groups (as stated earlier) were from comparable low-income, inner-city schools (86% of the treatment children and 83% of the control children received free or supported lunch). Prior to the intervention, the children in the two groups did not differ on age, sex, race, SES, phoneme segmentation, letter name knowledge, letter sound knowledge, or reading (as measured by the Word Identification Subtest of the Woodcock Reading Mastery Tests–Revised). In addition, both groups had extremely limited knowledge of the alphabet prior to the intervention, demonstrating knowledge on our pretest of an average of only two letter sounds. Yet, after the intervention, the treatment children significantly outperformed the control children on phoneme segmentation, letter name knowledge, letter sound knowledge, two of three reading measures, and a measure of invented spelling. Specifically, the treatment children were able to read more phonetically regular real words and nonwords (added to control for the small pool of real words some children were exposed to during the last few weeks of the intervention) and to represent more of the sounds in the five words dictated on our developmental spelling measure (lap, sick, pretty, train, and elephant). Thus, the treatment children were able to apply their skill in phoneme awareness, along with their awareness of how the sound segments connect to print, to beginning reading and writing activities. For example, when asked to spell the word *sick*, although none of the treatment or control children spelled it correctly, 32% of the treatment children represented all of the phonemes with conventional letters (e.g., *sik, sic*). None of the control children achieved this level of representation. The treatment children appeared to have at least a beginning understanding of how print maps to speech—an understanding that had yet to be achieved by the control children. Perhaps most important is the fact that the treatment children were taught in their regular classrooms by their kindergarten teachers and teaching assistants, as part of an otherwise typical kindergarten curriculum, before any of the children had an opportunity to fail in reading and spelling.

After Phonological Awareness—Then What?

Once a level of phonological awareness has been achieved (as measured, for example, by the ability to segment one-, two-, and three-phoneme items), where do we go next? We chose to follow our kindergarten phoneme awareness program with a first grade reading program that would explicitly build on this awareness (Blachman et al. in preparation). After a review of the segmentation and blending activities introduced in kindergarten, our first graders followed a five-step, code-emphasis reading lesson that had been used successfully in other inner-city schools (Blachman 1987). This program was developed specifically to provide classroom teachers with an alternative to programs, such as a traditional basal program, which often ignore the alphabetic principle.

The treatment children met with their first grade teachers each day and participated in a five-part reading lesson.

1. First, teachers briefly reviewed sound-symbol associations with the children (spending only two or three minutes on this activity). It was during this part of the lesson that a new sound was introduced.
2. Next, the teacher emphasized phoneme analysis and blending skills using a technique suggested by Slingerland (1971) to help children synthesize sounds without resorting to letter-by-letter blending. Each child used a small pocket-chart, called a sound board, to manipulate letters. The teacher slowly pronounced a word, such as *sat*, emphasizing the medial vowel. The child repeated the word, listened for the vowel, and then selected the appropriate letter (the vowels were color-coded to facilitate recognition) from the top pocket and moved it to the lower tier of the chart. The teacher then repeated the entire word and asked the child to locate the letter that represented the initial sound and then locate the letter that represented the final sound. The child then read the entire word. The teacher might then ask the children to change *sat* to *sam*, *sam* to *sad*, and *sad* to *mad*. Once new vowels were introduced, the children might be asked to change *sat* to *sit* and later, when blends were introduced, change *sit* to *slip*. Although one child was called on initially, all children in the group could make the words at the same time on their sound boards.
3. Once children could construct a pool of phonetically regular words

on the sound board (e.g., closed syllable words, such as *tag* and *lap*), these words were put on flash cards to be practiced for automatic recognition. High-frequency sight words (e.g., *said*) were also introduced at this point in the lesson. Again, as with the review of sound-symbol associations (step 1 in this lesson plan), this step of the lesson was also meant to be a brief review (2 to 3 minutes) to help children get ready to read these words in context.

4. The next step in the lesson was story reading. This step was emphasized, both in terms of time spent reading each day and also opportunities to read. For example, if a teacher had time to do only part of the lesson on a given day, story reading was the recommended focus of that lesson. The children used phonetically controlled readers (*Primary Phonics* series from Educators Publishing Service), stories from basal readers (the workbooks were not used), and popular trade books.

5. Finally, each lesson ended with a written dictation activity using words that had been produced earlier on the sound board and also words and sentences from the phonetically controlled readers. Once the children could comfortably read closed syllable words (e.g., *jet, hat*), the other five syllable patterns were introduced one at a time (i.e., open syllables, such as *be* and *my*; final "e" syllables, such as *hike* and *plane*; vowel team syllables, such as *rain, coat,* and *moist*; vowel plus "r" syllables, such as *car* and *corn*; and consonant *le* syllables, such as ta*ble* and han*dle*). The control children used a traditional basal reading program that emphasized whole-word memorization and did not provide the same systematic instruction in breaking the code.

At the end of the first grade year, the treatment children, who had now completed both the kindergarten phoneme awareness program and a first grade reading program that emphasized the alphabetic code, significantly outperformed the control children on posttest measures of phoneme segmentation, letter names, letter sounds, three measures of reading, our developmental spelling test (expanded to ten words), and a standardized spelling measure. In addition, fewer children in the treatment group were retained at the end of first grade, and fewer treatment children were referred for Chapter I remedial reading classes. Children who completed the code-emphasis program (either at the end of first grade or during their second grade year) were then placed in the basal program used by the school district. Thus, once the code-emphasis program was completed, our original treatment children began to receive the same reading instruction as the control children. We are continuing to monitor the reading achievement of the children who were in our original treatment and control groups. Our preliminary results from testing, conducted at the end of the second grade year, indicate that the significant reading superiority of the treatment children has been maintained. For the children involved in our study (a population of low-income children from inner-city schools, who had limited knowledge about the alphabet prior to their kindergarten participation in this study), an early emphasis on phonological awareness, followed by a code-emphasis approach to reading in first grade, has resulted in reading achievement that is significantly greater than that of the children who did not participate in this program.

PROVIDING FOR INDIVIDUAL
DIFFERENCES IN PHONOLOGICAL AWARENESS

There are, of course, many options for the type of reading program that follows an early emphasis on phonological awareness, and more of the options need to be carefully evaluated. What would appear to be crucial, however, is that "teachers understand the need to provide for individual differences in the phonological abilities that are required for reading in an alphabetic system" (Liberman and Shankweiler 1991, p. 14). This means, for one thing, making sure that all children learn about the segmental nature of speech and how print maps to speech. Although many children will make these discoveries on their own, by playing oral language games, such as rhyming (Maclean, Bryant, and Bradley 1987; Bryant et al. 1989), by repeated opportunities to connect printed and spoken words when being read to, and by opportunities to write, many other children will not be so fortunate. Some children will not have the necessary preschool exposure to language play and early literacy experiences that trigger these associations. Still other children, because of differences or deficiencies in phonological ability (many of whom may be labeled learning or reading disabled), will not discover the connections between print and speech on their own, *even* if they have the important preschool literacy experiences and opportunities to play with oral language. We have a responsibility to teach both groups of children, as well as those who are fortunate enough to learn to read regardless of the method.

An early emphasis on phonological awareness, using some of the activities described in this chapter, appears to put children in a better position to take advantage of reading and spelling instruction. Children who understand the segmental nature of speech, and who understand how the phonological segments are represented by the letters of an alphabetic writing system, have been shown repeatedly to be more successful in reading and spelling acquisition than children who lack this awareness. As Juel (1988) found when she followed the reading development of 54 children from first to fourth grade, the poorest readers at the end of fourth grade were the ones who began first grade with little phonemic awareness. As a result, they did not develop good decoding skills in first grade. Without good word recognition skills, Juel found that these children were the ones who disliked reading and did less of it, losing valuable opportunities for vocabulary growth and for exposure to new concepts and ideas. This vicious cycle (described eloquently by Stanovich 1986) is what we would like to try to prevent, by making sure that all children develop the phonological awareness that will enable them to understand how print maps to speech.

REFERENCES

Adams, M.J. 1990. *Beginning to Read: Thinking and Learning about Print.* Cambridge, MA: The MIT Press.

Anderson, R., Hiebert, E., Scott, J., and Wilkinson, I. (Eds.). 1985. *Becoming a Nation of Readers: The Report of the Commission on Reading.* Washington, DC: National Institute of Education.

Ball, E.W., and Blachman, B.A. 1988. Phoneme segmentation training: Effect on reading readiness. *Annals of Dyslexia* 38:208–25.

Ball, E.W., and Blachman, B.A. 1991. Does phoneme awareness training in kindergarten make a difference in early word recognition and developmental spelling? *Reading Research Quarterly* 26(1):49–66.

Benton, A.L. 1975. Developmental dyslexia: Neurological aspects. In *Advances in Neurology,* Vol. VII, ed. W.J. Friedlander. New York: Raven Press.

Blachman, B. 1984. Relationship of rapid naming ability and language analysis skill to kindergarten and first-grade reading achievement. *Journal of Educational Psychology* 76: 610–22.

Blachman, B.A. 1987. An alternative classroom reading program for learning disabled and other low-achieving children. In *Intimacy with Language: A Forgotten Basic in Teacher Education,* ed. R. Bowler. Baltimore: The Orton Dyslexia Society.

Blachman, B. 1989. Phonological awareness and word recognition: Assessment and intervention. In *Reading Disabilities: A Developmental Language Perspective,* eds. A.G. Kamhi and H.W. Catts. Boston: College-Hill Press.

Blachman, B.A. In press. Early intervention for children's reading problems: Clinical applications of the research in phonological awareness. *Topics in Language Disorders.*

Blachman, B. A., Ball, E., Black, S., and Tangel, D. 1991. Promising practices for improving beginning reading instruction: Teaching phoneme awareness in the kindergarten classroom. Manuscript submitted for publication.

Blachman, B.A., Ball, E., Black, S., and Tangel D. In preparation. Promising practices for beginning reading instruction in first and second grade classrooms.

Blachman, B., and James, S. 1986. A longitudinal study of metalinguistic abilities and reading achievement in primary grade children. Paper presented at the meeting of the International Academy for Research in Learning Disabilities, Northwestern University, October 1986, Evanston, IL.

Bradley, L. 1988. Making connections in learning to read and spell. *Applied Cognitive Psychology* 2:3–18.

Bradley, L., and Bryant, P. 1983. Categorizing sounds and learning to read: A causal connection. *Nature* 30:419–21.

Bradley, L., and Bryant, P. 1985. *Rhyme and Reason in Reading and Spelling.* Ann Arbor: University of Michigan Press.

Bryant, P.E., Bradley, L., MacLean, M., and Crossland, J. 1989. Nursery rhymes, phonological skills and reading. *Journal of Child Language* 16:407–428.

Chall, J.S. 1989. Learning to read: The great debate 20 years later: A response to "Debunking the great phonics myth." *Phi Delta Kappan* 70:521–38.

Cunningham, A.E. 1990. Explicit v. implicit instruction in phonemic awareness. *Journal of Experimental Child Psychology* 50(3):429–44.

Durkin, D. 1989. *Teaching Them to Read.* Boston: Allyn and Bacon.

Elkonin, D.B. 1963. The psychology of mastering the elements of reading. In *Educational Psychology in the U.S.S.R.*, eds. B. Simon and J. Simon. London: Rutledge & Kegan Paul.

Elkonin, D.B. 1973. U.S.S.R. In *Comparative Reading*, ed. J. Downing. New York: MacMillan.

Feitelson, D., and Goldstein, Z. 1986. Patterns of book ownership and reading to young children in Israeli school-oriented and nonschool-oriented families. *Reading Teacher* 39:924–30.

Fox, B., and Routh, D.K. 1984. Phonemic analysis and synthesis as word attack skills: Revisited. *Journal of Educational Psychology* 76(6):1059–1061.

Freebody, P., and Byrne, B. 1988. Word-reading strategies in elementary school children: Relations to comprehension, reading time, and phonemic awareness. *Reading Research Quarterly* 23(4):441–53.

Gleitman, L.R., and Rozin, P. 1973. Teaching reading by use of a syllabary. *Reading Research Quarterly* 8:447–83.

Goodman, K.S. 1986. *What's Whole in Whole Language: A Parent-Teacher Guide.* Portsmouth, NH: Heinemann.

Goodman, K.S., and Goodman, Y.M. 1979. Learning to read is natural. In *Theory and Practice of Early Reading*, Vol. 1, eds. L.B. Resnick and P.A. Weaver. Hillsdale, NJ: Lawrence Erlbaum Associates.

Heath, S.B. 1983. *Ways with Words.* Cambridge: Cambridge University Press.

Juel, C. 1988. Learning to read and write: A longitudinal study of 54 children from first through fourth grades. *Journal of Educational Psychology* 80(4):437–47.

Juel, C., Griffith, P., and Gough, P. 1986. Acquisition of literacy: A longitudinal study of children in first and second grade. *Journal of Educational Psychology* 78:243–55.

Kamhi, A.G., and Catts, H.W. (eds.). 1989. *Reading Disabilities: A Developmental Language Perspective.* Boston: College-Hill Press.

Kantrowitz, B. 1990, Fall/Winter. The reading wars. *Newsweek* (Special Issue), pp. 8, 9, 12, 14.

Kavanagh, J.F., and Mattingly, I.G. (Eds.). 1972. *Language by Ear and by Eye: The Relationships Between Speech and Reading*. Cambridge, MA: The MIT Press.

Larsen, S.C., and Hammill, D. 1975. The relationship of selected visual perceptual abilities to school learning. *Journal of Special Education* 2:281–91.

Liberman, A.M., Cooper, F.S., Shankweiler, D., and Studdert-Kennedy, M. 1967. Perception of the speech code. *Psychological Review* 74:731–61.

Liberman, I.Y. 1971. Basic research in speech and lateralization of language: Some implications for reading disability. *Bulletin of The Orton Society* 21:72–87.

Liberman, I.Y. 1983. A language-oriented view of reading and its disabilities. In *Progress in Learning Disabilities*, Vol. 5, ed. H. Myklebust. New York: Grune & Stratton.

Liberman, I.Y., and Liberman, A.M. 1990. Whole language vs. code emphasis: Underlying assumptions and their implications for reading instruction. *Annals of Dyslexia* 40:51–76.

Liberman, I.Y., and Shankweiler, D. 1991. Phonology and beginning reading: A tutorial. In *Learning to Read: Basic Research and Its Implications*, eds. L. Rieben and C.A. Perfetti. Hillsdale, NJ: Lawrence Erlbaum Associates.

Lundberg, I., Frost, J., and Peterson, O. 1988. Effects of an extensive program for stimulating phonological awareness in preschool children. *Reading Research Quarterly* 23(3):263–84.

Lundberg, I., Olofsson, A., and Wall, S. 1980. Reading and spelling skill in the first school years predicted from phonemic awareness skills in kindergarten. *Scandinavian Journal of Psychology* 21:159–73.

MacLean, M., Bryant, P., and Bradley, L. 1987. Rhymes, nursery rhymes, and reading in early childhood. *Merrill-Palmer Quarterly* 33:255–81.

Mann, V. 1984. Longitudinal prediction and prevention of early reading difficulty. *Annals of Dyslexia* 34:117–36.

Mann, V.A., and Liberman, I.Y. 1984. Phonological awareness and verbal short-term memory: Can they presage early reading problems? *Journal of Learning Disabilities* 17:592–99.

Olofsson, A., and Lundberg, I. 1983. Can phonemic awareness be trained in kindergarten? *Scandinavian Journal of Psychology* 24:35–44.

Shankweiler, D., and Liberman, I.Y. 1989. *Phonology and Reading Disability: Solving the Reading Puzzle*. Ann Arbor: The University of Michigan Press.

Share, D.J., Jorm, A.F., Maclean, R., and Mathews, R. 1984. Sources of individual differences in reading achievement. *Journal of Educational Psychology* 76(6):466–77.

Slingerland, B.H. 1971. *A Multi-sensory Approach to Language Arts for Specific Language Disability Children: A Guide for Primary Teachers*. Cambridge, MA: Educators Publishing Service.

Spache, G. 1961. Children's vision and their reading success. *Journal of the California Optometric Association* 29(5):3–4.

Stanovich, K.E. 1986. Matthew effects in reading: Some consequences of individual differences in the acquisition of literacy. *Reading Research Quarterly* 21:360–407.

Stanovich, K.E., Cunningham, A.E., and Cramer, B.B. 1984. Assessing phonological awareness in kindergarten children: Issues of task comparability. *Journal of Experimental Child Psychology* 38:175–90.

Stedman, L.C., and Kaestle, C.E. 1987. Literacy and reading performance in the United States from 1880 to the present. *Reading Research Quarterly* 22:8–46.

Teale, W.H. 1986. Home background and young children's literacy development. In *Emergent Literacy: Writing and Reading*, eds. W.H. Teale and E. Sulzby. Norwood, NJ: Ablex Publishing Corporation.

Torneus, M. 1984. Phonological awareness and reading: A chicken and egg problem? *Journal of Educational Psychology* 76(6):1346–1358.

Treiman, R., and Baron, J. 1983. Phonemic-analysis training helps children benefit from spelling-sound rules. *Memory & Cognition* 11:382–89.

Vellutino, F.R. 1977. Alternative conceptualizations of dyslexia: Evidence in support of a verbal-deficit hypothesis. *Harvard Educational Review* 47:334–45.

Vellutino, F.R. 1979. *Dyslexia: Theory and Research.* Cambridge, MA: The MIT Press.

Vellutino, F.R. 1987. Dyslexia. *Scientific American* 256(3):34–41.

Vellutino, F.R., and Scanlon, D.M. 1987. Phonological coding, phonological awareness, and reading ability: Evidence from a longitudinal and experimental study. *Merrill-Palmer Quarterly* 33(3):321–63.

Williams, J. 1979. The ABD's of reading: A program for the learning disabled. In *Theory and Practice of Early Reading*, Vol. 3, eds. L.B. Resnick and P.A. Weaver. Hillsdale, NJ: Lawrence Erlbaum Associates.

Williams, J. 1980. Teaching decoding with an emphasis on phoneme analysis and phoneme blending. *Journal of Educational Psychology* 72:1–15.

Williams, J. 1987. Educational treatments for dyslexia at the elementary and secondary levels. In *Intimacy with Language: A Forgotten Basic in Teacher Education*, ed. R. Bowler. Baltimore: The Orton Dyslexia Society.

Chapter • 3

Acquiring the Linguistic Code for Reading
A Model for Teaching and Learning

Ellis Richardson and Barbara DiBenedetto

Considered from a simple perspective, language communication occurs in two directions, input and output, and in two modalities, visual and auditory. We speak of expressive language (output) and receptive language (input). Expressive language may be oral (spoken) or visual (written) while receptive language involves either audition (listening) or vision (reading).

The acquisition of oral language, the development of phonological awareness, and the relationship of these two skills to reading are discussed in the preceding two chapters of this volume. For our purposes, there are two points worth raising regarding the development of the language processes: (1) Children acquire language through a complex interactive and integrated process, and (2) Children learn to understand language input and express themselves orally without formal instruction.

At five or six years of age, the child in our culture is expected to begin to acquire facility with language in the visual modality (reading and writing). While it is clear that there are important differences between learning to understand spoken language and learning to read (Wardhaugh 1976), some children come to the task of learning to read better equipped than do others. The reasons for this are wide and varied, but verbal stimulation is clearly among them (Milner 1963). Children who come from enriched verbal environments have been read to often, have experienced extensive verbal interaction with adults, and are better prepared for learning to read than are those who have had less language exposure. Those who are unusually talented may appear to acquire the ability to read through simple exposure in the same way that they acquired auditory language. The type of formal instruction that such children receive, indeed, instruction itself, seems to be irrelevant.

Unfortunately, this is not the case with most of the children in our nation. Many have never listened to adults read or learned the alphabet, and, among those who have, the vast majority are not so talented that they can learn to read in this manner. Exposure to visually encoded language is extremely limited as compared to exposure to auditory language. Furthermore, written language is a great deal more formally constrained than is spoken language and serves different functions (Vygotsky 1962). Thus, children do not acquire the ability to read and write in the spontaneous way that they learn to listen and speak. It falls on the educational system to devise some formal method of teaching children to read and write. The process is generally begun in kindergarten (at five years of age) where children begin to learn about the alphabet (e.g., that letters have names and sounds, that letters are used to form words). The formal task of teaching children to read usually begins in the first grade and continues over the next few years. However, history has shown us that it is not easy to devise a formal method for teaching all children to read and write.

HISTORICAL PERSPECTIVE

A History of Reading Failure

At the beginning of this century there was a heavy emphasis on letter sounds and phonics. Children were taught to respond to individual letter units. By the 1930s, in response to developments in the field of educational psychology, phonics approaches fell into disfavor. How was a child expected to become excited about this new language modality with such meaningless material? (For example, "In Adam's fall we sinned all.") This gave rise to an emphasis on graphic processing (the sight-word approach) and a near complete abandonment of attention to letter-sound units as a key to learning how to read. The sight-word approach allowed educators to provide initial reading experiences that were thought to be richer than those provided by the phonics approach.

After Flesch (1955) made public the abysmal failure of the sight-word approach in his book, *Why Johnny Can't Read,* a number of new phonics programs were developed. Linguistic programs, which stressed letter sounds in spelling patterns as opposed to individual sound units, also appeared in our schools. The standard basal-reader programs began to offer token phonics as a part of their sight-word approaches, but there was no systematic attempt to convert these big money makers into programs that were really based on letter sounds as an instructional method. Still, all too many Johnnys (and Susys) were not learning how to read and the educational world searched for yet another answer to the problem.

More recently, whole language approaches have purported to be the solution. The whole language philosophy stresses reading as a complex meaningful act involving the interaction of thought and language, the intent of which is the reconstruction of meaning (i.e., the message in the graphic input) (Goodman 1976a). Thus, whole language approaches to teaching reading emphasize the context and intent of ongoing text rather than individual words or letters. Furthermore, as the term *whole language* implies, such approaches emphasize reading as a function that is interactive with all other language processes—not a distinctly separate behavior.

All of these approaches to teaching reading have strong points. Phonics and the ability to sound out words certainly help a learner in the mammoth task of mastering reading. Sight words can be readily learned even by reading disabled children (Rozin, Poritsky, and Sotsky 1971) and this approach does have the potential for generating more interesting early reading matter. Linguistic approaches take into consideration the fact that sounds shift according to spelling pattern. Finally, there is great value in the recognition that reading is, in the end, a naturalistic language act that can follow from and build upon the rich language base that children bring to the first grade.

However, despite years of shifting approaches to the teaching of reading, many children in our schools are simply not learning how to read. Why have we failed so many children for so many years? Although a wide variety of contributory factors may be cited, we believe that there are three general reasons:

1. Each of the approaches that has held sway over the years has strong points, but none takes into account the full range of fundamental processes that are involved in and required for learning to read effectively.
2. In the face of failure, the teacher has been blamed and reading programs have increasingly sought to relieve teachers of the responsi-

bility for teaching. Such programs require teachers to follow elaborate procedures and specific scripts that are designed to do the job. This deprives teachers of the ability to teach effectively, especially with regard to their ability to address the needs of individual children.

3. While much noise is generated as a result of the perception that so many children are not learning how to read, little attention is paid to the individual child who is failing. Year after year, children receive labels based on standardized test scores that are virtually useless from a diagnostic-prescriptive point of view. Children are then passed on from grade to grade or, finally, if they fall so far behind that their test scores cannot be located on the norm-referenced table, placed in special education environments. By this time, the deficits are so great as to be overwhelming to both teacher and student.

We believe that if the first problem is addressed effectively, and in such a way that the second problem is avoided, the severity of the third problem will be greatly reduced. That is, if the teaching of reading is approached from a broad perspective that integrates all of the fundamental processes involved in reading, and if the approach is flexible enough to allow teachers the freedom to teach, the specific needs of individual children will be met and far fewer children will emerge from their elementary school years as reading failures.

Reading-Process Models

Interest in models designed to explicate the basic processes involved in reading began to develop in the late 1960s as a result of the recognition of the fact that large numbers of otherwise normal children were failing to learn how to read. Kavanagh (1976) proposed that "An understanding of what may interfere with normal reading might be achieved through a better understanding of the basic processes involved and by determining how this complex language-related skill is normally acquired" (p. vii).

By the 1980s, a large array of reading-process models had emerged. Such models came from a wide variety of perspectives: psycholinguistic, developmental, information processing and, more recently, neurological (see Duffy and Geschwind 1985). Given that the mission of model builders has been to explicate this complex language-related skill as a basis for research, such models are generally (and necessarily) extremely detailed and complex.

As with everything related to the field of reading, model building has generated a great deal of controversy. For example, we have two seemingly diametrically opposed models: On the one hand, there are the word-by-word, left-to-right, serial models, such as Gough's (1976) model. On the other, we have Goodman's (1976b) "psycholinguistic guessing game," which appears to dismiss the notion that reading involves the apprehension of individual letters or words in any seriate fashion. More recently, interactive information processing models have been studied (see Lesgold and Perfetti 1981). This research has moved us considerably closer to the goal cited at the outset of the development of reading-process models that was outlined by Kavanagh almost 20 years ago (i.e., a better understanding of what *goes wrong* when people fail to learn how to read).

However, despite this wide variety of models, there is no model, to our knowledge, that has been used to generate a *specific* approach to the teaching of reading. The first problem with translating most existing reading-process models into instructional procedures is their complexity. For example, how does a teacher make use of the knowledge that communication occurs on three structural levels (surface, semantic, and deep) as depicted in Ruddell's (1976) Systems of Communication Model? Similarly, what is a teacher to make of the "spreading activation mechanism" explicated by Rumelhart and McClelland (1981)? These detailed model components serve useful theoretical and research functions, but they are of questionable value with regard to instructional application. This is not the fault of the model builders. The purpose of constructing models has not been instructional application and, without such models, more simplified instruction-oriented models could not be constructed.

The second problem with translating existing reading models into instructional practice concerns the more global question of conflicting overall perspectives. Given that two or more informed sides in any controversy (and the sides in this controversy are informed) usually have something to contribute to a realistic assessment of reality, one might look for a model perspective that incorporates the best features of opposing positions.

In order for a reading-process model to have a useful instructional application it must be: (1) simple enough so that teaching behaviors can be linked to its components, and (2) eclectic enough so that most of what can be agreed upon regarding the processes of reading and learning how to read can be incorporated into its structure. Therefore, a detailed model of the reading process, although appropriate for theory-based research, is inappropriate as a basis for an instructional model.

In this chapter, we present a simplified model of the reading process that satisfies the above two criteria and can be used as a guide to teaching reading. We call this model-based approach to teaching reading the Integrated Skills Method (ISM) (Richardson 1989a). We then show how this model has been applied to the practical matter of teaching reading. Finally, we present results that have been obtained with the ISM in three different settings: (1) a clinic setting, (2) a special program for children identified as dyslexic, and (3) an elementary school setting.

A READING-PROCESS MODEL FOR INSTRUCTION

Figure 1 presents a model that can be used for understanding the most important facets of what happens when a person reads. We have used this model in teacher training and we always stress its logic and simplicity. Logically, reading must start with printed language, which is labeled as Graphic Input in the figure. That is, reading must start as a bottom-up process. No amount of cognition, prediction, or premonition will enable a reader to read without receiving graphic input. From an instructional point of view, we can manipulate a number of variables related to the graphic input (font, type size and style, lighting, distance). However, there are little hard data to guide us in making decisions regarding how to set these variables to maximize effective reading instruction. Nevertheless, if we are to teach someone to read, we must have graphic input—something for them to read.

Next, this graphic input must be received by the eye (Visual Reception in figure 1). Light patterns reflected from the graphic input are received by the eye where they pass through the lens, to the retina, and are encoded as neural impulses. Learners who have defective lenses will experience difficulty at this juncture. Alert teachers who are paying attention to the process of teaching, as opposed to performing required rituals, can recognize when a learner may be having difficulty seeing the graphic input and recommend that the learner be examined for corrective lenses.

There are some who feel that the coordination and strength of the eye muscles may interfere with visual reception of the graphic input. Programs of eye exercises have been used to try to improve the student's ability to learn to read. Others aver that defects in scotopic vision may have adverse effects on visual reception. They recommend that tinted glasses be worn. Clearly, sharp and unequivocal images of the graphic input must be received by the retina for reading to proceed.

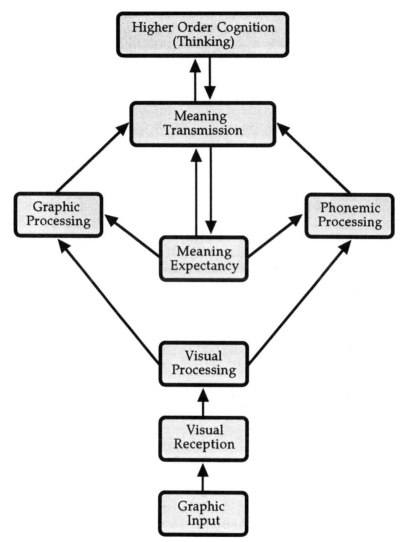

Figure 1. The ISM reading-process model.

Those of us who have suffered temporary reading impairment from developing far sightedness can appreciate the importance of this. However, with the important exception that a teacher may detect problems in visual reception in some learners, this aspect of the process is not in the teacher's control and has little to do with teaching reading.

Having impinged on the retina, the graphic input is encoded as neural impulses that travel along the optic nerve to the occipital lobe of the brain. Here they must be recognized as visual linguistic information and forwarded to the language centers of the brain. Very little is known about how this is accomplished. Some theories of reading disability and dyslexia have posited that faulty visual processing is a primary cause of the difficulty many children have in learning how to read (see Vellutino 1979). Given that available research has failed to reveal a link between reading disabilities and deficiencies in visual discrimination (see Liberman 1985), it is difficult to see such theories as credible. In any case, as the process of reading continues through visual processing, it is still essentially a bottom-up process and outside the control of the teacher.

Having reached the language centers of the brain, the information must be decoded as specific word units or phrases, at least to the degree that some sense can be made of the ongoing text. That is, sufficient amounts of text must be decoded so that meaning can be ascribed to the information that is received by the language centers. We know of only two ways in which this can be accomplished. The information may be recognized immediately as a meaningful word or phrase (Graphic Processing in figure 1), or it may be processed as letter sounds or letter-sound patterns to derive a meaningful word sound (Phonemic Processing in the figure). It is at this point that instructional methodologies enter the picture and that teachers may exert an influence on the learner (i.e., teach).

It is clear that words may be recognized with minimal regard for the sounds associated with the letters composing them. When we see the word *cafe*, for example, we are rarely tempted to pronounce this word as though it rhymed with *safe*. We know the word, we know what it sounds like, and we know what it means. In figure 1, we refer to this as Graphic Processing. It is this facility for learning and recognizing words that is stressed by the sight-word approaches. In spite of the apparent failure of this methodology to teach everyone to read effectively, the power of this tool for teaching reading must not be passed over lightly.

Words that are not immediately recognized as having associated meanings must be processed through their constituent letters and associated sounds (Phonemic Processing in figure 1). The result of grapheme-phoneme processing is some hypothesis regarding word meaning. According to this model, when this meaning hypothesis has been formulated (Meaning Transmission in the figure), it is transmitted to Higher-Order Cognition, a fancy way of saying *thinking*.

Up to this point, we have been describing a purely bottom-up process. Much has been said in the reading-model literature about the distinction between various types of interactive and serial-stage models (see Levy 1981). The question seems to center on whether top-down and bottom-up processes occur simultaneously (e.g., Rumelhart 1977), in successive stages where information from one stage forms the data base for the next stage (e.g., LaBerge and Samuels 1976), or whether serial stages overlap to allow for interaction between lower-order feature processing and higher-order cognitive processing at some point during the reading process (e.g., Massaro 1977).

The model we describe may appear to have more in common with the serial-stage models because we describe lower-order processing as occurring prior to higher-order processing. However, we view this model as a combination of serial-stage and interactive models, as shall become apparent.

Once the meaning hypothesis has been transmitted for higher-order analysis, top-down processing has begun. The meaning hypothesis must be integrated into ongoing thought processes. It may be changed slightly to fit into the context of the ongoing thought or it may be evaluated and even rejected as not feasible within the context of ongoing thought. However, this is just the beginning of a very powerful aspect of reading as a process. Having received a meaning hypothesis and integrated it into ongoing thought, the higher-order center begins to send information down that influences the way the meaning transmission process responds to information received from graphic and phonemic processing. The meaning transmission process is given a framework for evaluating incoming information.

At this point, the top-down and bottom-up processes function interactively. The top-down information is used to create a set for receiving further inputs, called Meaning Expectancy in figure 1. Meaning expectancy exerts a powerful influence on the speed and accuracy of graphic and phonemic processing. Thus, the bottom-up processes that analyze the graphic input are driven by the top-down process of meaning expectancy. Words are not processed as isolated units, but rather as a part of an integrated flow of information.

This is not a process that must be taught. Children with normally developing speech are experts at this when communication is by ear. To illustrate this point, we give you a sound:

wa

This is a meaning unit, a word, but you have no context in which to interpret it. When we add the sound *'dle*:

wa 'dle

. . . you may ascribe a meaning. *Waddle,* something a duck does. Now we add another unit, *e* (long *e* sound):

wa 'dle e

This blows the hypothesis about the duck and we are again stuck with what appears to be nonsense. Now one more unit: *doo.*

wa 'dle e doo

If you have failed to form stable hypotheses regarding the meanings of each of the four sound units at this point, we can insure that you form accurate hypotheses by giving these sounds more context:

wa 'dl e doo if he looses his job?

Now the meaning unit associated with each sound unit becomes apparent:

What Will He Do?

We are usually unaware that we are formulating hypotheses regarding the utterances we hear. The sounds are unconsciously mapped onto the segmented bits of language that we understand as words and this allows us to derive meaning. It is the *expectancy of meaning* that drives the process of comprehending what we hear.

Meaning expectancy functions in an integrated way with bottom-up (graphic and phonemic) processes in reading in a way that parallels its function in listening. In teaching reading, we want to teach beginners how to derive meaning from visual input. Children use meaning expectancy as a tool for understanding what they hear even before they learn to speak. However, the application of meaning expectancy to visual language reception is new to beginning readers. What must be taught is the bottom-up process and how to integrate this new source of language information with the already well-developed skill of applying meaning expectancy to incoming linguistic information. Children must be taught to recognize printed words as meaningful units (graphic processing), to use the sound information encoded in letter strings to generate meaningful units (phonemic processing), and to apply their well-developed language skills to drive these processes (meaning expectancy).

If one ignores the function of meaning expectancy in teaching reading (as do many approaches that focus on the decoding of individual words—and this includes both whole-word and phonics approaches), one is ignoring a part of the language communication process that is absolutely essential in both reading and listening. However, on the opposite extreme, if one ignores the graphic and phonemic processes in teaching reading (as some proponents of whole language approaches seem to advocate), the learner lacks substance upon which to formulate the original meaning hypothesis. That is, there are insufficient data to be tested or retested by meaning expectancy.

The teacher must also recognize that these processes function interactively and, to a large degree, simultaneously. Although the model shows graphic and phonemic processing occurring *prior* to the top-down processes that feed meaning expectancy, this is only true to the degree that it is necessary to perceive graphic input before higher-order processors can come into play. Higher-order cognition frequently primes meaning expectancy even before graphic input begins to be perceived. (It's a book about horses. It's a newspaper article about the gubernatorial election. It's a sign directing us to a much-needed comfort station.) Furthermore, when print is difficult to read, the more information we have to create meaning expectations, the better we perceive the actual input. (Again, far-sighted individuals will appreciate the truth of this point immediately.) Meaning expectancy functions as an essential component of what, in computer programing terminology, we call a feed-back loop. Thus, there is no denying that, to a large degree, what we see when we read is what we expect to see. However, proficient reading is also largely a question of how accurately we are able to process the original input. If the salient characteristics of the data base (i.e., the actual letters and words) are processed inaccurately, expectations will necessarily be inaccurate.

One final point should be made with regard to this model's application, particularly because it is the source of so much acrimonious controversy in recent years (see Edelsky 1990; McKenna, Robinson, and Miller 1990a, 1990b). This has to do with what we will dub "the war between the skill-builders and the whole-language theorists." Any model that posits subcomponents of the reading act that function sequentially leads to an instructional model that includes teaching reading sub-skills. At the most atomized extreme, this would be a program that "builds skills" and assumes that Skill A (e.g., letter-shape discrimination) must be learned before Skill B (e.g., the names of all 26 letters), Skill B before Skill C (e.g., the sounds of the consonants), and so on. (Basal-reader programs tend to function this way as do many phonics programs.) One consequence of this approach is that children may be required to spend months practicing "prereading" skills before they are permitted to do anything that resembles reading text. Another consequence is that teachers may be required to engage in elaborate teaching routines to teach skills that are not prerequisite to, or even in evidence in, the materials that the students are to read for that lesson.

When one views the reading performance of proficient readers, the subskills or components of the reading process posited by the skill builders are not very much in evidence. Proficient readers do not sound out words nor do they appear to perceive accurately and precisely each word individually while engaged in the reading of ongoing text. These observations have led to the view that reading subskills are not important. Some advocates of whole language approaches seem to suggest that subskills should not be taught *at all*.

However, as Lesgold and Curtis (1981) have stated, a lower-order skill does not need to be included in the performance of a higher-order function for it to be prerequisite to the performance of that function. It may be prerequisite to the *efficient* performance or to the *learning* of that function. Given so much evidence that poor readers exhibit weak phonological encoding skills (Vellutino 1979), we feel that this is undoubtedly the case with regard to the subcomponents of our model, particularly phonemic processing.

How does this relate to the model's application to teaching reading? First, we recognize that certain subskills are prerequisite to both learning to read and efficient reading. These are represented by graphic and phonemic processing in the model. However, the skills involved in using these processes should not be taught in a fragmented or sequential way. That is, they should not be viewed as isolated functions divorced from the total reading act. Reading and, *indeed,* learning to read, even at the most rudimentary levels, involve all of these functions simultaneously. Six-year-old children being taught to read the simplest sentences should learn, at the outset, to use the entire microcosm of skills that are employed by the proficient reader.

APPLYING THE MODEL TO INSTRUCTION

To illustrate how this model is applied in instruction, we turn to a procedure we use in teacher training (Richardson 1989b). We place you in a position of being unable to read and then teach you to read. If you avoid translating these symbols into the letters that you already know, you will be able to better understand the task that a beginning reader faces.

We start by teaching you something about phonemic processing. This letter, ➤, makes a long *e* sound. If we put an /s/ sound symbolized by ▲, in front of two ➤s, we get the word, ▲➤➤. Pronounce the word, stressing the sounds, ▲▲▲➤➤➤.

Now we will add two words for graphic processing: the word *I* (☆) and the word *can* (✛●■). Now we can ask a question:

✛●■ ☆ ▲➤➤?

. . . and we can answer the question.

☆ ✛●■ ▲➤➤.

Let's add a name for fun. (The name is printed in standard orthography to simplify the demonstration.)

✛●■ Susan ▲➤➤? Susan✛●■ ▲➤➤.

✛●■ ☆ ▲➤➤ Susan? ☆ ✛●■ ▲➤➤ Susan.

Now we add another word for phonemic processing. This letter, ◯, makes the sound /m/, so when it comes before ➤ we get ◯➤. Pronounce it, stressing the sounds, ◯◯◯➤➤➤. This will help you remember it.

☆ ✛●■ ▲➤➤ Susan. ✛●■ Susan ▲➤➤ ◯➤?
Susan ✛●■ ▲➤➤ ◯➤.

Now we add another sight word for graphic processing. This word, ☐◆■, says *run*. Now you can read this:

✛●■ ☆ ☐◆■? ☆ ✛●■ ☐◆■.

✛●■ ☆ ▲ ➤➤ Susan ☐◆■? ☆ ✛●■ ▲➤➤ Susan ☐◆■.

✛●■ Susan ▲➤➤ ◯➤ ☐◆■? Susan ✛●■ ▲➤➤ ◯➤ ☐◆■.

If you have been following carefully, you should be able to read the above sentences with ease. In training workshops, we devote about six 15-minute sessions to this training exercise. Between these brief reading lessons we present material related to program design, teaching techniques, and classroom management. Figure 2 shows an example of a page of text that teachers can read when they have completed these six 15-minute sessions. In the process, the teachers learn a great deal about how children go about the difficult task of learning to read and they are able to teach better.

There are many reasons for including this exercise in teacher training. The teachers use many of the same learning tools that come naturally to the children and this helps them understand how to help the children learn more effectively and efficiently. The primary reason for

Figure 2. Page 12 of *Learning to Teach by Learning to Read* (reprinted from Richardson 1989b).

including it here is to illustrate the model in a graphic way. As you were learning to read, you were able to see the importance of both graphic and phonemic processing and the great advantage of putting words into a meaningful context immediately. This allows meaning expectancy to support word recognition at the outset. It is hoped that you also have seen how natural it is to invoke this language skill when reading is being learned and how it is necessary to integrate this process with bottom-up processing. That is, meaning expectancy should support the graphic and phonemic processes but not preempt them.

THE ISM INSTRUCTIONAL PROGRAM

The Three ISM Components

Now we turn our attention to an instructional program through which the teaching model is expressed, the Integrated Skills Method (ISM), which has evolved substantially since we first published an article describing it (Richardson and Bradley 1975). The program, which is described in detail by Richardson (1989a), includes three components (see figure 3): a component to teach the basic mechanics of reading and writing, another to encourage enjoyment in reading, and a third to teach children to apply their reading skills to other academic tasks.

The Linguistic Pattern Series. The primary *how to* of reading is handled by the *Linguistic Pattern Series* (Richardson 1989c), which we

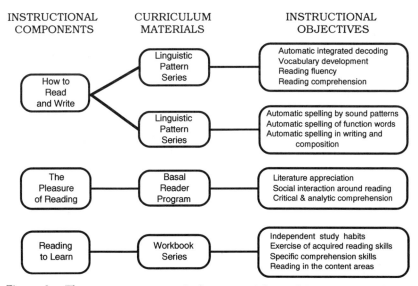

Figure 3. The components, curriculum materials, and instructional objectives of the ISM (reprinted from Richardson 1989a).

explore in some depth later. At this point, we direct the reader's attention to the instructional objectives of the *Linguistic Pattern Series*. The first objective is automatic, integrated decoding. That is, students are taught to integrate the bottom-up and top-down processes for automatic decoding. The series is also used to teach comprehension, vocabulary development, spelling, and writing.

The Basal Readers. Despite the general shortcomings of basal-reader programs, basal readers themselves are used to encourage reading for pleasure. Most contemporary basals include good stories that children can enjoy if they are not struggling with the text and if the stories are presented with spontaneity and animation. The vocabulary control feature of basal readers allows the teacher to select materials that are appropriate to the individual child's level of development. While we do not recommend that vocabulary control be taken to an extreme, it is important that the child be able to read enough of the words easily so that reading is not fragmented and, as a result, unpleasant. Thus, an appropriate level of text is one in which the vast majority of words are: (1) quickly recognized because they have been encountered previously and read numerous times, or (2) easily decoded because of previously acquired phonological information.

In ISM instruction, the readers are used purely as a source of literature. Accompanying teacher's guides and workbooks are not used. Progress in the basal readers can be coordinated with progress in the *Linguistic Pattern Series* in such a way that students will have little difficulty with the basal reader material. In the *Linguistic Pattern Series*, the students learn to integrate effectively graphic and phonemic processing with meaning expectancy in learning new words. This process is easily transferred to the basal readers where new words are learned as they arise in the context of the stories.

The Workbook Series. The third component of the ISM, which we have called Reading to Learn in figure 3, is supported by a series of workbooks. We use the the Barnell-Loft *Specific Skill Series* (Boning 1982) for several reasons. This series addresses nine skill areas (e.g., Drawing Conclusions, Using the Context), each of which is covered in a 50-page exercise book at each level of the program (see table I). The tasks presented by this series are encountered often in the content areas and they are similar to problems posed by most standardized tests.

The other advantage of the *Specific Skill Series* is the large amount of material that is keyed to specific reading levels, particularly the first-grade levels. A set of skill books is directed at each of the first-grade

Table I.   Specifications of the *Specific Skill Series*

The Sequence	
Picture Level	Preprimer
Preparatory Level	Primer
Level A	First Grade
Level B	Second Grade
Level C	Third Grade
Level D	Fourth Grade
Level E	Fifth Grade
. . . .	
Level L	Twelfth Grade

Skills Taught
1. Working With Sounds
2. Following Directions
3. Using the Context
4. Locating the Answer
5. Getting the Facts
6. Drawing Conclusions
7. Getting the Main Idea
8. Detecting the Sequence
9. Identifying Inferences

reader levels (preprimer, primer, and first reader), for a total of 27 books for first-grade instruction. This provides the teacher with reinforcing materials for students working at levels where such materials are difficult to find. After the first-grade levels, the series includes a single set of nine skill books for each grade level up through high school, so it is also quite comprehensive. Thus, this component helps students to cope in the content areas and to perform efficiently on standardized tests. It also presents students with a wealth of material that can be used for independent practice of newly acquired reading skills.

The Linguistic Pattern Series

The Content Sequence.   Because the teacher's primary task in reading instruction is to teach children how to read, the primary component of the ISM is the *Linguistic Pattern Series*. The *Linguistic Pattern Series* is organized into a number of levels that are defined by curriculum objectives rather than by grade level. Table II presents examples of the content taught by the *Linguistic Pattern Series* at each successive level. There is a readiness sequence called "Getting Ready" that

Table II.   Examples of Letters and Words Taught in the Curriculum Sequence of the Linguistic Pattern Series

Sequence		Level Content
Getting Ready	I	Letters: A, C, D, E, F, G, I, M, N, R, S, U Sight-Words: can, run, ride, see, sing, I
	II	Letters: B, H, J, L, O, P, T, W Pattern Words: see, he, me, we, be, bee, she, tree Sight-Words: horse, jump, play, fish, bicycle
Beginner	A	Pattern Words: see, he, me, we, be, bee, she, tree, free, Dee, Lee Sight-Words: can, run, ride, sing, I, jump, play, fish, bicycle
	B	Pattern Words: play, may, say, way, day, hay, today, away, stay, bay Sight-Words: the, not, you, did, like, do, all, that, from, in, up, down, by, at
	C	Pattern Words: my, by, why, lie, tie, try, pie, cry, sky, fly, spy, die, sly, shy Sight-Words: his, her, boy, girl, big, little, but, of, want, arm, is, are, could
	D	Pattern Words: king, sing, ring, wing, being, saying, trying, running, wanting Sight-Words: look, some, thing, something, stop, please, where, there
Introductory	1	flee, plea, meet, heed, sleep, screen, leak, meal, streak, bleak, squeal, scream
	2	leaning, screaming, speaking, sneaker, beaver, faster, steeper, sweeter, eager
	3	clay, spray, shook, brook, player, swaying, layer, ban, spun, tanner, stunning
Short Vowel I	4	scat, cram, scrap, shack, shatter, trapper, stand, brass, master, swagger
	5	steeple, baffle, straggle, dreamy, shaggy, crabby, gladly, vastly, happily
	6	chin, twig, skipper, glitter, ripple, slick, thick, bicker, picky, tickle, fiddle
	7	throb, chop, plod, shock, blond, throttle, jockey, snobbery, clodhopper, gossip
Short Vowel II	8	strut, snug, pluck, strum, chuckle, muggy, trumpet, stumble, crusty, mumble
	9	misconduct, disrupt, mansion, division, deduct, respond, abscond, adaption
	10	fret, wet, speck, swept, confession, dressy, member, objection, impending
	11	express, exceed, expensive, exaggeration, indestructible, expendable, prefix

teaches letter sounds and a few sight words and introduces the process of decoding words by sound patterns.

Children who are starting first grade and who have some idea about letter sounds and printed words would begin in the *Beginner Sequence*. In Level A, the students are taught to use initial consonants in decoding pattern words with the long *e* sound and they are taught a few sight words that are necessary for writing materials with a modicum of interest value. The long *e* pattern was selected as a starting point for two reasons. First, many fundamental vocabulary words are based on this pattern (*me, he, she,* etc.), and, second, it is easy for beginning readers to blend initial consonants with long vowel sounds. The primary guideline for selecting sight words for the *Beginner Sequence* was to introduce words that were required for using the pattern words in context. This way, when the more difficult-to-learn function words (e.g., *the, is, on, there*) are introduced, they are predictable from the meaning of the text and the learner's meaning expectancy aids in their acquisition. Level A also introduces a few sight words to form a basis for ideas, especially action words (e.g., *run, jump, sing*). Thereafter, most sight words are introduced for utility value (i.e., they are needed to provide a context for reading the pattern words).

Level B of the *Beginner Sequence* introduces a long *a* pattern using *ay* (see table II). Again, the automatic blending of initial consonants with the long vowel sound is the simplest approach to teaching children how letter sounds function in reading and many high-frequency basic vocabulary words use this pattern (e.g., *day, may, say*). Sight words continue to be introduced primarily to generate interesting and natural sentences for reading. It is important to recall in reviewing the curriculum sequence of the *Linguistic Pattern Series* that most of the teaching and learning occurs in the context of meaningful sentences, not in rote drilling.

Level C continues to teach the use of initial consonants in long vowel patterns by introducing long *i* patterns, but now the student is taught that two spellings are possible (*y* = long *i* and *ie* = long *i*). Again, these patterns generate many high-frequency words. In Level D, the *ing* pattern is introduced. Our experience has shown that this is a simple sound pattern for learners, it generates many useful and motivating words, and it provides a means of introducing polysyllabic word forms (e.g., *playing, seeing, crying, running*).

By the end of the *Beginner Sequence*, the student has a good idea of why letter sounds are important in reading, understands that letter sounds do not apply only to words that conform to a specific pattern (as in the short vowel trigram), and has learned a large number of the basic fabric words of the language. In brief, the beginning reader now has a very good idea of what learning to read is all about.

The *Introductory Sequence* is used with students who have already acquired a high first-grade reading level and, of course, with students who have completed the *Beginner Sequence*. The first two levels of this sequence are devoted to teaching the students to process long *e* words with two spellings (*ee* and *ea*) and with the final syllables (*er* and *ing*, see table II). Emphasis on vocabulary development is increased with attention to words such as *heed* and *bleak*. The third level of the *Introductory Sequence* teaches the idea that well-known sight words can be used to generate a host of other words (e.g., *look* helps us read *brook*, *shook*, and *nook*). One objective of this sequence is to teach the learner that all of the letters in words are important. Students learn to process initial consonants and blends, to process final consonants and blends, and to attend to final syllables. Most programs that stress letter sounds teach students to sound out short vowel trigrams. In contrast, the *Linguistic Pattern Series* teaches students to integrate the use of letter sounds with all other aspects of reading.

The next sequence, *Short Vowel I*, teaches the use of the short vowel patterns involving *a*, *i*, and *o*. It also introduces additional final syllables (*y*, *ly*, and *le*). Consistent with the philosophy of the ISM, virtually every word in the English language that conforms to these patterns is introduced. This sets the occasion to emphasize vocabulary development with words such as *baffle*, *throttle*, *shaggy*, and *twitter*. The sequence exploits prior knowledge by adding the previously learned *er* and *ing* syllables to the new short vowel material and by adding the new final syllables (*y*, *ly*, and *le*) to the previously learned long *e* pattern words.

The last two short vowel patterns (*u* and *e*) are introduced in the *Short Vowel II Sequence*. In this sequence, students learn that there are many common prefixes and suffixes that conform to the short vowel pattern. Students begin to explore morphemes as a source of vocabulary building (e.g., *mismatch*, *misconduct*, *mistake*). Students who complete this sequence are able to read fourth-grade level readers with ease and can cope with instruction at a fifth-grade level.

At this point, two additional sequences are under development, one to present the use of vowel digraphs and another to deal with the many variations in vowel spellings.

How the Linguistic Pattern Series *Works.* The *Linguistic Pattern Series* includes three types of teaching materials:

1. *Book of Lessons:* A series of lessons that introduces sets of pattern words for decoding, vocabulary development, and comprehension.
2. *Read Aloud Story Book:* A set of stories that is keyed to the lessons and stresses the pattern words covered in each lesson.
3. *Fun Book:* A series of exercises also keyed to the lessons that reinforces the lesson material.

Naturally, the skill emphasis varies across the levels of the program, which spans about five years of elementary reading instruction. In the early levels, the focus is on reliable word recognition. That is, teaching graphic and phonemic processing and synchronizing them with meaning expectancy. Thus, the *Beginner Sequence* stresses the use of initial consonants in combination with long vowel sounds, introduces a variety of basic fabric words, and teaches students that the goal of reading is to derive meaning from print. Emphasis begins to shift to vocabulary development (i.e., learning new word meanings) in the *Introductory Sequence* while the students also learn to pay attention to consonant endings and common suffixes. In the more advanced sequences (Short Vowel I and II), there is increased emphasis on vocabulary development, learning to process complex polysyllabic word forms, and learning to apply more advanced cognitive skills while reading.

The Book of Lessons. Each lesson consists of a list of new pattern words, about 20 sentences that use the pattern words, two limericks, and space for spelling and writing with the new pattern words. We have selected material from Level 5 to illustrate how the *Linguistic Pattern Series* is used. The first part of Lesson 5.1 (the first of five Level 5 lessons) is illustrated in figure 4. Teachers begin a lesson by going over the pattern words at the top of the page. Note that some of these words may be unfamiliar to many second-grade students. (This lesson is at a high second-grade level.) There may even be a few words that are unfamiliar to the teacher (e.g., *beadle*).

In introducing the words, the teacher has the children read the words and follows this with a brief discussion of the meaning of each word. The teacher explains less familiar words (e.g., *mingle, baffle*) by giving contextual examples and solicits interpretations from the students of the more familiar words (e.g., *needle, battle*). The teacher does not drill the students in word meaning but rather leads and participates in interactive discussion. In keeping with the ISM instructional model, the focus of this exercise is on deriving the meanings of the words by using them in context and on bringing them into the children's lexicons through familiarization during conversation. This

---

Lesson 5.1

Adding "le" endings

needle	beadle	candle	handle
battle	apple	cattle	steeple
dabble	babble	rabble	baffle
paddle	saddle	rattle	crackle
mingle	jingle	beetle	tackle

1. _____ Why would a brook be called a "babbling brook"?

2. _____ Do you like to mingle with a mass of people at a shopping center?

3. _____ How old are most babies when they start to babble?

4. _____ Do cowboys put saddles on cattle and ride after their horses?

5. _____ What is a jingle and where are you likely to hear one?

Figure 4. The top third of one page of Lesson 5.1.

phase of the lesson should be brief and the teacher should move quickly to the sentences where the students exercise their phonemic decoding skills and meaning expectancy in the act of reading.

The sentences are framed as questions (see figure 4) to provoke an automatic comprehension response. (It is difficult to read a question without answering it.) Sentences are also constructed to reinforce vocabulary development. For example, in the first sentence the meaning of the word *brook*, learned in an earlier level, must be related to the meaning of the new word *babble* in order to answer this question. Some of the sentences are designed to be humorous or absurd (see Sentence #4). There are 20 questions in each lesson designed to reinforce the use of the new pattern and to foster discussion that will support vocabulary development and encourage students to think.

The second page of each lesson at this level (not shown in the figure) includes two limericks or short poems to further reinforce the use of letter sounds in reading and to provide additional amusement. The bottom half of the page provides space for a spelling exercise and a dictation or composition exercise. The students learn to spell the words they have been reading and to use sound patterns to assist them in learning to spell.

Read Aloud Story Book. Each lesson is accompanied by material in a *Read Aloud Story Book.* A sample from the Lesson 5.1 story is shown

... and the men who raised the cattle were called cowboys.

Also, next to each of the shacks on the Crandle Ranch there were two or three apple trees. Now this baffles me because, as far as I know, apple trees do not grow in Texas. But the apples from these trees were about the best you could find anywhere.

It was said that a man named Johnny Appleseed had been there many years before and had planted apple seeds near the shacks. It was said that Johnny Appleseed planted some very special apple seeds and that this is why the apple trees had grown in Texas. Now this baffles me too, because I do not see why a man would run around planting apple seeds all over the country, which is what people said Johnny Appleseed did. But that is another story. No one knew for sure who planted the apple trees on the Crandle Ranch, but the apples on every single one of these trees were the best. So, the cowboys would grab an apple or two from a tree before they saddled up and rode off to look after the cattle.

Figure 5. Part of a page from the *Read Aloud Story Book* designed to reinforce the pattern introduced in Lesson 5.1.

in figure 5. This is a rather lengthy story that extends across five chapters (one chapter for each lesson in Level 5). The figure shows only a few paragraphs of the six pages of text that constitute Chapter 1. Note the high density of pattern words in the text. The name *Crandle* and the words *baffle, apple, saddle,* and *cattle* all conform to the Lesson 5.1 pattern. Also, the continued focus on vocabulary development can be seen in the treatment of the word *baffle* in this bit of text. Finally, the attempt to treat cultural knowledge should be noted in the reference to Johnny Appleseed.

The *Read Aloud Story Books* are consumable. Comprehension exercises in the form of cloze tasks, true/false questions, and questions for group discussion are included in the books. The pictures are designed to be colored and sometimes space is provided for students to draw their own illustrations. When students complete a *Read Aloud Story Book,* they take the book home. This feature of the program is particularly important to students who come from poor neighbor-hoods where little reading material may be available in the home.

The Fun Books.   *The Fun Books* provide game-like problems that reinforce the patterns taught in the lessons. Standard types of word games such as crossword puzzles, matching, and word finding are in-cluded as well as some less conventional types of problems. Many of the exercises are designed to provoke a variety of possible answers. The student's task is to be able to explain why a particular answer was given. This was done to provide some break in the pervasive right/wrong orientation students acquire from most academic exercises.

Three *Fun Book* exercises accompany Lesson 5.1. One is a word matching exercise that requires the student to match words with their definitions. The second is a scrambled word exercise which includes items such as:

> I am afraid of snakes that make a _____. [T A R T L E]

The third *Fun Book* exercise for Lesson 5.1 is entitled "You Can Say That." Following is one of the three items in this exercise:

> I am not really keen on the game of football. Why people like this game baffles me. I dabble in other sports, but not football! What is so great about watching a tackle? A bunch of big lads fall on top of each other, that's all! The only thing I like about football is that, if you go to a game instead of watching it on TV, you get to mingle with people and eat lots of hot dogs.

From the passage you can say that:

O—I dislike all sports.
O—I must be a girl.
O—I like meeting people at games.
O—I like watching people get hurt.

Note the stress on the pattern words (*tackle, baffle, dabble, mingle*), particularly those that may have been unfamiliar to the students prior to this lesson.

The ISM in Practice

In keeping with the objectives of this chapter, we now describe how a hypothetical first-grade class is taught throughout the school year and follow their acquisition of the linguistic code for reading. We will as-sume that we have students who know at least half of the consonant sounds, can write all of the letters of the alphabet, and can read and write their own names. In following this hypothetical scenario, the reader should bear in mind that there is tremendous flexibility in the application of the ISM. The events we describe are what one teacher might do; the variety of actual events is virtually limitless.

Classroom Management. Before describing how the students will be taught, it is necessary to consider how the program fits into the larger scheme of classroom management. In order to be effective with *all* students, the teacher must conduct small group lessons (four to seven students per group). Unless the classroom routines and arrangement permit independent student activities, the teacher will be unable to teach in small groups. In regular classrooms where the ISM has been applied, the room is divided into learning centers. There may be centers for reading, math, art, listening, social studies, and other areas. The centers may provide books for the students to look at or read, games related to the curriculum, materials for small group or individual learning activities, etc.

The ISM reading program is a part of the Interdependent Learning Model sponsored by Fordham University. The Interdependent Learning Model is an early childhood education model that is one of the national Follow Through program models for improving the education of children living in neighborhoods below the poverty level (National Diffusion Network 1990; Rath et al. 1976). In addition to providing a system of learning centers as described above, the Interdependent Learning Model emphasizes student choice in academic activities, self-evaluation, the use of games as a vehicle for curriculum content, and an atmosphere where students are encouraged to learn from each other (i.e., interdependent learning).

For discussion, we will posit a first-grade classroom with 25 students, a teacher, and a paraprofessional. The students are divided into four groups for reading lessons (three groups of six and one of seven) and the groups are balanced for factors such as personality, gender, and loquaciousness. A one and one-half hour session is scheduled each morning for direct reading instruction, and the teacher allocates approximately 20 minutes to each of the four reading groups. During the time for direct instruction, children who are not actively involved in lessons are in the learning centers where they may be playing reading games or doing other exercises related to the reading curriculum. Table III outlines the progress of the students through each of the ISM components during 32 weeks of a school year.

Teaching the Linguistic Code for Reading

The first week. During the first week of school, instruction focuses exclusively on Lesson A.1. On the first day, the teacher presents

Table III.   Activities Across 32 Weeks of ISM Instruction

Period	LPS	Basal	SSS	Estimated Vocabulary
First Month				
Week 1	A.1	—*	—	5 words
Week 2	A.2	—	—	9 words
Week 3	A.3	—	—	15 words
Week 4	A.4	—	—	20 words
Second Month				
Week 5	A.5	—	—	25 words
Week 6	B.1	—	—	30 words
Week 7	B.2	PP1	—	45 words
Week 8	B.3	PP1	—	60 words
Third Month				
Week 9	B.4	PP1	—	75 words
Week 10	B.5	PP2	—	90 words
Week 11	C.1	PP2	—	105 words
Week 12	C.2	PP3	—	120 words
Fourth Month				
Week 13	C.3	PP3	Pict.	140 words
Week 14	C.4	PP3	Pict.	160 words
Week 15	C.5	Primer	Pict.	190 words
Week 16	D.1	Primer	Pict.	220 words
Fifth Month				
Week 17	D.2	Primer	Pict.	250 words
Week 18	D.3	Primer	Pict.	280 words
Week 19	D.4	Primer	Prep.	310 words
Week 20	D.5	Primer	Prep.	340 words
Sixth Month				
Week 21	1.1	Primer	Prep.	370 words
Week 22	1.2	Primer	Prep.	400 words
Week 23	1.3	First	Prep.	450 words
Week 24	1.4	First	Prep.	500 words
Seventh Month				
Week 25	1.5	First	A	550 words
Week 26	2.1	First	A	600 words
Week 27	2.2	First	A	650 words
Week 28	2.3	First	A	700 words
Eighth Month				
Week 29	2.4	First	A	750 words
Week 30	2.5	First	A	800 words
Week 31	3.1	First	A	850 words
Week 32	3.2	First	A	900 words

*A dash indicates that the program component is not yet applicable.

Lesson A.1

"e" and "ee" Can Say E

e	ee
me	see

I	can
run	_____
	name

1. _____ I can run.

2. _____ _____ can run.
   name

3. _____ I can see.

4. _____ _____ can see.
   name

5. _____ Can _____ run?
   name

6. _____ _____ can run.
   name

7. _____ Can I run?

8. _____ I can run.

9. _____ Can _____ see?
   name

10. _____ _____ can see.
    name

11. _____ Can I see?

12. _____ I can see.

Figure 6a. The first page of Lesson A.1 from the *Book of Lessons*.

the first part of the lesson (see figure 6a). Before starting the lesson, the teacher assists the students in writing their own names and the names of a few close friends in the spaces provided for names. This should take about 3 to 5 minutes. Then the teacher spends about 2 to 3 minutes introducing the words. Sounds are stressed for the pattern words *me* and *see* and also for the initial consonant in the word *run*.

The teacher proceeds quickly to the sentences, for this is where the words will actually be learned. As the first student reads, the teacher points for that student. Students who are not reading aloud are asked to point to each word as it is read to ensure that they are following. The teacher provides letter sound and meaning prompts to assist the students. A brief discussion follows the reading of each sentence to ensure comprehension. A sentence may be read by two or three different students. The number of times a sentence is read is based on the teacher's judgment of the students' needs. The teacher may also spot a student who is having more difficulty than the others and can provide that student with extra assistance and opportunities to read. As the group completes each sentence, the students place a check in the space next to that sentence. This will serve as a record of how many times the material has been covered by each student. The reading of the sentences is stopped after 10 minutes to ensure that there is time to teach all four groups. The first session may end before all of the Lesson A.1 sentences have been read and before the spelling and dictation exercises shown in figure 6b have been introduced.

During the second reading session, the teacher quickly reviews the lesson words and moves directly into the sentences. This is the children's second exposure to these sentences and the session should proceed quickly. All 21 of the sentences may be completed in less than 15 minutes, leaving about 5 minutes for the teacher to conduct spelling and dictation exercises (see figure 6b). For spelling, the teacher asks the students to write a word (e.g., *see*) in the first space. While the students are writing, the teacher observes and provides individual assistance to students who need it. Note that the words are visually available to the students in the lesson material. The students should be encouraged to look back if they need to. After they have written three or four of the lesson words, brief sentences are given for dictation (e.g., *I can see.*). The students are required to listen to an entire sentence and hold it in memory before they begin writing. The objective of the dictation exercise is to teach the students to maintain complete ideas in active memory while they engage in the arduous tasks of spelling and writing. There should be time remaining for writing two or three sentences within the 20 minutes allocated for the lesson.

On the third day, the teacher may quickly review the five words and dictate two or three more sentences. This should take no more than 5 to 7 minutes. The teacher may then have the students read the story for Lesson A.1 in the *Read Aloud Story Book* (see figure 7). The entire story, consisting of only 36 words, can be read by a student in less that 2 minutes. Thus, no more than 12 to 15 minutes may be con-

13. _____ Can _____ see me?
name

14. _____ _____ can see me.
name

15. _____ I can see _____.
name

16. _____ Can _____ see me?
name

17. _____ _____ can see me.
name

18. _____ Can I see _____ run?
name

19. _____ I can see _____ run.
name

20. _____ Can _____ see me run?
name

21. _____ _____ can see me run.
name

SPELLING

1. _____ 3. _____ 5. _____

2. _____ 4. _____ 6. _____

DICTATION

_____

_____

_____

_____

_____

Figure 6b.   The second page of Lesson A.1 from the *Book of Lessons.*

sumed in this phase of the lesson. Note that the word *yes*, which is underlined the first time it occurs, has not been taught in Lesson A.1. This sets the occasion for teaching the students to use meaning expectancy in decoding and learning to recognize new words in context. This skill is emphasized throughout the *Linguistic Pattern Series* and

Story for Lesson A.1

Can I?

Can I run?	Yes, I can!
<u>Yes</u>, I can.	Yes, I can!
I can run.	
	I can run.
Can I see?	I can see.
Yes, I can.	See me run!
I can see.	See me run!

Figure 7. The *Read Aloud Story Book* story for Lesson A.1.

forms the basis for learning words in context when the second ISM component, the basal reader, is introduced at a later point.

The fourth session is devoted to teaching the children how to do the exercise in the *Fun Book* (see figure 8). This is a cloze exercise that includes all of the words covered in the A.1 materials. Teaching stu-

Can You See What I Say? (A.1)

DIRECTIONS: Fill in each blank with a word to finish each sentence.

---

me   see   I   can   run   yes

---

1. Can _____ run?

2. I _____ run.

3. Can _____ see?

4. I _____ see.

5. Can _____ run?

6. Yes, I can _____.

7. _____ I see?

8. Yes, _____ can see.

9. _____ I run?

10. _____, I can run.

Figure 8. The *Fun Book* exercise for Lesson A.1.

dents to perform a cloze exercise is not a difficult task. Teachers who use the ISM rely on their own understanding of the task, as opposed to following elaborate procedures in a teacher's guide. This can be accomplished easily within the 20 minutes allocated for the session.

Thus far, we have described a group of six first-grade students that has received a total of one hour and twenty minutes of direct instruction. During this time, each student has probably had the opportunity to read aloud each of the five lesson words 20 to 30 times and to read them silently as many as 200 times while other students were reading. If the classroom is set up properly, these students have had many additional opportunities to read these words while playing games or simply looking at the classroom walls, where the words and many of the sentences are prominently displayed. Even the moderately reading disabled students are certain to learn these five words from this kind of exposure.

The second through fourth weeks. During the second week, the teacher presents the material for Lesson A.2. On the first day, the pattern words *he* and *we* and the sight words *play* and *jump* are presented. Initial consonants are stressed both for the pattern words and for the two sight words. At this point, the students are becoming accustomed to the lesson routines and the lesson proceeds quickly. Sentence reading requires just over 10 minutes and the teacher is able to conduct spelling and dictation exercises within the 20 minutes allocated for the session.

On the second day, the students read the stories for Lesson A.2. This includes three pages of text with approximately 100 words per page. Paragraphs are read two or three times. The teacher asks students who need extra practice to reread paragraphs immediately after another student has read. The *Fun Book* exercise for A.2 is presented on the third day. At this point, the objective is to teach the children to work independently. As the more able students complete this exercise, they are released to independent activities. This gives the teacher more time for individualized instruction with those who need it.

On the fourth and fifth days of this week, the paraprofessional conducts the reading lessons, repeating Lesson A.2 on the fourth day and leading the students in the *Read Aloud Story Book* for A.2 on the fifth. The teacher uses this time to observe students in independent activities and to teach them to use this time more efficiently. The teacher provides individualized instruction for the two to four students in the class who are having the most difficulty and for students who have been absent for one or more reading sessions.

The teacher maintains the pace and covers the material for successive lessons through the fourth week. By the end of the first month, *all* of the students in the class are able to read a total of 20 words, but they have learned a great deal more than this about reading and learning to read. They have learned to write and spell all 20 of these words. They have learned to attack unfamiliar words automatically in context by starting at the beginning sound and using meaning expectancy to help them identify words as they are reading. They have learned that reading is about deriving meaning and that letter sounds and meaning expectancy are used in this process.

We feel that we have described a first month of reading instruction that differs from what children generally experience. The teacher has worked in small groups where the difficulties of individual students were observed and corrected before they became a problem. The teacher has had the freedom to exercise a full range of teaching talents and techniques, unconstrained by a detailed teacher's guide.

The second month. In the fifth week of school, the long *e* pattern words are completed in Lesson A.5. All of the students are now able to read approximately 25 words. The Level A Read Aloud book is completed and the students take their books home where they can demonstrate their newly acquired reading skills for parents and other significant people in their lives. The teacher writes brief rewarding notes to the students and parents inside the readers. This serves as a means of reinforcing the student and communicating with the parents.

Level B is started in the sixth week of school. In this level, pattern words with *ay* spelling (e.g., *may, say, way, day*) are presented. This is the first time the students have been asked to discriminate between two vowels (both spellings and sounds). However, because the students have been processing some 10 or 12 long *e* pattern words, this should present no particular problem. By the end of week six, the estimated vocabulary count is up to 30 words.

During the seventh week, the teacher introduces the basal readers. For our example, we use the Macmillan *Series "r"* readers (Smith and Wardhaugh 1980), but almost any basal program might be used. The children read the first story following procedures that are very similar to those used in *Linguistic Pattern Series* lessons. The teacher points for the child who is reading. The other children follow, pointing in their own readers. Each page contains only a few words and may be reread several times, especially by students who need the extra practice. The first story is based on a total of eight words, but five of these are old friends from the *Linguistic Pattern Series.* The teacher goes on to the next story, which presents four new words, only one of which is new to our students.

The first two stories in the first preprimer, which introduce 12 words, cover 15 pages in the book. The total word count across these 15 pages is only 60. This is in contrast to the 80 to 100 words on every page of the *Linguistic Pattern Series* readers. Nevertheless, the students are now skilled at using context to help them learn new words, and they will be able to learn the four words that are new to them in these stories with relative ease.

On the second day of this week, the teacher introduces Lesson B.2. The third session is devoted to the *Read Aloud Story Books.* In the fourth session the first two basal reader stories are reviewed and the third story is introduced. Six additional words are introduced in this story but only three are new to these students. The students are now familiar with the *Fun Book* procedures and they have completed the *Fun Book* exercises in independent activities with the help of the aide. The aide conducts sessions on the last day of the week. The *Read Aloud Story Books* for B.2 and the three basal stories are reread in this session. The aide gains experience in using the basal reader and the teacher is free to direct independent activities and provide extra assistance for students who need it.

During the eighth week of school, the material for Lesson B.3 is covered and two more stories in the basal are read. Although the basal reader lists 22 new words for this story, only 7 of these are new to the students. The students complete their second month of school with an estimated reading vocabulary of 60 words. Their ability to use letter sounds and context to support the development of their reading vocabulary has been substantially strengthened, and they have learned that their reading skills can be applied to new and interesting materials (i.e., the basal readers).

The third month.   In the third month, Level B of the *Linguistic Pattern Series* is completed and Level C, which presents long *i* pattern words, is begun. The first and second preprimers are completed and the third preprimer is begun. The management of these two ISM components, the basal and the *Linguistic Pattern Series*, proceeds as described above. The number of words that the children can read has doubled during this third month.

Before continuing, let us consider three important factors that have ensured the students' success up to this point: (1) the role of the paraprofessional, (2) the classroom environment and independent reading activities, and (3) the identification and treatment of children who are having difficulty.

The paraprofessional has been conducting reading lessons almost from the outset of instruction. At first, the aide presented review lessons, but as the year proceeded, the aide acquired the skills to introduce new lessons. This has a number of advantages. By conducting lessons, the aide gains a good understanding of the curriculum and how it relates to independent activities. The aide also becomes familiar with the problems of each student and can provide more effective individualized assistance. When the teacher is absent, the aide can conduct reading sessions and avoid one of the problems that can interfere with the continuity and consistency of reading program management.

Independent activities in the learning centers reinforce the reading curriculum. Games that use the program content are available in the game center. These are updated as the children progress through the curriculum. The books that the children are reading in lessons (*Read Aloud Story Books* and basal readers) are available in the library center together with other books that are of interest to them. The art center contains templates for painting the lesson words and materials for coloring and illustrating the *Read Aloud Story Books*. A variety of wall decorations have been developed by the teacher, aide, and students, so that new curriculum material is prominently displayed around the classroom.

Finally, and perhaps most importantly, the children are monitored continually so that those who are having difficulty may be identified and given extra help. The teacher and the aide listen to every child read every day. In lessons, children with difficulties are given extra opportunities to read and individualized feedback while they are reading. During independent activities, these children are assisted by the teacher or aide, assigned to group activities in which other students can help them, and given special exercises designed to correct their problems. A student would have to be severely learning disabled to fail to learn to read in this environment. This environment is designed to detect and correct early problems before they develop into learning disabilities.

The fourth month.   During the fourth month the students complete Level C of the *Linguistic Pattern Series.* In these lessons, the students learn that the spelling of the vowel sound can vary (*by, my, why, lie, pie*). They move into the primer level of the basal readers where new words are introduced more rapidly and where the stories resemble more closely those in library books. The children are able to acquire new words at this more rapid pace because they now have the processes depicted in the ISM reading-process model (see figure 1) well integrated into their learning behavior.

Also during the fourth month, the teacher introduces the *Specific Skill Series,* which is the third component of ISM instruction (see figure 3). At this level, very little reading is actually required because the question and answer options are repetitive (i.e., the same question appears on each page). The teacher has no difficulty teaching the children to read this simple material and the children now have a new source of productive independent activities.

The fifth through eighth months. The remaining months of the school year proceed as previously described. The teacher and aide conduct daily, small-group instruction. During reading time, while students are not receiving direct instruction, they are engaged in relevant and productive independent and interdependent reading activities. The teacher and aide continue to spot children who are having difficulty, provide assistance in the form of individual instruction, and assign special activities.

As can be seen in table III, Level D, the last level of the Beginner Sequence of the *Linguistic Pattern Series,* is completed in the fifth month while the students continue working in the primer of the basal readers and graduate to the Preparatory level of the *Specific Skill Series.* By the end of this month, the students have an estimated reading vocabulary of 340 words.

In the sixth month, the students begin Level 1 of the Introductory Sequence of the *Linguistic Pattern Series,* which teaches them to apply phonemic processing to final consonants. The basal reader primer is completed and the first reader is begun. By the end of the sixth month, the students have an estimated reading vocabulary of 500 words. With the skill base that they have developed for learning new words, they learn an additional 400 words during the seventh and eighth months. They complete Level 2 and start Level 3 of the Introductory Sequence, finish the first reader in the basal program, and work in Level A of the *Specific Skill Series* throughout these two months.

APPLICATIONS AND RESULTS

In this section, we discuss results obtained with ISM instruction in three different settings: clinic, special program, and regular school.

Clinical Applications

Clinical applications of the ISM generally involve the parent or significant other in the instructional process. Diagnosis usually involves only the *Decoding Skills Test* (DST) (Richardson and DiBenedetto 1985) to assess the child's word-recognition ability and phonological development. Sometimes, the *Gates-MacGinitie Reading Test* (MacGinitie 1978) is given to obtain standardized reading test scores. DST results are used to place the child in the ISM instructional sequence and active instruction is begun in the first session. Thereafter, the child and parent attend weekly sessions at the clinic. During these sessions, a trained ISM therapist administers a lesson (which may involve several of the various activities described in the previous section), makes recommendations regarding procedures to be used at home, and lays out a series of five sessions that the parent and child are to complete during the ensuing week.

Students at a wide range of ages and with varying degrees of deficits have been treated using this model. We focus here on those who were unable to read at all when they enrolled in the program. These are generally children nearing the end of first grade. However, one of the most remarkable cases is that of a brain-injured adult who was a licensed nurse when she completely lost the ability to read or even recognize letters. She remained in this state for six years before she began working in the ISM program. After two years of extremely hard work on her part (averaging three hours per day), she is now reading third-grade level material with relative ease and is continuing her efforts to regain her lost reading skills.

We were fortunate to have participated in a study at a major New York State children's psychiatric center in which the investigators were studying the differential effects of psychotropic medication on learning in children with conduct disorder. The design required daily, one-to-one sessions of ISM instruction over a period of three weeks. One of three children who had completed the study protocol at the time that this chapter was being prepared was an eight-year-old, bilingual child who had had two and one-half years of reading instruction but was a nonreader prior to study participation. Although this child was not a typical clinic case, the results are similar to those obtained with most nonreaders who have been treated in our clinics. Furthermore, because this child was participating in a formal research study, we can report systematic data.

Two measures of reading achievement were obtained before and after instruction: Subtest I of the DST and the Mastery Test for Level A. DST Subtest I, Basal Vocabulary, is an individually administered, oral word-reading test, which consists of 11 word lists designed to assess mastery of basal vocabulary at a particular reader level (preprimer, primer, first reader, etc.). The Mastery Tests are used with the *Linguistic Pattern Series* to assess mastery of material as students progress from level to level. The Level A Mastery Test has three sections: Sentence Completion (a cloze task), Evaluating Questions (10 questions that re-

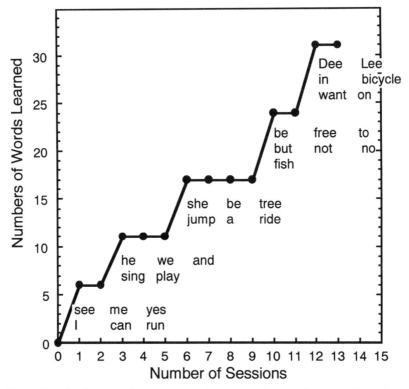

Figure 9. Reading acquisition curve of a non-reader taught across 13 sessions with the *Linguistic Pattern Series*.

quire *Yes* or *No* responses), and Picture Descriptions (10 four-option, multiple-choice items that require the selection of the sentence that best describes a picture).

Figure 9 shows the child's progress across 13 sessions. Lesson A.1 material was introduced in the first session (*see, me, yes, I, can,* and *run*) and reinforced in the second session. Three sessions were devoted to Lesson A.2 and four sessions to Lesson A.3. At this point, the child had acquired a reading vocabulary of 17 words. Lesson A.4 was presented in two sessions and two sessions were devoted to Lesson A.5, giving the child a reading vocabulary of 30 words. Because the ISM is a mastery approach to learning, the therapist made the decisions as to when to introduce new lessons based on the strength of the child's performance with prior lessons.

At pretest, this child obtained a score of zero on the DST (indicating that he could not read words such as *the, yes,* or *and*) and a score of

24% (near chance level) on the Level A Mastery Test. Both scores indicate that the child was a nonreader. At posttest, the child obtained a score of 9 on the DST (indicating that he was able to read essential pre-primer words) and a score of 76% on the Level A test, which meets the minimum criterion for mastery at that level.

Special Program Applications

In 1985, the Texas Legislature passed two laws mandating the identification and treatment of dyslexic children in the mainstream school population. The first requires school districts to develop a program of inservice training for teachers in the recognition of dyslexia and related disorders, and the second requires that the districts adopt procedures for identifying dyslexic students and provide them with appropriate reading instruction. In response to this legislation, the El Paso Independent School District (EPISD) adopted the DST as the primary test for identifying dyslexic students and the ISM for providing appropriate instruction.

Program design. The procedures for identifying and diagnosing the children as dyslexic are described more fully by Richardson and Reinhart (1989a, 1989b). Students are referred for the program and screened with the DST during late spring or early fall. Teachers receive a full day of training in ISM procedures and provide daily 45-minute sessions in a special pull-out program. The student-teacher ratio is limited to 12:1. Direct teaching sessions are conducted with 2 to 6 students while other students in the group are engaged in independent activities (e.g., *Fun Book* or the *Specific Skill Series* workbooks). A student may be released from the program at any time based on the recommendation of the ISM teacher in consultation with the child's regular classroom teacher and the parent. At the end of each school year, all students who are still participating in the program are given Subtests I and II of the DST to evaluate progress and to provide the next year's teacher with information for continuing instruction.

The program was initiated in the 1987–88 school year with a group of 276 second and third graders (Cohort 1). During the 1988–89 school year, the program was expanded to include fourth and fifth graders. During the most recent school year (1990–91) the program served approximately 1,200 students, including first graders who had been held over and children from the district's large bilingual population.

Subject sample. Evaluating results for a program that was designed primarily for service and not for research is extremely complex.

By the Spring of 1991, we had accumulated data from nearly 1,500 children. Here we present results obtained from two samples. The first, Cohort 1, includes 55 children of the original sample of 276 who were enrolled in the program in the first year. This group was selected because it enables us to trace progress across four years of program participation. The second sample, Cohort 4, includes 484 children who were newly enrolled in the fourth year of the program (the 1990–91 school year). This group was the largest of the four cohorts and the data set was the most complete because few of these children were released in the single year of program participation.

Instruments. The DST is the primary measure used for identifying dyslexic students and for evaluating progress in the El Paso program. The DST was developed under a contract with the National Institute of Child Health and Human Development to provide a measure for research on developmental dyslexia. It includes three subtests, each designed to measure a different aspect of decoding.

Subtest I, Basal Vocabulary, is described above in the section on Clinical Applications. In addition to yielding a Raw Score, Subtest I provides an Instructional Level Grade Equivalent, which is a grade equivalent estimate of the basal program level at which a student will benefit most from instruction. Subtest II, Phonic Patterns, is composed of 60 lists of 5 words each (i.e., a total of 120 items) selected to conform to common orthographic patterns. Half of these items are words that are representative of the second through sixth grade curriculum and the other half are nonsense words formed by changing one or two letters in the real words. Subtest II provides a profile of decoding abilities that is used by EPISD in identifying dyslexic students. Subtest III, Contextual Reading, is used in identifying students but is not used in follow-up testing.

In addition to the DST scores, the school district supplied us with results on the *Iowa Test of Basic Skills* (ITBS) (Hieronymous, Hoover, and Lindquist 1986), which is administered to all students in second grade and above every March to assess district-wide student achievement.

Results. At the end of the 1990–91 school year, 55 of the original 276 Cohort 1 children remained in the sample. Many students had been released from the program because they were deemed capable of achieving at a normal pace. Others were promoted to the sixth grade where the program is not available. Therefore, it is likely that the remaining 55 Cohort 1 students are among the most severely dyslexic in the original sample. Of these, 19 (34%) were retained once during the course of the four-year program but none were held over twice. Of the

55 children in the final sample, 35% were girls. When these children began the program in 1987 they were placed in the second or third grade. By 1991, after four years in the program, they were placed in the fourth or fifth grade.

To assess the effects of the program across the four years of the project, distributions of DST Instructional Level scores, shown in figure 10, were developed. Reference to the figure reveals that in 1987 (light bars in the figure), prior to starting the program, most of these students scored at first-grade levels on the DST. In 1989 (grey bars), following two years of ISM instruction, only one student scored at a first grade level (Primer) while most scored at a high second-grade level (Two-two) or above. By 1991 (dark bars), following four years of ISM instruction, none scored at first-grade levels, only 5 scored at second-grade levels, and most scored at fourth- and fifth-grade levels on the DST.

ITBS results were difficult to analyze for Cohort 1. Many of these students had been in first grade in 1987 and were not given the test that year. However, the data set included scores for 53 of the 55 students in 1988, after one year in the program, and in 1991. The gains in national percentile scores on Reading, Vocabulary, and Spelling were all about

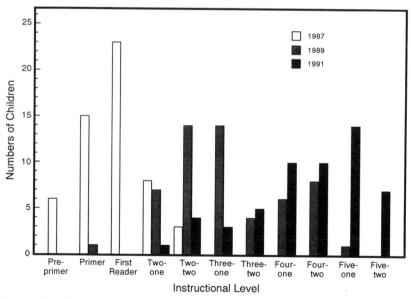

Figure 10. Distributions of DST Instructional Level Scores for 55 Cohort 1 children at three test points.

Table IV.   Means, *SD*s and *t* Tests of Changes from 1988 to 1991 on ITBS Reading, Vocabulary, and Spelling for Cohort 1 Students (*n* = 53)

Subtest		Year		*t* value
		1988	1991	
Reading	Mean	21.6	31.1	3.68**
	SD	14.6	16.5	
Vocabulary	Mean	23.8	33.9	2.98*
	SD	16.0	16.1	
Spelling	Mean	21.6	31.7	5.12**
	SD	13.9	17.7	

*p < .01. **p < .001.

10 points and were all significant (see table IV). Furthermore, while 37 (70%) of these students scored below the 25th percentile in 1988, only 16 (30%) scored that low in 1991.

While many of these children were still deficient in reading following four years of program participation, all had learned to read well enough to cope with material written at second-grade levels and many were functioning at or near the level expected at their current grade placement. Given that these students are among the most severely reading disabled students placed in mainstream classrooms, there is little doubt that the program had a positive impact on their reading achievement. In fact, many of these students might have been placed in special education environments without the aid of the program.

In the 1990–91 school year, the program was expanded to include bilingual children and first graders who had been retained. A total of 484 new students (Cohort 4) were admitted to the program that year. Table V reports the means and *SD*s for the 1990 (pretest) and 1991 (posttest) on selected DST scores. With the exception of the 41 first grade retainees, results show gains of approximately 25 points on the Subtest I Raw Score (of a possible 110), gains of just over one year on the Instructional Level Grade Equivalent score, and gains of about 30 points on the Phonic Patterns Total Score (of a possible 120). All gains were significant (*p* < .001). These data suggest that these dyslexic students had begun to achieve at a normal pace in reading as a result of ISM instruction.

The ITBS data set on Cohort 4 included 241 of the 484 Cohort 4 students. None of the first graders and only 14 students who were held over in second grade were represented in the data set for 1990 since EPISD does not administer the ITBS to first graders, but 88% of the

Table V. Means, *SD*s, and *t* Tests of Changes from 1990 to 1991 on Selected
DST Scores for Cohort 4 Students in Grades 1 through 5

Grade	n	Subtest	Score		1990	1991	t value
					Year		
1	41	Basal Vocabulary	Raw Score	Mean	15.8	36.0	14.22*
				SD	7.4	12.3	
			Instr. Level	Mean	1.23	1.82	8.28*
				SD	0.23	0.49	
		Phonic Patterns	Total Score	Mean	1.4	18.7	6.14*
				SD	4.5	19.5	
2	183	Basal Vocabulary	Raw Score	Mean	29.8	57.3	25.80*
				SD	10.5	16.9	
			Instr. Level	Mean	1.61	2.65	20.35*
				SD	0.43	0.77	
		Phonic Patterns	Total Score	Mean	10.4	46.7	24.58*
				SD	13.2	24.8	
3	134	Basal Vocabulary	Raw Score	Mean	48.0	74.0	20.67*
				SD	14.8	16.9	
			Instr. Level	Mean	2.23	3.32	14.88*
				SD	0.65	0.90	
		Phonic Patterns	Total Score	Mean	33.0	65.2	18.95*
				SD	21.4	24.1	
4	79	Basal Vocabulary	Raw Score	Mean	62.0	86.0	19.58*
				SD	19.3	17.2	
			Instr. Level	Mean	2.75	3.90	14.09*
				SD	0.84	1.02	
		Phonic Patterns	Total Score	Mean	48.2	76.0	18.55*
				SD	23.1	23.5	
5	47	Basal Vocabulary	Raw Score	Mean	68.4	89.7	13.75*
				SD	15.8	13.1	
			Instr. Level	Mean	3.06	4.10	8.55*
				SD	0.80	0.89	
		Phonic Patterns	Total Score	Mean	49.9	76.7	13.67*
				SD	20.4	18.8	

*$p < .001$

remaining sample of third through fifth graders had ITBS scores for
both 1990 (pretest) and 1991 (posttest). Table VI reports the means, *SD*s
and *t* values assessing changes in the percentile scores on Reading,
Vocabulary, and Spelling from 1990 to 1991. Inspection of these data
reveals gains of from 5 to 7 percentile points, all of which are significant
($p < .001$). This suggests that these students' reading levels are beginning to improve with respect to the normal distribution.

Table VI. Means, SDs and t Tests of Changes from 1990 to 1991 on ITBS Reading, Vocabulary, and Spelling for Cohort 4 Students ($n = 241$)

Subtest		Year		
		1990	1991	t value
Reading	Mean	23.9	29.3	4.69*
	SD	17.9	20.1	
Vocabulary	Mean	25.0	31.9	4.85*
	SD	19.6	22.2	
Spelling	Mean	25.3	32.2	5.08*
	SD	18.1	21.7	

*$p < .001$.

Regular Classroom Applications

The main classroom use of the ISM has been in the Interdependent Learning Model (ILM) classrooms. Here we present results from a school in a neighborhood designated as below poverty level by the federal government. In addition to the ISM, the classroom teachers were trained in and implemented the ILM. The program is implemented in the primary grades (kindergarten through third grade) and there are four classrooms at each grade level (i.e., from 80 to 100 children per grade level). Each classroom has at least a half-time paraprofessional, and the children use learning centers and a choice-board for selecting the learning center that they go to at designated periods (Bowles, Freeman, and Jarvis 1981). Games are also a part of the ILM and children may receive reinforcement of various reading skills through Table Games (Atlanta Follow Through Program 1985), Conversation Games (Freeman 1981), and Street/Folk/Musical Games (Hilary, Simmons, and Freeman 1982).

The Atlanta Public School System (APS) administers the ITBS every March to assess student achievement. Although the teaching teams had been using the ILM in their classrooms for a number of years and had been using a phonics program developed over a decade ago by the senior author (Richardson 1974), the *Linguistic Pattern Series* and the ISM did not become a part of the total program until the 1988–89 school year.

Results presented here were taken from a report issued by the APS Division of Research and Evaluation (Harris and Lewis 1990). In evaluating schools in their system, the APS focuses on the percentage of children who score at or above the 50th percentile on the various subtests of the ITBS. Figure 11 reports the percentages of children in the first, second, and third grades who scored at or above the 50th percentile in reading on the ITBS in 1988 (before ISM implementation), 1989 (following one year of program implementation), and 1990 (following two years). Reference to the first-grade results in the figure reveal that in 1988 about 45% of the students scored at or above the 50th percentile in ITBS Reading. In 1989, this number had risen to 70% and by 1990 it was 85%. That is, 85% of the first-grade students in a school that serves inner-city, poverty level families scored above national norms on a widely used standardized test. We feel that these results are most remarkable.

The second-grade results (see figure 11) show that about 40% of these samples scored at or above the 50th percentile in ITBS Reading in both 1988 and 1989. It should be noted that the 1988–89 school year was the first year of ISM implementation in that school and that the second

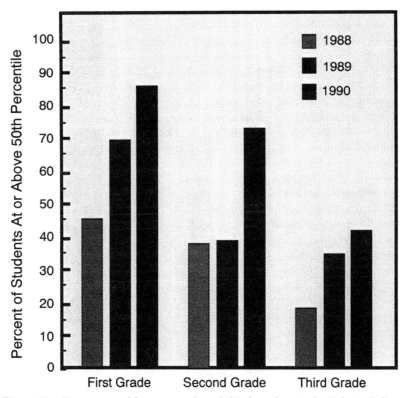

Figure 11.   Percentage of first, second, and third graders in the Atlanta Follow Through program scoring at or above the 50th percentile on ITBS Reading in 1988 (prior to ISM implementation) and after one (1989) and two (1990) years of ISM implementation.

graders had not received the benefit of ISM instruction in the first grade. However, about 70% of the second graders in the 1990 sample, many of whom had received two years of ISM instruction, scored at or above national norms. The third-grade results reported in figure 11 are not so remarkable. However, in 1988 only about 15% of the students scored at or above the 50th percentile, while in 1989 and 1990 this number rose to about 35% and 45%, respectively. We have every reason to believe that the effects observed in the first- and second-grade samples for 1990 will carry over into the third-grade results in future years.

For evaluating special programs, the APS compares results obtained from special program schools with those obtained from comparable schools and from the system at large. Figure 12 shows the per-

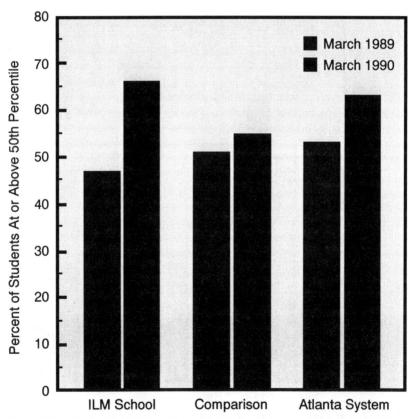

Figure 12. Percentage of first through third graders in the ILM school, a group of seven Comparison schools, and the entire Atlanta Public School System scoring at or above the 50th percentile on ITBS Reading in 1989 and in 1990.

centage of children, in a combined sample of first through third graders, who scored at or above the 50th percentile on ITBS Reading in 1989 and 1990 from three samples: the ILM school, a group of seven schools located in comparable low-income neighborhoods (labeled Comparison in the figure), and the total APS. Reference to the figure reveals that in 1989, only about 47% of the students in the ILM school scored at or above the 50th percentile, while about 51% of the Comparison and 53% of the Atlanta System students scored at that level. However, by 1990 the situation had changed dramatically. In that year, there was an increase of nearly 20% in the number of students who scored at or above the 50th percentile in the ILM sample, while the improvement in the Comparison schools was marginal (about 3%). Although the improvement in the Atlanta System was large (about 10%), it did not approach the improvement demonstrated in the ILM school.

CONCLUSIONS

Over the years, numerous programs and methodologies for teaching reading have held sway. Unfortunately, none of these has been able to solve the critical problem of teaching all of our children to read, and it appears unlikely that the currently popular methodology, the whole-language approach, will be the answer. Although each of the approaches has strong points, each focuses on one or two specific aspects of learning to read and none takes into account the full range of fundamental processes that must be taught to children who have inadequate language experience, who lack talent for translating visual images into language, or who may suffer from dyslexia. Many programs in current use deprive the teacher of the flexibility needed to address individual children's needs because they dictate narrowly focused and sequenced teaching routines that cannot be modified. In the end, the children who fail to learn to read are blamed and our schools continue to turn out a high percentage of reading failures.

Models of the reading process have led to productive research over the past two decades. However, these models are too complex to be of much use to teachers, and they generally present a one-sided perspective (that of the model) of how reading is accomplished. We have presented a simplified model of reading (see figure 1) that incorporates the essential features of most of the models in the literature and we have shown how this model may be used as a basis for an instructional approach that can help students develop more effective strategies for learning to read. We propose that a teacher who has a good understanding of this model and who is provided with sufficient, well-structured reading materials can effectively teach all children to read.

The ISM as described in this chapter constitutes a total program for teaching reading and spelling. We do not believe that this is the only program that is capable of accomplishing the objective of ensuring that all children learn to read. However, we do believe that any program that incorporates all of the essential features of the ISM can be successful with all children. These essential features are: (1) a reliance on the teacher to organize teaching and learning activities, (2) a carefully structured approach for teaching the phonetic code in reading, (3) an approach to teaching reading subskills in which students are immediately given the opportunity to apply these subskill in active contextual reading, (4) an abundance of reading material that is geared to the skill levels of the students, (5) an emphasis on oral reading in context during lessons so that the teacher can observe the behavior of individual students, provide appropriate feedback, and program corrective measures before problems arise, and (6) the use of content mastery as a basis for progression in the curriculum sequence.

In the clinic setting, we have found that parents are able to understand the model and, with the guidance of someone trained in ISM procedures, they are able to teach their own children to read. We have seen many children (first, second, and third graders), who were unable to read *any* words when they arrived at the clinic, acquire effective reading vocabularies of 20 to 30 words within a single month of ISM instruction. In the EPISD program, we have demonstrated that children who are experiencing difficulty in learning to read can be identified in a mainstream program and taught successfully by teachers who have received only one day of special training in the program procedures. Finally, in Atlanta, we have shown that children who are at high risk for reading failure can learn effectively in the context of a regular classroom program.

At this point in our history, when so much is known about the process of learning to read as well as how to teach reading, we feel that there is no excuse for failing our children. However, the following conditions must be met to ensure that all children learn to read:

1. *Money:* Classrooms must be adequately staffed (i.e., have the support of a paraprofessional) so that reading instruction can be provided to small groups. Classrooms must be fully stocked with books and supplies.
2. *Teacher Education:* Teacher education programs must be geared toward training teachers to become independent professionals who are capable of teaching without scripts and elaborate program im-

plementation guides. Public school systems must recognize the professional status and capability of their teachers and gear their teacher evaluation programs to this.

3. *Student Monitoring:* Public school systems must devise and implement programs of student progress monitoring, such as the one described by Richardson and Freeman (1976), that rely on content- and criterion-referenced instruments and teacher placements of students in the curriculum rather than standardized tests. (Standardized tests are designed so that 50% of all children will always score below national norms and tell us next to nothing about the academic development of an individual child.) Progress monitoring should begin early and occur frequently so that problems may be identified and corrected before they become severe.

If these three conditions are met, it is certain that there would be a large increase in the numbers of children who learn how to read effectively in the elementary grades with a consequent reduction in adult illiteracy in our population over the next 10 years. Unfortunately, there is little hope that these conditions will be met on a nation-wide basis in the near future. However, we can hope that a few pioneering communities and school districts will demonstrate the courage and concern required to meet these conditions. If this happens, the effects on reading achievement in these communities could not be ignored by the nation at large, and it is possible that our vision of an educational system that teaches all children to read will occur at some time in the not too distant future.

REFERENCES

Atlanta Follow Through Program. 1985. *Games Children Play.* Atlanta, GA: Atlanta Public School System.

Boning, R.A. 1982. *Specific Skill Series.* Baldwin, NY: Barnell Loft.

Bowles, E., Freeman Jr., H.F., and Jarvis, C. 1981. *Classroom Management Manual.* New York: Fordham University.

Duffy, F.H., and Geschwind, N. (Eds.). 1985. *Dyslexia: A Neuroscientific Approach to Clinical Evaluation.* Boston: Little, Brown and Co.

Edelsky, C. 1990. Whose agenda is this anyway? A response to McKenna, Robinson, and Miller. *Educational Researcher* 19(6):7–11.

Flesch, R. 1955. *Why Johnny Can't Read.* New York: Harper and Row, Inc.

Freeman Jr., H.F. 1981. *Conversation Games (Vols 1, 2, & 3).* New York: Fordham University.

Goodman, K.S. 1976a. Behind the eye: What happens in reading. In *Theoretical Models and Processes of Reading*, eds. H. Singer and R.B. Ruddell. Newark, DE: International Reading Association.

Goodman, K.S. 1976b. Reading: A psycholinguistic guessing game. In *Theoretical Models and Processes of Reading,* eds. H. Singer and R.B. Ruddell. Newark, DE: International Reading Association.

Gough, P.B. 1976. One second of reading. In *Theoretical Models and Processes of Reading,* eds. H. Singer and R.B. Ruddell. Newark, DE: International Reading Association.

Harris, J., and Lewis, S. 1990. *Follow Through Performance Report.* Atlanta, GA: Atlanta Public School System.

Hieronymous, A.N., Hoover, H.D., and Lindquist, E.F. 1986. *The Iowa Test of Basic Skills.* Chicago: Riverside Publishing Co.

Hilary, M.A., Simmons, P.M., and Freeman Jr., H.F. 1982. *A Guide to the Use of Street/Folk/Musical Games in the Classroom (Vols. 1, 2, and 3).* New York: Fordham University.

Kavanagh, J.F. 1976. Foreword. In *Theoretical Models and Processes of Reading,* eds. H. Singer and R.B. Ruddell. Newark, DE: International Reading Association.

LaBerge, D., and Samuels, S.J. 1976. Toward a theory of automatic information processing in reading. In *Theoretical Models and Processes of Reading,* eds. H. Singer and R.B. Ruddell. Newark, DE: International Reading Association.

Lesgold, A.M., and Curtis, M.E. 1981. Learning to read words efficiently. In *Interactive Processes in Reading,* eds. A.M. Lesgold and C.A. Perfetti. Hillsdale, NJ: Lawrence Erlbaum Associates.

Lesgold, A.M., and Perfetti, C.A. (Eds.) 1981. *Interactive Processes in Reading.* Hillsdale, NJ: Lawrence Erlbaum Associates.

Levy, B.A. 1981. Interactive processing during reading. In *Interactive Processes in Reading,* eds. A.M. Lesgold and C.A. Perfetti. Hillsdale, NJ: Lawrence Erlbaum Associates.

Liberman, I.Y. 1985. Should so-called modality preferences determine the nature of instruction for children with reading disabilities? In *Dyslexia: A Neuroscientific Approach to Clinical Evaluation,* eds. F.H. Duffy and N. Gescwind. Boston: Little, Brown and Co.

MacGinitie, W.H. 1978. *Gates-MacGinitie Reading Tests.* Boston: Houghton Mifflin.

McKenna, M.C., Robinson, R.D., and Miller, J.W. 1990a. Whole language: A research agenda for the ninties. *Educational Researcher* 19(6):3–6.

McKenna, M.C., Robinson, R.D., and Miller, J.W. 1990b. Whole language and the need for open inquiry: A rejoinder to Edelsky. *Educational Researcher* 19(6):12–19.

Massaro, D.W. 1977. *Reading and Listening.* (Tech. Rep. No. 423). Madison, WI: Research and Development Center for Cognitive Learning.

Milner, E. 1963. A study of the relationship between reading readiness in grade one school children and patterns of parent-child interaction. In *The 62nd Yearbook of the National Society for the Study of Education.* Chicago: University of Chicago Press.

National Diffusion Network 1990. Interdependent Learning Model. In *Education Programs at Work:* (p. f 9, 16th ed.). Longmont, CO: Sopris West, Inc.

Rath, S.W., O'Neil, B.B., Gedney, B.D., and Osorio, J. (Eds.) 1976. The interdependent learning model in follow through. In *A Resource Guide to Sponsor Models and Materials.* Portland, OR: Nero & Associates, Inc.

Richardson, E. 1974. *A Direct Approach to Decoding.* New York: Interdependent Learning Model, Fordham University.

Richardson, E. 1989a. *ISM Implementation Guide.* Mt. Vernon, NY: ISM Teaching Systems, Inc.

Richardson, E. 1989b. *Learning to Teach by Learning to Read.* Mt. Vernon, NY: ISM Teaching Systems, Inc.

Richardson, E. 1989c. *Linguistic Pattern Series.* Mt. Vernon, NY: ISM Teaching Systems, Inc.

Richardson, E., and Bradley, C. 1975. The ISM: A teacher-oriented method of reading instruction for the child-oriented teacher. *Journal of Learning Disabilities* 7:341–352.

Richardson, E., and Freeman, H. 1976. *The Reading Progress Feedback System.* Interdependent Learning Model. New York: Fordham University (ISBN-0-939632-32-2).

Richardson, E., and DiBenedetto, B. 1985. *Decoding Skills Test.* Parkton, MD: York Press.

Richardson, E., and Reinhart, J. 1989a. *Diagnosing Dyslexia in a Large City School District: The El Paso Project* (ISM Technical Bulletin No. 1). Mt. Vernon, NY: ISM Teaching Systems, Inc.

Richardson, E., and Reinhart, J. 1989b. *Diagnosing and Treating Dyslexia in a Large City School District: The El Paso Project, Year 2.* (ISM Technical Bulletin No. 3). Mt. Vernon, NY: ISM Teaching Systems, Inc.

Rozin, P., Poritsky, F., and Sotsky, R. 1971. American children with reading problems can easily learn to read English represented by Chinese characters. *Science* 71:1264.

Ruddell, R.B. 1976. Psycholinguistic implications for a systems of cummunication model. In *Theoretical Models and Processes of Reading,* eds. H. Singer and R.B. Ruddell. Newark, DE: International Reading Association.

Rumelhart, D. E. 1977. Toward an interactive model of reading. In *Attention and Performance,* Vol. 6, eds. S. Dornic and P. Rabbit. Hillsdale, NJ: Lawrence Erlbaum Associates.

Rumelhart, D.E., and McClelland, J.L. 1981. Interactive processing through spreading activation. In *Interactive Processes in Reading,* eds. A.M. Lesgold and C.A. Perfetti. Hillsdale, NJ: Lawrence Erlbaum Associates.

Smith, C.B., and Wardhaugh, R. 1980. *Series "r".* New York: Macmillan Publishing, Inc.

Vellutino, F.R. 1979. *Dyslexia: Theory and Research.* Cambridge, MA: MIT Press.

Vygotsky, L.S. 1962. *Thought and Language.* Cambridge, MA: MIT Press.

Wardhaugh, R. 1976. Theories of language acquisition in relation to beginning reading instruction. In *Theoretical Models and Processes of Reading,* eds. H. Singer and R.B. Ruddell. Newark, DE: International Reading Association.

Chapter • 4

Language Comprehension and Text Structure

Joanne F. Carlisle

Although children are said to understand the language structures used by adult speakers by the time they start school, they go on learning about language and acquire very important kinds of control over aspects of language comprehension through the school years. The growth of their language comprehension is fostered by the quality and kinds of experiences they have with both oral and written language texts. The level of proficiency they achieve is also affected by their language-learning capabilities, so we cannot assume that every child will make the same progress if offered the same instruction.

Language comprehension entails not simply adequate processing of basic language components, such as syntax and semantics, on a sentence-by-sentence basis (microstructures), but also understanding of the rhetorical structures used to frame the presentation of ideas and the relationships that interconnect ideas in texts (macrostructures). The term *text*, as it is used here, means the use of more than one sentence in a unified speech act, whether oral or written. In such a speech act, sentences must be related to one another in some way in order to convey a message. Thus, it is likely that comprehension of texts will be

This research reported herein was supported by a grant from the Northwestern University Grants Committee.

Gretchen Mitman and Karen Schoenhals deserve credit for their work on this project. Specifically, they provided invaluable assistance analyzing the passages and the students' performances. I am also grateful for the comments of Addison Stone and John Pfeiffer on earlier drafts of this chapter.

dependent upon students' awareness of the ways that ideas can be related to one another to achieve some communicative purpose.

The nature of text structures and the effects of text structure on comprehension and recall have become an area of active research interest only in the last twenty years (see Horowitz 1987). Much of the research to date has focused on adults; some studies have been concerned with developmental issues, including the extent to which school-age children understand and use text structure in remembering text passages. Regardless of the considerable interest in these issues, there is much that is still poorly understood about text structures and their effects on comprehension. Certainly, little is known about the degree to which comprehension of text structures constitutes a specific deficit for children with significant language comprehension problems. We are just beginning to realize that it is important to understand poor comprehenders' problems with both microstructural and macrostructural aspects of text comprehension.

The purpose of this chapter, then, is to discuss understanding of text structure as a factor in the language comprehension of good and poor comprehenders. The first section focuses on the relationship between comprehension of microstructures and macrostructures in text comprehension. The second section looks at the problems poor comprehenders might have understanding texts, and the third section focuses on texts, tasks, and modality of presentation as they affect understanding of text structures. These are followed by a section that presents the results of a study focused on the comprehension of sentences at different levels of importance in texts. The last section focuses on current issues of potential significance to researchers and practitioners.

At several points in the discussion, illustrations will be drawn from a study of students' performances on passages presented for reading and listening, in which comprehension and recall of the ideas of text sentences were analyzed as a function of their importance in the text. This study involves a re-analysis of an existing data base. The original study concerned differences in performances on different types of test sentences by students who were good at listening and reading, poor at reading, poor at listening, or poor at both. One hundred sixty-six fourth, sixth, and eighth graders from regular classes were presented with short expository passages at three levels of difficulty—one two grade levels below their grade, one on grade level, and one two grade levels above their grade. Comprehension was tested by sentence verification, following a system devised by Royer and his colleagues (Royer, Hastings, and Hook 1979; Royer et al. 1986). This meant that, after reading or listening to each passage, the students responded to twelve sentences, indicating whether the idea of the sentence had been in the passage. Four types of test sentences were used: *Originals* (sentences taken exactly from the passage), *Paraphrases* (sentences with the same meaning but shifts in word choice and word order), *Meaning Changes* (sentences like Originals except for the substitution of one or two words), and *Distractors* (sentences with information on the topic not mentioned in the passage). Examples of these types of test sentences can be seen in Appendix A to this chapter. The student who has grasped the intended meaning of the author responds "yes" to Originals and Paraphrases and "no" to Meaning Changes and Distractors. This method tests comprehension of sentences within a text passage and so may help us understand the interrelations of microstructural and macrostructural levels of language comprehension. The method is thought to assess language comprehension without taxing higher-level reasoning abilities (Royer 1986).

With the initial analysis of the students' performances new questions arose. One was the degree to which errors on the four different types of sentences might be attributable to characteristics of the passages from which they had come. The present research report involves re-analysis of the students' performances, but now focused on aspects of text structure that might affect sentence comprehension. Readers interested in the development of the Listening and Reading subtests or in the initial research report are referred to Carlisle (1989a, 1989b) and Carlisle and Felbinger (1991).

LANGUAGE COMPREHENSION

Comprehension at Microstructural Levels

Children become increasingly adept at understanding language, oral and written, over the school years (Doehring et al. 1981; Morice and Slaghuis 1985). Growth of students' language comprehension is supported by an increasingly sophisticated understanding of the ways that language is appropriately used in different contexts (Prutting 1982). Also evident is growth in their ability to reflect on and with language. They become more sensitive to words and sentences with more than one meaning, they understand and use figurative language more fully, and they detect inconsistencies and inaccuracies of language use (Menyuk 1984). Their cognitive and linguistic development fosters the development of metalinguistic capabilities (Tunmer 1989). Over time they gain proficiency in making accurate judgments about language use and manipulating aspects of language (e.g., sounds in words or word order in sentences), and they learn to interrelate language and thought processes (Bashir, Wiig, and Abrams 1987). Because so many aspects of linguistic and metalinguistic capabilities develop so rapidly between ages 6 and 16, language comprehension in listening (as also in reading) of older students is qualitatively different from that of younger students.

Language comprehension seems to be most commonly understood as the processing of linguistic information of words, phrases, and sentences. Typically, published tests of language comprehension focus predominantly on comprehension of words and sentences. Students are asked to remember and repeat sentences, to judge whether or not the sentences are grammatical, and to manipulate colored blocks or point to pictures that correspond to word or sentence meanings. Processing of linguistic information at the sentence level has been referred to as requiring microstructural analysis (Kintsch and van Dijk 1978; Pearson and Camperell 1985). However, because language comprehension in normal contexts involves extended discourse, language comprehension also includes processing at a macrostructural level (Kintsch and van Dijk 1978; Pearson and Camperell 1985). This macrostructural level entails awareness and analysis of the relations among ideas in the full communicative act, sometimes referred to as rhetorical structures or text structures (Horowitz 1987; Meyer and Rice 1984). The text structure constitutes a sort of mental map by which readers or listeners are able to construct a mental representation of the writer's or speaker's intended meaning. Readers or listeners may perceive the logical connections among sentences and the relative importance of different ideas to the main argument or purpose. Thus, for example, in the passage called "Ice Boxes" in Appendix A, readers initially encounter the apparent purpose of the passage—to consider how people kept food from spoiling before refrigerators were invented. Readers sensitive to text structure would anticipate finding out how this problem was solved. When they have finished reading, they ideally will have extracted the two solutions mentioned—ice boxes and cellars—, and they may remember some or all of the details used to describe these methods of keeping food from spoiling.

Relationship of Sentence and Text Comprehension

In extended discourse, ideas may be related to one another in a number of different ways. Children are used to hearing explanations, descriptions, accounts of events, and stories before they enter school.

Presumably they become attuned to relationships between the purpose and structure of these forms of discourse. Once children start school, they encounter different types of discourse. The nature of texts and the ways teachers and scholars talk about texts gradually introduce new ways to organize ideas and events, new logical relations, and rhetorical devices. Awareness of expository text structures may begin at about a third-grade level (Gillis and Olson 1987; Rasool and Royer 1986). Over time, students become increasingly familiar with different types of expository text structures; they learn to use text structures to understand and remember ideas and information.

Initial encounters with text structures, therefore, may come through listening or reading. Oral texts may be loosely organized, characterized by coordination of ideas; in comparison, written texts may seem to be tightly organized and may be characterized by subordination of ideas to the central point. If these characterizations are correct, it is possible that students learn more about the full range of expository text structures from reading than they do from listening. The extent to which comprehension of text structures transfers from one modality to another is at this point largely a matter of speculation (Horowitz 1987). However, older students and adults, at least, are able to perform equally well on narrative and expository passages presented for listening and for reading (Smiley et al. 1977; Sticht and James 1984).

Students' awareness and knowledge of text structures might influence their understanding and memory for sentences. If so, we might expect the comprehension of sentences to differ, depending on their importance in the text structure and their relationship to one another. If we could compare comprehension of a sentence in isolation with comprehension of that sentence in a text, we could imagine two different outcomes. A sentence might be less well understood or remembered because the passage context (meaning and structure) made its meaning more obscure, or a sentence might be more easily understood because the passage context prepared the listener/reader to understand it.

In the research study referred to at the beginning of this chapter, our initial analysis of the data compared students' responses on different types of test sentences. However, as we looked at the data, we realized that the error rate seemed to vary on *each* type of test sentence, as well as across sentence types. Because the students were making their sentence judgments after reading or listening to short expository passages, the text structure might have affected their comprehension of individual sentences. If this were the case, it would constitute evidence that text structure influenced sentence comprehension. Following this line of reasoning, we looked to see if students had different error rates on the simplest kind of test sentence—those taken directly from the passage (Originals). Remember that the students were asked to read or listen to a passage and then to judge whether or not each test sentence contained an idea from the passage.

The analysis of errors on Originals turned out as we had expected. The students' sentence judgments were inconsistent: they made virtually no errors on some Originals, but many errors on others.

The sentences in figure 1 illustrate these results. They were taken from two passages listened to or read by the fourth graders and sixth graders. Having listened to a passage called "Sled Dogs," these students generally recognized the idea of sentence #10 as having been in the passage, but about a third of them responded incorrectly to sentence #3. The fact that the fourth and sixth graders had similar response patterns suggests that the result is not group-specific. Furthermore, the same sort of inconsistency can be seen in the students' responses to Originals after reading a passage, as illustrated by the differences in percent of errors on sentences #6 and #9, following the reading of "Mountain Climbing." In each of these cases (and on a number of the other passages), there is nothing about the sentence structure itself that would lead us to expect more errors on the one sentence than on the other. The most likely explanation is that charcteristics of the text affect sentence comprehension and recall, not just characteristics of the sentences themselves.

Listening Passage—"Sled Dogs" (Fourth-grade reading level)

3. Eskimo sled dogs are raised to work.
   Fourth grade error rate = 36%
   Sixth grade error rate = 27%

10. One dog may snap at another who is not pulling his share.
    Fourth grade error rate = 7%
    Sixth grade error rate = 2%

Reading Passage—"Mountain Climbing" (Sixth-grade reading level)

6. When the leader starts up a steep area, the next man "belays" him by fastening the rope around a rock in case he should fall.
   Fourth grade error rate = 14%
   Sixth grade error rate = 6%

9. They must also watch out for snow slides and large cracks hidden under the snow.
   Fourth grade error rate = 32%
   Sixth grade error rate = 24%

Figure 1. Error rates on originals from a listening and a reading passage.

The influence of text structure on sentence comprehension has been demonstrated in another way. Some researchers have given students two types of passages to read—passages with sentences in an orderly sequence, bearing a logical relation to one another, and passages in which the sentence order has been scrambled so that the text structure is disorganized (Danner 1976; Hinchley and Levy 1988; Taylor and Samuels 1983; Richgels 1987). When they tested the students' comprehension and recall, they found that performances on the well-structured passages were superior to performances on the scrambled passages. Such results suggest that some students, at least, are aware of the structural patterns of different passages and use this awareness to organize and retain the ideas of the passage. When extended discourse lacks apparent structure, the ideas of sentences are harder to understand and remember.

How Text Structure Might Come to Affect Comprehension and Recall

As we have noted, for older students and adults, text structure may aid comprehension and memory through mapping out the logical relations among the ideas presented in that text. Presumably, as authors write, they organize their ideas in particular ways. This organization can include an overall rhetorical pattern, as well as various methods to show the logical relations among ideas and events. In many passages there is a kind of hierarchy of ideas at decreasing levels of thematic importance, wherein the topic sentence (which often provides a clue to the overall rhetorical device) is explicated and extended, and these secondary ideas are supported by details (Meyer 1984; Meyer and Rice 1984). From experiences with texts, students become familiar with both general rhetorical structures and particular devices for linking ideas. As they start to read a passage in their textbooks or listen to a teacher's lecture, the initial sentences may activate an awareness of a given rhetorical or logical relationship. From this awareness, the students develop an expectation about how the subsequent information will be organized and presented. The organizational structure serves as a framework on which the listener or reader builds meaning. As Horowitz says, "Decisions about structure ultimately influence decisions about thinking, ways of knowing, and the different realities that readers or writers construct" (1987, p. 119). One important question, however, is the way young children learn about text structures.

Children learn about text structures from experiences with them. Some structures are grasped earlier than others, perhaps because some structures are common in young students' schoolbooks, while others are not. Along with experience, cognitive development may play a role in students' growing awareness and use of text structures. This may be because some structures require an understanding of more complex logical relations than others. For instance, understanding of comparisons may be dependent on the student's ability to understand transitive reasoning.

Both factors, experience and cognitive development, suggest that older students should be more sensitive to text structures than younger students and that older students should perform better on the more complex structural relations than younger students, as in fact research studies have found. Thus, some but not all third graders have been found to be sensitive to enumeration (e.g., "One kind . . . A second kind . . .") or sequences of ideas (e.g., "First . . . Then . . .") (Englert and Hiebert 1984). In contrast, sixth graders showed clear sensitivity to enumeration and sequencing structures but performed less well on comparisons (Englert and Hiebert 1984; Englert and Thomas 1987). Students appear to have continuing difficulties recognizing cause-effect structures, even in the fifth or sixth grades (Richgels et al. 1987; Zinar 1990).

Another issue involves students' awareness of the logical and linguistic cues that link sentences and reveal the relative importance of sentences in the overall framework, sometimes referred to as the hierarchical structure. The premise is that older students, who are more attuned to text structures, are more likely than younger students to recall thematically important information from the top level of the hierarchy (main idea) better than information from the lower levels (supportive ideas and details). Studies have provided some empirical support for this developmental pattern. For example, Taylor (1980) found that 12% of a fourth-grade group used the top-level structure in recalling passages, while 47% of a sixth-grade group did.

One other developmental issue involves the role of metacognition in text comprehension. Many researchers seem to feel that awareness is the cornerstone of effective use of text structure knowledge. However, children could have an implicit understanding of the text structure but not think to use this understanding in free recall conditions. Richgels et al. (1987) investigated the issue of awareness by using a variety of measures—use of organization in written recalls, use of organization in a composition, and indications of awareness in an interview. They found that students' interviews showed more awareness of the structures they were investigating (i.e., collection, comparison/contrast, causation, and problem-solution) than their recall protocols did.

Students differed in their ability to formulate an explanation of the structure of passages (e.g., "They show likenesses and differences" for a comparison).

Another method for determining students' sensitivity to text structures is detection of intrusions. For instance, Smith and Hahn (1989) used "macrostructural intrusions" in paragraphs presented to fourth, sixth, and eighth graders. These were sentences that would fit a different type of paragraph structure (e.g., a sentence from a sequence paragraph placed in a descriptive paragraph). The researchers found that the students occasionally commented on the intrusion, usually did not include the intrusion in their paragraph recalls, but almost always identified the violation of text structure when asked the question, "What is the problem with this paragraph?" The exception was with the comparison paragraphs, where even eighth graders showed minimal sensitivity to the text structure. The results of these two studies suggest that it is not possible to infer students' awareness of text structures from performances on recall tasks; instead, more direct forms of inquiry need to be used. Further, students may be aware of the text structure but not use it in retelling the passage. This may be because retelling of passages requires kinds of knowledge other than awareness of the text structure.

POOR COMPREHENDERS' UNDERSTANDING OF TEXTS

Possible Reasons for Problems Comprehending Text Structures

It is likely that most children with significant comprehension problems (either in oral language or in reading) have difficulty gaining understanding of text structures and using them efficiently to construct meaning from texts. There are several possible reasons for such an expectation. One is that children with all kinds of comprehension problems might be less proficient at microstructural processing levels, and so might bring less linguistic competence to the macrostructural aspects of texts as well. Another reason is that poor comprehenders might develop awareness of text structures more slowly, possibly because they read fewer books and simpler books than their peers. This reason is akin to what Stanovich (1986) calls the Matthew effect, wherein good readers become increasingly able and poor readers suffer from increasing decrements in the development of reading and reading-related skills. Poor comprehenders may also be in educational settings where teachers do not present information for learning via extended discourse. A third possibility is that comprehension of text structure involves a higher level of cognitive development, because it presupposes an ability to understand various logical relations among ideas. Thus, some poor comprehenders might have little or no difficulty with microstructural processing but extensive difficulty using text structures as a means for understanding and remembering texts. Each of these explanations could apply to some subset of the broad group identified as "poor comprehenders."

Types of Poor Comprehenders

At present we have little support for any of these possible explanations, in part because researchers tend not to sort their subjects into different groups on the basis of comparisons of their comprehension of oral and written language. Most typically, poor readers are distinguished from good readers on a test of reading comprehension only. However, unless we know more about the nature of the students' deficits in oral as well as written language, we may not learn whether or why poor comprehenders have problems with the interrelation of microstructural and macrostructural linguistic processing. The inaccurate identification of "poor comprehender" groups constitutes a significant problem for the interpretation of the results of a large number of research studies.

Commonly, comprehension studies compare performance of good and poor readers. Poor readers are identified as performing somewhere below grade level (the discrepancy varying with the study) on a test of comprehension (Berger 1978; Hinchley and Levy 1988; Weisberg 1979; Zinar 1990). In some cases, the students are also identified as receiving special services of some kind, including Title I (Smiley et al. 1977) or Learning Disabilities (Guthrie and Taylor 1976).

The problem with this approach to identifying poor comprehenders is that students can do poorly on reading comprehension tests for several different reasons. One reason is that they have significant language comprehension problems. If their listening comprehension were tested, as well as their reading comprehension, these students would show deficits in both areas. A second reason, however, is poor word recognition skills. Students with good language comprehension, as shown by adequate performance on a listening comprehension test, might nonetheless appear to have language comprehension difficulties on a reading test if they are having significant problems with accurate and efficient word recognition. Because these students can perform well on the same passages presented orally, it is evident that they do not *really* have comprehension problems, even though their reading comprehension test scores seem to suggest that they do!

In studies that use only a measure of reading comprehension to define good and poor readers, groups of poor readers may contain different numbers of these two types of poor reading comprehenders. It is no wonder, then, that different studies have yielded different results, particularly when they compare listening and reading performances. Thus, for example, Berger (1978) found that good readers were better than poor readers at recalling passage information in both listening and reading. In contrast, Horowitz and Samuels (1985) found that the good readers differed from the poor readers in reading but not in listening. It is hard to reconcile differences in results when we suspect that they are attributable to unspecified differences in the nature of the reading problems of the "poor readers."

Researchers may recognize the importance of controlling for poor decoding skills when they are comparing groups of students on passage comprehension, but adjusting for low levels of decoding skill does not eliminate the possibility that groups differ in language comprehension. For instance, one way to control for possible group differences in word recognition skills is to use passages that are very easy for the reading disabled or learning disabled students. This approach was used by Englert and Thomas (1987) when they compared learning disabled (LD) and nondisabled students on their awareness of text structures and their ability to use text structures in writing. The students were in two grade-level groups, one representing younger students (third and fourth graders) and the other representing older students (sixth and seventh graders). The LD students were matched on IQ and reading level to low-achieving children in the third or sixth grades, and a normal-achieving control group was also used. The LD groups' performance on both reading and writing tasks was significantly worse than that of both the normal-achieving peers and the low-achieving group. The researchers suggest that the poor performance of the LD group cannot be explained by their reading ability, because the passages were at a grade level below their reading capabilities and because the reading passages were read aloud to them. Instead, the researchers suggest that the LD students lacked the metacognitive skills needed to recognize text structures. It is possible, however, that at least some of these students had significant receptive language difficulties. If so, controls for decoding difficulty would not make the passages equally accessible to the different groups of students.

There are good reasons to expect that more precise characterization of the comprehension problems of poor readers would clarify our understanding of students' problems in understanding texts. The research literature largely supports the view that the reasons for poor performances on text comprehension tests differ for "poor readers" with and without listening comprehension problems. A model for the relationship between listening and reading has been offered by Gough and Tunmer (1986). They argue that a simple view of reading comprehension is that it is the product of listening and decoding (word recognition). This model can account for the dyslexic student, who is usually found to be poor in word recognition but not deficient in listening or general language comprehension capabilities. It can also account for students whose oral language disabilities affect their listening comprehension. Whether their word recognition skills are poor or not, their reading comprehension is seriously affected.

Research studies have provided support for assumptions about the relationship of reading and listening that underlie this model. There are indications that students weak in language comprehension are also poor reading comprehenders. Some of these are undoubtedly children who were diagnosed as having language impairments in the preschool years. Such children are very likely to develop problems with reading comprehension in the school years (Aram and Nation 1975). In one study (Stark et al. 1984), 14 normal and 29 specifically language-impaired (SLI) children were assessed at the ages of 4½ to 8. They were reassessed four years later, when they were 8 to 12 years old. The reassessment indicated that all of the children were developing their language skills, but the language development of the SLI children was taking place at a slower rate. Furthermore, 80% of the SLI children were found to have significant problems with reading comprehension, while none of the normal children did. The language-learning problems that children have in their preschool years are chronic; quite consistently there is a pattern of underachievement in school, particularly in language-related areas of learning such as reading.

Researchers who seek to identify the nature of reading disabilities generally distinguish two types of reading problems—those that are specific to reading and those that are attributable to more general language comprehension deficiencies. The specifically disabled readers (sometimes synonymous with dyslexia) are commonly described as having adequate listening comprehension capabilities (Conners and Olsen 1989). Their poor performances in reading comprehension are attributable to poor word recognition processes. The students with general comprehension deficits may fall into the category of "garden-variety" poor readers (Gough and Tunmer 1986), a group that also has been referred to as "generally backward" readers (Rutter 1979).

Aaron, Kutcha, and Grapenthin (1988) have shown that these groups are distinguishable. These researchers gave a group of 38 reading-disabled students in the fourth through eighth grades tests of reading and listening comprehension. They separated the students into two groups—those with poor performances in listening comprehension and those with adequate performances in listening comprehension. Then they gave both groups tests of word recognition and comprehension. The poor readers who had not shown comprehension problems with listening did have significant difficulties with the word recognition tests. They did not perform poorly on the comprehension exercises. In contrast, the students with both reading and listening comprehension weaknesses performed poorly on the comprehension exercises.

Unless we make an effort to distinguish specifically disabled readers from students with general language comprehension deficits, we may not be able to interpret sensibly the results of studies investigating individual differences in comprehension at the microstructural and macrostructural levels.

TEXTS, TASKS, AND MODALITY OF TEXT PRESENTATION

Along with proper identification of the nature of students' comprehension problems, there are other factors affecting our ability to understand poor comprehenders' understanding of text structures. In particular, the types of texts that we present to them, the tasks we use to assess their comprehension and recall, and the modality of presentation may affect what we learn about their problems understanding texts. These factors affect the outcome of research studies and may also be relevant to teachers who wish to help students learn about text structures.

Assessing Listening and Reading

Research on text structure has been carried out sometimes by asking students to listen to passages and sometimes by asking students to read passages. A cursory glance at the research on expository text structures suggests that most studies require the students to read the passages. This may be because well-organized texts are thought to be more characteristic of written language than of oral language; written texts also may be considered representative of the cognitive and linguistic demands that content-area textbooks place on students. However, if awareness of text structure aids comprehensibility and recall, this should presumably be the case whether children are listening to or reading texts. Language comprehension is a unitary process, whether the input is visual or auditory (Sticht 1979; Royer 1986).

Comparisons of students' comprehension of texts through listening and reading might provide valuable information about the development of students' comprehension capabilities. That is, students can normally comprehend higher level passages through listening than reading in the first few years of school. This is because their word recognition skills are not proficient enough to allow them to read passages as complex as those they can understand by listening. However, by about the sixth grade, the correlation between listening and reading comprehension performances is much stronger (in the order of .60), suggesting that students' word recognition skills are accurate and efficient enough so that they can understand texts of comparable levels of difficulty through listening and reading (Sticht and James 1984). Older students may be better at reading than listening, because they have more control over the speed and strategies they use in trying to understand complex texts. Developmental differences in the relationship between listening and reading performances may have diagnostic implications. If a seventh-grade student were found to be significantly weaker in listening to or reading passages than his or her peers, the deviance from the normal pattern should be noted and investigated further.

In addition, examination of listening and reading is potentially useful as a way to help us learn more about children's developing awareness of text structures of different kinds. For example, Hinchley and Levy (1985) studied the comprehension of well-organized and poorly organized stories by third and sixth graders. The children were asked to read aloud, read silently, and listen to such stories. Sensitivity to text structure was inferred by comparing performances on the well-organized and poorly organized stories. The researchers found that the students at both grade levels were equally competent in listening and reading. However, they also found a small group of students at each grade level who were insensitive to story structure in both listening and reading. Investigation of the difficulties of these students might help us understand the reason or reasons for failures to understand text structures.

Some comparisons of listening and reading performances have been carried out using expository text passages. A noteworthy example is a study by Horowitz and Samuels (1985) in which sixth graders both read and listened to expository passages. The researchers found no difference in listening for good and poor readers for either easy or hard texts. Reading was tested not by silent reading but by oral reading; using this procedure, they found that the poor readers recalled less than the good readers on both easy and hard texts. They concluded that the decoding problems of the poor readers affected their performances in reading. The similar performances on the listening task suggested that the poor readers did not have general language problems. This sort of experimental control is helpful in interpreting the results. We might infer that the poor readers are in fact not deficient in their knowledge of text structures, because they did as well as the good readers on the listening task. If this is a reasonable interpretation, it contrasts with the findings of many other studies that have not used both listening and reading tasks but have nonetheless suggested that poor readers are deficient in the knowledge of text structures (e.g., Englert and Thomas 1987).

Studies that include modality comparisons may be particularly important for understanding the problems of the two types of poor comprehenders discussed earlier (those with comprehension problems in reading only and those with general language-comprehension problems). Quite possibly, these two groups have different problems developing competence in understanding text structures.

Tasks and Characteristics of Texts

A further methodological problem encountered in investigations of children's comprehension of texts is choice of task and of text passages. Because students become more able to use different text structures as they grow older, selection of appropriate texts becomes an issue. Furthermore, tasks that emphasize receptive language capabilities should be used, but rarely are.

The most common way researchers test awareness and use of text structure has been free recall, which entails asking the student to tell the examiner as much of the passage as possible after reading or listening to it (Smith and Hahn 1989). The expectation is that students who understand and use the text structure to construct the meaning of the passage will use the same structure to organize their retellings. While this task does seem to show us the relative importance of the ideas students recollect, it may also underestimate how much of the intended meaning of the text they have understood. Free recall is problematic because it is an expressive language task used to assess a receptive language activity. Typically, in either oral or written free recall, children tell less than they actually can remember. That is, if they are asked specific questions about the passage after they have completed a free recall task, they are apt to show that they remember additional ideas and details. The task may be more appropriately used with older students and students with good oral language capabilities than with younger or language-impaired students.

Two other methods used to assess awareness and use of text structures are the writing of texts and judgments of the appropriateness of sentences, in both cases given paragraph "starters." Both of these methods were used by Englert and Thomas (1987) in the study described earlier. The students were asked to judge the appropriateness of sentences that were candidates to follow a paragraph "stem" (i.e., a topic sentence and follow-up sentence that suggested the structure of the paragraph). An example of a stem for a "description" paragraph is:

The Mako shark looks frightening. Its nose comes to a point.

Students then were asked to decide which sentences could be included in this paragraph. Two of the choices were "target sentences":

   a.   The Mako shark's eyes are set back deep in its head.
   b.   The Mako shark's mouth has several rows of teeth.

Two of the choices were "distractor sentences":

   a.   There are several steps to catching a shark.
   b.   First, it is important to find an area of the ocean where sharks live.

For the writing condition, students were presented with the same kinds of two-sentence paragraph starters and were asked to add two sentences that fit closely with the topic. The writing task has the same problem as the free recall task discussed above, in that success is to a large extent dependent on the students' expressive language capabilities. An additional problem is that students can have extreme difficulties with writing for reasons other than their knowledge of text structures (e.g., fine motor or attention deficits). The researchers read the paragraph starters to the students and, when necessary, allowed the LD students to dictate their answers instead of writing them. Such adjustments eliminate some of the possible reasons for failure (e.g., handwriting and spelling) but not others (e.g., difficulties with oral language formulation).

The sentence judgment task appears to be a more appropriate way of assessing awareness of text structures, in that successful performance seems to depend on receptive language processing and metacognitive awareness. As the example above shows, the paragraph starters suggest an organizational structure that the reader must assume will be used for the remainder of the paragraph. We can probably infer that, if the student correctly distinguishes the two sentences that fit from the two that do not, he or she is sensitive to that type of expository structure. In this sense, the task will provide information about awareness of text structures. It introduces another problem, however. This is the use of artificially simple texts as a means of assessing knowledge of text structures. In naturalistic situations, texts do not have such simple and/or clear-cut organizational structures. Thus, students' performances on such a task may not help us understand whether these students, or others like them, are likely to use cues that signal text structures under normal listening and reading circumstances.

An indication that simplified texts may yield misleading results comes from a study in which "contrived texts," those written to be good examples of particular text structures, are compared to "less constrained texts," those more closely resembling passages from typical reading materials that students encounter. Hare, Rabinowitz, and Schieble (1989) studied the effects of these two types of texts on main idea comprehension. Their subjects were fourth, sixth, and eleventh graders who were reported to have no difficulties with decoding or overall reading capabilities. They found that students inferred fewer main ideas from the "less constrained" texts than from the "contrived" texts. They suggest that the relatively predictable structure of contrived texts made it easier for students to infer the main idea, if it was implicit. Natural texts may contain partial or irregular overlap of thematic material. Students may not be able to abstract a single main idea, because different bits of information seem salient but are not related to one another in a single way.

It is possible that understanding the top-level structure may not be sufficient for understanding the full passage. First of all, the choice of structure may either interfere with or facilitate the understanding of the particular content of the passage (Horowitz 1987). Second, the overall rhetorical structure may not be the only logical relation connecting ideas. When texts are not written to be exemplary models, supportive ideas may be linked in a number of different ways, and the number as well as the complexities of these linkages may place substantial hurdles in the way of the young or less able student. An additional problem is that the cues focusing attention on the relations of ideas may or may not be explicit. The presence of different types of logical relations to support and build on the main idea in a passage, as illustrated by Meyer and Rice (1984), contrasts with the simple texts devised for some research projects, in which one and only one type of structure connects ideas throughout a given passage (see Richgels et al. 1987).

An example of the complexity of relations within a relatively simple passage can be seen by looking again at the passage called "Ice Boxes" in Appendix A. This paragraph was constructed from information in an encyclopedia; its hierarchical structure was subsequently analyzed, using Meyer's system (Meyer 1984; Meyer and Rice 1984). The first sentence serves as the cue to the rhetorical device called *problem-solution*. However, the paragraph (supportive ideas and details) also includes causation and description relations. An example of causation can be found in the middle of the paragraph where the difficulty of using an ice box in warm winters or in warm climates is discussed. In addition, a good part of the paragraph involves description of the ice box and the process by which the ice is provided for ice boxes. It is possible that, for passages of this type, awareness of the top level rhetorical structure may be less demanding than grasping the logical relations at lower levels. Furthermore, it is possible that there is a trade-off between levels of thematic importance and the number of ideas at each level. For instance, in "Ice Boxes," there is just one sentence that sets up the problem-solution pattern. However, there are a handful of sentences that provide a description of ice boxes and that show the causation pattern. Could numbers of ideas and levels of thematic importance vie for salience in the children's process of understanding and remembering such a passage?

In content area textbooks (e.g., science, social studies, and history), many passages may not follow one rhetorical pattern and may not make the various rhetorical devices clear because of inadequate signaling and other such problems. In fact, the structural unity of passages is a problem discussed by researchers interested in "readable textbooks" (Anderson and Armbruster 1986). Because contrived texts may provide a misleading view of the complexities of understanding text structures, it seems clear that we need to know more about how children construct meaning when passages are characterized by the interplay of different logical relations.

Sentence Comprehension as a Function of Text Structure

As so often happens in a relatively new area of research, initial hypotheses often suggest appealingly simple and straight-forward explanations of students' behaviors, but these become less clear as we come to appreciate the complexities of the problems that need to be understood in order to test the hypotheses. It is apparent at this point that certain aspects of research methodology may be affecting our understanding of text structures and the problems of language comprehension associated with them. In fact, as researchers make different decisions about kinds of texts and tasks and so on, a number of the initial assumptions about the nature of text structures in comprehension processing are being challenged (see Smith and Hahn 1989; Zinar 1990). That appears to be the case in the study we undertook in re-analyzing students' performances on expository passages. Following the work of Meyer and others (see Meyer 1984; Meyer and Rice 1984), we asked whether students' test performances would reflect the thematic importance of the sentences in the test passages, but we used somewhat different methods and ended up with different results. Our approach involved the identification of students with specific comprehension problems in listening or reading or in both areas, the use of relatively natural passages, and the use of tasks that tested receptive language comprehension. Some of the particulars of our methodology need more complete explanation.

As the earlier description of this project suggested, sentence verification was used as the method of assessing comprehension of passages. This is a recognition measure, one that is believed to assess language comprehension without tapping complex metacognitive capabilities or test-taking strategies (Royer 1986). The passages were originally developed to represent explanations of events or phenomenon that are generally familiar to school-age children. The information and structure of the passages were adapted from entries in encyclopedias found in school libraries (see Carlisle 1989b, and Carlisle and Felbinger 1991, for further details about the test materials).

For this study, the passages were analyzed by the author and by a research assistant to determine the thematic importance of each of the sentences, using Meyer's hierarchical system (1984). Comparisons of our hierarchical structures yielded a number of differences labeling the logical relatives of ideas subordinate for the main idea (Level 2); these were resolved by discussion and mutual agreement. However, in several cases, it seemed that the internal structure of the passages could be represented in several different ways, (a problem also noted by Hare, Rabinowitz, and Schieble 1989). For the Listening subtest, all of the passages had a top-level structure of description (Level 1); at Level 2, however, there were several different logical relations, as table I shows.

On the Reading subtest, a variety of top-level structures were found, but all of the passages had description as one of the Level 2 relations, as table I also shows. All of the passages had originally been selected because they conformed to the general category of "explana-

Table I. Rhetorical Structure at Levels 1 and 2 for Listening and Reading Passages

Grade Level	LISTENING	
	Level 1	Level 2
2	Description	Antecedent/Consequent, Description
4	Description	Collection, Description
6	Description	Antecedent/Consequent, Description
8	Description	Description, Comparison
10	Description	Collection, Description
	READING	
2	Comparison	Description
4	Problem/Solution	Antecedent/Consequent, Description
6	Description	Antecedent/Consequent
8	Comparison	Description, Collection
10	Comparison	Description

tions" of some event or phenomenon. It is interesting, therefore, that this post-hoc analysis showed description to be the prevailing pattern, as description includes what Meyer calls explanation. Given the similarity of the top-level structures for listening, we felt we could compare students' performance across grade levels and comprehension ability groups. The same approach would not yield interpretable results from Reading, since the top-level structures differed. That is, a clear effect for thematic importance might not emerge if different overall rhetorical structures were used. The reading passages, then, would allow us to ask whether levels of thematic importance based on different rhetorical devices affect comprehension the same way. This question was left for another report, and analysis of the Listening passages only are included here.

As noted earlier, the students at each grade level were presented with passages two grade levels below their grade placement, passages on grade level, and passages two grade-levels above their grade level. This being the case, we did not expect to find, and did not find, differences across grade levels in the students' mean performances on the passages on the Listening and Reading subtests. Using the grade level means and standard deviations, we identified students who were good at both listening and reading (henceforth, Good Both), poor at listening but not poor at reading (Poor Listeners), poor at reading but not poor at listening (Poor Readers), and poor at both listening and reading (Poor Both). In the three grades, there were 128 Good Both, 15 Poor Listeners, 13 Poor Readers, and 10 Poor Both. Word recognition tests (both standardized and experimental) indicated no significant differences, with the exception of the Poor Both being marginally weaker than the Good Both on the Wide Range Achievement Test, Reading subtest. Thus, while the students were not classified as reading disabled or language impaired, some had weak comprehension capabilities in listening, reading, or both in comparison to their peers.

Our first question, then, was whether students at the three grade levels would show an effect of level of thematic importance on the sentence verification tests, following Listening. Because the students at each grade level read or listened to passages appropriate for their grade level, we did not expect to find differences in their overall levels of performance. Instead, we were curious to see whether the older students would recall comparatively more main ideas (Level 1) than supportive sentences and details (Levels 2 and 3), in contrast to the younger students. However, we did not find the typical "staircase" pattern that other studies have found (see Meyer 1984; Meyer and Rice 1984), as figure 2 shows. That is, we did not find a step down (decrease in accuracy) from Level 1 to Level 2 and from Level 2 to Level 3 at any grade level.

The students at all grade levels did better on Level 1 sentences than Level 2 sentences, but their performances on Level 3 sentences were also better than those on Level 2! A repeated measures multivariate analysis showed that the grade-level effect was not significant, but that the effect for Levels was. (See Appendix B for the results of the statistical analyses.) Separate one-way analyses of variance showed that Level 1

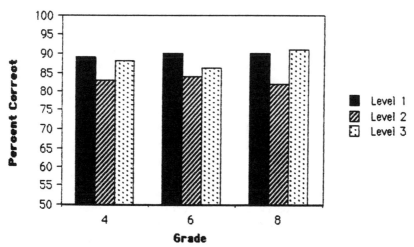

Figure 2.   Listening comprehension as a function of thematic importance: grade-level comparisons.

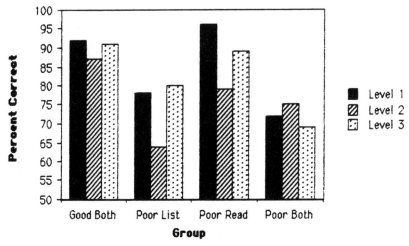

Figure 3. Listening comprehension as a function of thematic importance: comparisons of good and poor listeners and readers.

and 2 did not differ significantly by grade; performances did differ on Level 3, as the eighth graders apparently remembered details at this level better than the sixth graders did. The interaction was not significant.

The second question was whether students with different comprehension capabilities would show the effect of thematic importance on their sentence responses on the Listening subtest. If the Poor Listeners and Poor Both did not show an effect on levels of thematic importance, we might infer that they were less able than their peers at using thematic importance to understand and remember these passages. The results, shown in figure 3, do indicate that the Poor Listeners and the Poor Both performed more poorly in general. The Poor Listeners had the same pattern of performances that we saw across grade levels in figure 2, but the drop in performance on Level 2 sentences is considerably more pronounced. The Poor Both group had significantly more difficulty with Level 1 sentences, which may reflect difficulties understanding and remembering the main ideas of the passages. A repeated measures analysis of variance showed significant differences across groups and levels; the interaction was also significant.

What might all of this mean? One finding that stands out is the students' greater accuracy for remembering details (Level 3 sentences) than has emerged in other studies of thematic importance. Two aspects of this study may explain this unusual finding. One is the nature of the passages. At Level 2 one (and sometimes two) different forms of logical relations are often introduced. The students may have had particular difficulty seeing the relationships between ideas (and remembering them), because of the newly introduced complexities at this level. The second is the nature of the test. The sentence verification technique might have facilitated recall of the detail, perhaps because it does not require the formulation of sentences, as free recall does. These results certainly suggest that differences on recall and recognition tasks should be explored further.

A second interesting finding is the differences in performances on the Listening passages for students who have specific weaknesses in listening or in both listening and reading. The Poor Listeners have a more aggravated problem with the Level 2 sentences than their Poor Reader peers. The Poor Both students, on the other hand, seem to be having difficulties with even main idea comprehension. The students in this study were not identified by their school as having specific reading or language learning disabilities, so that differences in performances on these passages may show that there is a fair amount of variation in normal groups of students in the mastery of text structures when they listen to and read expository texts. Comparisons of the patterns of performance of previously diagnosed poor comprehenders of different types might be one way to determine why they have difficulties with language comprehension of expository texts.

CURRENT ISSUES

Despite the fact that comprehension of text structures has been a popular area of research for about twenty years, there continue to be many aspects of students' understanding of text structures that are not well understood. Because comprehension of texts and text structure is of interest to educators and special educators, speech-language pathologists, reading researchers, linguists, and psychologists, research studies will undoubtedly continue to be multifaceted in their concerns, but review of the work to date indicates that there are a number of issues of importance to all interested parties. For the sake of clarity of focus, I have chosen four such issues that seem particularly crucial if our goal is to understand the problems students might have with text structures and text comprehension.

A Broader View of Text Comprehension

In some respects, studies of text structures have had a relatively narrow focus. At present, we know very little about children's understanding of texts in relation to their linguistic and cognitive capabilities. It seems clear that comprehension of text structures draws on various aspects of linguistic knowledge, but sensitivity to text structures may also be related to cognitive development as well. This may be because of the importance of students' understanding of logical relations. Both the linguistic capabilities and the cognitive capabilities of students would seem to be natural areas of investigation, of course in relation to text comprehension performances.

Furthermore, Horowitz (1987) suggests that rhetorical structures interact not only with other linguistic and cognitive factors but also with social-contextual factors that are related to text comprehension. The knowledge that children bring to the understanding of texts and the contexts in which they engage in the process of understanding texts may influence what they come to understand from them. There are complex interrelations between expectations, prior knowledge, and text structure, all of which may have an impact on comprehensibility of texts. For instance, the overriding text structure and the logical organization expected by the students may be in conflict with one another. What a person knows about a topic and the way this knowledge is organized in memory may not be reflected in the way a given author discusses that topic (Horowitz 1987). Thus, Roller (1990) suggests that further research is needed in order to understand the ways in which prior knowledge and text structures interact. It may be that passages on familiar topics are understood primarily in relation to knowledge structures, whereas passages on unfamiliar topics are comprehended in relation to the structure provided by the text itself.

Complexities and Interrelations

A second issue involves the complexities of understanding text structures. We have discussed overall rhetorical structures, the logical relations of ideas used to explicate and support the major theme, and the use of various devices and cues to help readers and listeners follow the relations of ideas as they are conceived by the speaker or writer. We believe that the kinds of text structures commonly used by speakers and writers represent the ways people think and order their knowledge about the world. However, in some respects, we may not yet appreciate all of the complexities and interrelations of the knowledge of text structure and knowledge of topics and perceived purposes of communication. Certainly, the use of tidy passages that conform to a single type of text structure will not help us understand such complex interactions. For this reason, more naturalistic passages may provide the kinds of insights we seek. There are particular reasons to believe that processing of text structures may not be a simple matter. We need to understand more fully the difficulties posed by the introduction of different logical relations as a way to explicate and support the main idea of a passage. The integration of these different supportive ideas might be more challenging than recognition of the main idea itself. Furthermore, does subordination of ideas or sentences make passages harder or easier to understand than coordination of ideas? Is subordination more difficult for younger and less linguistically able children to understand? These and similar questions need to be answered.

We know little about naturalistic forms and uses of texts, oral and written. Are teachers' lectures characteristically more loosely structured than the textbooks' passages? Are textbooks written with concern for the types and complexities of the structural relations and rhetorical devices? Interest in such issues has resulted in studies of textbooks. We need to learn about the texts students interact with and the ways they learn about text structure from their experiences in schools.

Texts and Tasks

A third issue involves the problems of selecting appropriate tasks and passages both for research and diagnostic purposes. To learn about language comprehension at both microstructural and macrostructural levels, passages should present an overriding rhetorical structure and specified relations among the ideas used to explicate or support the main theme. We will not learn about text-processing capabilities of students if the texts assess primarily microstructural aspects of language comprehension. Along the same lines, the method of testing ideally should require attention to the text structure as a device to aid comprehension and recall of passage information.

Unfortunately, selection of appropriate texts and tasks continues to be a problem. For instance, Spring and French (1990) have chosen to use the two or three sentence "passages" of the Peabody Individual Achievement Test, Reading Comprehension (Dunn and Markwardt 1970) subtest, as the basis for their comparison of listening and reading comprehension performances. They have sorted odd and even items on this subtest to make two tests, one for use as a test of listening comprehension and the other as a test of reading comprehension. The short length of the passages is unlikely to require much, if any, structural analysis. Furthermore, because picture recognition is the method by which students' demonstrate comprehension, only passages whose "meaning" can be depicted in a single picture can be included. This method may not require attention to text structures. Somewhat similarly, Aaron (1991) has used two forms of the Woodcock Reading Mastery Test: one for assessing listening and one for assessing reading comprehension. Again, passages are relatively short. The method of assessing comprehension on the Woodcock is a modified cloze procedure. As on the PIAT, text-level processing is generally not required. As with other cloze procedure tests, it is likely that linguistic analysis solely at a microstructural level (sentence comprehension) is being assessed (see Kintsch and Yarbrough 1982).

The Problems of Different Types of Poor Comprehenders

A fourth issue is the distinction of different types of comprehension problems. It seems likely that students with specific problems in reading comprehension will differ from students with generalized language comprehension problems in their development of microstructural and macrostructural language comprehension capabilities. We must know the nature of students' comprehension problems in order to determine whether this expectation is a valid one. At present, we do not know enough to choose among the various possible explanations for poor comprehenders' difficulties developing sensitivities to text structures. For instance, microstructural levels of language comprehension may impede macrostructural processes; the reverse may be true. It may also be that long-term reading or language learning difficulties hinder the development of appropriate sorts of metalinguistic capabilities. It may be difficult for researchers and diagnosticians to identify students with different types of comprehension problems, but the effort seems necessary if we want to understand the developing text comprehension capabilities of these students.

Awareness of the problems different students have with text structures has important instructional implications. Anderson and Armbruster provide a helpful analogy when they compare reading of texts with driving through a city:

> For the most part, the flow of ideas from the page into and through the reader's mind is a smooth one. When barriers are encountered, the reader must know how to work around them. Likewise writers must know what to do to help increase the likelihood that his smooth flow of ideas is maintained. Thus, we see research on text variables as a way to forewarn authors about the potential rough spots for readers and a way to help teachers prepare readers to overcome these trouble spots (1986, p. 154).

APPENDIX A   ICE BOXES

How did people keep fresh food from spoiling before refrigerators were invented? Many people kept their fresh food in ice boxes. An ice box was a large chest with one space on top for a block of ice and a second space for the food. The ice came from frozen lakes and rivers in the winter. This ice was cut up with large saws and stored in ice houses. It was covered with sawdust to keep it from melting. For as long as the ice lasted, blocks of ice were brought to the homes of people who had ice boxes. But there was little ice for use in ice boxes in warm winters. And there was no ice for ice boxes in hot climates. Food spoiled quickly in such places, too! Where ice boxes could not be used, people kept potatoes and carrots in the cellars of their houses. Even with ice boxes and cool cellars, food could not be kept fresh for very long!

Examples of the four types of test sentences:

1. In the winter, ice was taken from frozen lakes and rivers. (Paraphrase)
2. It was covered with sawdust to keep it from freezing. (Meaning Change)
3. An ice box was a large chest with one space on top for a block of ice and a second space for food. (Original)
4. Large sleds or wagons were used to move the blocks of ice. (Distractor)

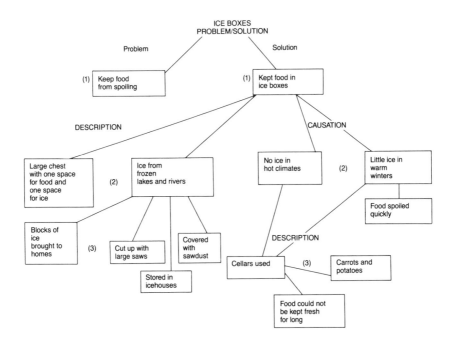

APPENDIX B   MULTIVARIATE REPEATED MEASURES ANALYSES FOR THE LISTENING SUBTEST

Grade-Level Performances on Test Sentences as a Function of Thematic Importance Levels

Grade	$F(2,150) = 0.424,\ p = .66$
Levels	$F(2,300) = 17.873,\ p < .001$
Interaction	$F(4,300) = 1.750,\ p = .14$

Good-Poor Comprehender Performances on Test Sentences as a Function of Thematic Importance

Group	$F(3,149) = 57.964,\ p < .001$
Levels	$F(2,298) = 10.887,\ p < .001$
Interaction	$F(6,298) = 3.750,\ p < .001$

REFERENCES

Aaron, P.G. 1991. Can reading disabilities be diagnosed without using intelligence tests? *Journal of Learning Disabilities* 24(3):178–87.

Aaron, P.G., Kuchta, S., and Grapenthin, C.T. 1988. Is there a thing called dyslexia? *Annals of Dyslexia* 38:33–49.

Anderson, T.H., and Armbruster, B.B. 1986. Readable textbooks, or, selecting a textbook is not like buying a pair of shoes. In *Reading Comprehension: From Research to Practice*, ed. J. Orsanu. Hillsdale, NJ: Lawrence Erlbaum Associates.

Aram, D.M., and Nation, J.E. 1975. Patterns of language behavior in children. *Journal of Speech and Hearing Research* 18:229–41.

Bashir, A.S., Wiig, E.H., and Abrams, J.C. 1987. Language disorders in childhood and adolescence: Implications for learning and socialization. *Pediatric Annals* 16(2):145–56.

Berger, N. 1978. Why can't Johnny read? Perhaps he's not a good listener. *Journal of Learning Disabilities* 11:633–38.

Carlisle, J.F. 1989a. Diagnosing comprehension deficits through listening and reading. *Annals of Dyslexia* 39:159–76.

Carlisle, J.F. 1989b. The use of the Sentence Verification Technique in diagnostic assessment of listening and reading comprehension. *Learning Disabilities Research* 5(1):33–44.

Carlisle, J.F., and Felbinger, L. 1991. Profiles in listening and reading comprehension. *Journal of Educational Psychology* 84(6):345–54.

Conners, F.A., and Olsen, R.K. 1989. Reading comprehension in dyslexia and normal readers: A component-skills analysis. In *Comprehension Processes in Reading*, eds. D.A. Balota, G.B. Flores d'Arcais, and K. Rayner. Hillsdale, NJ: Lawrence Erlbaum Associates.

Danner, F.W. 1976. Children's understanding of intersentence organization in the recall of short descriptive passages. *Journal of Educational Psychology* 68:174–83.

Doehring, D.G., Trites, R.L., Patel, P.G., and Fiedorowicz, C.A. 1981. *Reading Disabilities: The Interaction of Reading, Language, and Neuropsychological Deficits.* NY: Academic Press.

Dunn, L.M., and Markwardt, F.L. 1970. *Peabody Individual Achievement Test.* Circle Pines, MN: American Guidance Service, Inc.

Englert, C.S., and Hiebert, E. 1984. Children's developing awareness of text structures in expository materials. *Journal of Educational Psychology* 76:65–74.

Englert, C.S., and Thomas, C.C. 1987. Sensitivity to text structure in reading and writing: A comparison between learning disabled and non-learning disabled students. *Learning Disabilities Quarterly* 10(2):106–111.

Gillis, M.K., and Olson, M.W. 1987. Elementary IRIs: Do they reflect what we know about text type structure and comprehension? *Reading Research and Instruction* 27:36–44.

Gough, P.B., and Tunmer, W.E. 1986. Decoding, reading, and reading disabilities. *Remedial and Special Education* 7(1):6–10.

Guthrie, J.T., and Taylor, J.S. 1976. Psycholinguistic processing in reading and listening among good and poor readers. *Journal of Reading Behavior* 8:415–26.

Hare, V.C., Rabinowitz, M., and Schieble, K.M. 1989. Text effects on main idea comprehension. *Reading Research Quarterly* 24(1):72–88.

Hinchley, J., and Levy, B.A. 1988. Developmental and individual differences in reading comprehension. *Cognition and Instruction* 5(1):3–47.

Horowitz, R. 1987. Rhetorical structure in discourse processing. In *Comprehending Oral and Written Language,* eds. R. Horowitz and S.J. Samuels. NY: Academic Press.

Horowitz, R., and Samuels, S.J. 1985. Reading and listening to expository text. *Journal of Reading Behavior* 17(3):185–97.

Kintsch, W., and van Dijk, T. 1978. Toward a model of text comprehension and production. *Psychological Review* 85:363–94.

Kintsch, W., and Yarbrough, J.C. 1982. Role of rhetorical structure in text comprehension. *Journal of Educational Psychology* 74(6):828–34.

Menyuk, P. 1984. Language development and reading. In *Understanding Reading Comprehension,* ed. J. Flood. Newark, DE: International Reading Association.

Meyer, B.J.F. 1984. Organizational aspects of text: Effects on reading comprehension and applications for the classroom. In *Promoting Reading Comprehension,* ed. J. Flood. Newark, DE: International Reading Association.

Meyer, B.J.F., and Rice, G.E. 1984. The structure of text. In *Handbook of Reading Research,* ed. P.D. Pearson. NY: Longman.

Morice, R., and Slaghuis, W. 1985. Language performance and reading ability at 8 years of age. *Applied Psycholinguistics* 6:141–60.

Pearson, P.D., and Camperell, K. 1985. Comprehension of text structures. In *Theoretical Models and Processes of Reading,* 3rd ed., eds. H. Singer and R.B. Ruddell. Newark, DE: International Reading Association.

Prutting, C. 1982. Pragmatics as social competence. *Journal of Speech and Hearing Disorders* 47:123–34.

Rasool, J.M., and Royer, J.M. 1986. Assessment of reading comprehension using the sentence verification technique: Evidence from narrative and descriptive texts. *Journal of Educational Research* 79(3):180–84.

Richgels, D.J., McGee, L.M., Lomax, R.G., and Sheard, C. 1987. Awareness of four text structures: Effects on recall of expository text. *Reading Research Quarterly* 22(2):177–96.

Roller, C.M. 1990. The interaction of knowledge and structure variables in the processing of expository prose. *Reading Research Quarterly* 15(2):79–89.

Royer, J.M. 1986. The sentence verification technique as a measure of comprehension: Validity, reliability and practicality. University of Massachusetts, Unpublished manuscript.

Royer, J.M., Hastings, C.N., and Hook, C. 1979. A sentence verification technique for measuring reading comprehension. *Journal of Reading Behavior* 11(4):355–63.

Royer, J.M., Kulhavy, R.W., Lee, S., and Peterson, S.E. 1986. The relationship between reading and listening comprehension. *Educational and Psychological Research* 6:299–314.

Rutter, M. 1979. Prevalence and type of dyslexia. In *Dyslexia: An Appraisal of Current Knowledge,* eds. A.L. Benton and D. Pearl. NY: Oxford University Press.

Smiley, S.S., Oakley, D.D., Worthen, D., Campione, J.C., and Brown, A.L. 1977. Recall of thematically relevant material by adolescent good and poor readers as a function of written versus oral presentation. *Journal of Educational Psychology* 69:381–87.

Smith, J.F., and Hahn, A.L. 1989. Intermediate-grade students' sensitivity to macrostructure intrusions. *Journal of Reading Behavior* 21(2):167–80.

Spring, C., and French, L. 1990. Identifying children with specific reading disabilities from listening and reading discrepancy scores. *Journal of Learning Disabilities* 23(1):53–58.

Stark, R.E., Bernstein, L.E., Condino, R., Bender, M., Tallal, P., and Catts, H. 1984. Four-year follow-up study of language of impaired children. *Annals of Dyslexia* 34:49–68.

Stanovich, K.E. 1986. Matthew effects in reading: Some consequences of individual differences in the acquisition of literacy. *Reading Research Quarterly* 21(4):360–407.

Sticht, T.G. 1979. Applications of the audread model to reading comprehension evaluation and instruction. In *Theory and Practice of Early Reading*, Vol. 1, eds. L.B. Resnick and P.A. Weaver. Hillsdale, NJ: Lawrence Erlbaum Associates.

Sticht, T.G., and James, H.J. 1984. Listening and reading. In *Handbook of Reading Research*, ed. P.D. Pearson. NY: Longman.

Taylor, B.M. 1980. Children's memory for expository text after reading. *Reading Research Quarterly* 15:399–411.

Taylor, B.M., and Samuels, S.J. 1983. Children's use of text structure in the recall of expository material. *American Educational Research Journal* 20(4): 517–28.

Tunmer, W.F. 1989. The role of language-related factors in reading disability. In *Phonology and Reading Disability: Solving the Reading Puzzle*, eds. D. Shankweiler and I.Y. Liberman. Ann Arbor: University of Michigan Press.

Weisberg, R. 1979. A comparison of good and poor readers' ability to comprehend explicit and implicit information in short stories based on two modes of presentation. *Research in the Teaching of English* 18:337–51.

Zinar, S. 1990. Fifth-graders' recall of propositional content and causal relationships from expository prose. *Journal of Reading Behavior* 22(2):181–99.

Chapter • 5

Written Language

Doris J. Johnson

In 1967 I was asked to speak on the "Language Continuum" at the National meeting of The Orton Dyslexia Society in New York (Johnson 1968) and to discuss various hierarchies in the language acquisition process. At that time there was a growing awareness of childhood language learning disabilities. Now, nearly 25 years later, a great deal more has been learned about the relations between oral and written language, as well as the many variables that may have an impact on development.

In this chapter I have been asked to focus on one aspect of the language continuum—written language. However, it is necessary to review some of the complex relationships between oral language, reading, and writing, because the analysis of any written product requires an understanding of the characteristics of the learner, the home environment, schooling, type of instruction, and the activity of the learner.

My earliest perspective on the language continuum came from the work of Myklebust (1954) who suggested that during the course of development, children first accumulate experiences on which to base language. This he called *inner language*. Later, at about 9 months of age infants begin to understand words that represent experiences, such as, "ma-ma," "pat-a-cake," "all gone," and "bye-bye." Not long after, if the auditory-motor system is intact, children begin to use words meaningfully. Thus, expressive language begins. This is not to suggest, however, that infants are inactive expressively. On the contrary, as children babble and make sounds like the names for objects or experiences, someone in the environment reinforces the utterances, encourages the child to repeat them, and therefore enhances both receptive and expressive language. Thus, from the earliest stages, there are many reciprocal processes between cognition, language comprehension, and production. Following the acquisition of auditory language (although not necessarily fully developed) if children are exposed to print, they learn to read. This form of visual receptive language is followed by written expression if the visual motor system is intact and if the environment provides the necessary motivation and instruction.

Myklebust included bi-directional arrows in his hierarchy to show reciprocal patterns of development. For example, oral expressive language aids comprehension, as children learn to ask questions. In addition, reading enhances vocabulary growth and syntactic development along with an awareness of various forms of discourse. Finally, writing may change the way we think or organize ideas, and so it modifies our inner language. Thus, language development is not a simple continuum. Rather, it involves many complex interactions, any one of which may have gone awry among individuals with language learning problems.

The notion of a linear hierarchy has been questioned, particularly by researchers who report that some children write before they read. As one observes young children writing messages or journals with invented spelling, one sees that they do indeed write combinations of letters they cannot read. However, they have abstracted something from print in order to use invented spelling. If they had never been exposed to print or the idea that visual symbols represent sounds, it is doubtful that they would have a way to represent speech. In other words, although they may not be able to read in the purest sense, they have abstracted features from the orthography and retained some visual images, as well as phonological features, in order to begin the writing process. Thus, a certain amount of input is necessary for output. Similarly in the area of oral language, as children speak, their first communication attempts are not perfectly articulate (e.g., "mu" for milk; "ga-pu" for grandpa). If one played audio recordings of these utterances to the children, it is doubtful they would comprehend everything they had said. If there is no input, there will be little comprehension or expression. Thus, in order to write meaningfully children must be given the opportunity to hear and see many forms of language.

Recently I proposed a different language hierarchy (Johnson 1987) that suggests that the rudiments of all symbol systems including reading, writing, and mathematics begin very early in life, at least in literate cultures (see figure 1). Often the child's earliest toys are blocks with letters on them and picture books that provide an input for early literacy. Infants and toddlers also are given sets of graduated boxes or rings

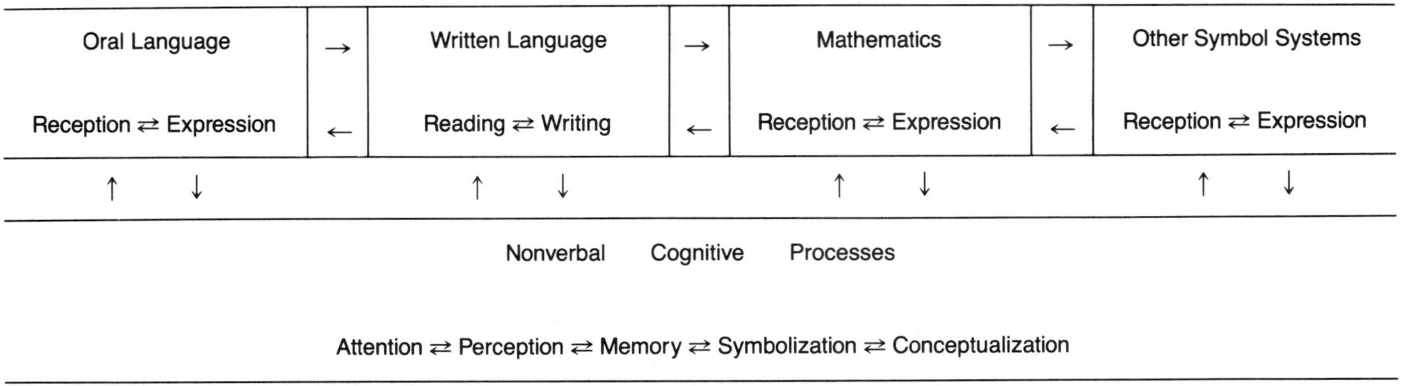

Oral Language		Written Language		Mathematics		Other Symbol Systems
	↑		↑		↑	
	↓		↓		↓	
Reception ⇄ Expression		Reading ⇄ Writing		Reception ⇄ Expression		Reception ⇄ Expression
→		→		→		→
←		←		←		←

Nonverbal   Cognitive   Processes

Attention ⇄ Perception ⇄ Memory ⇄ Symbolization ⇄ Conceptualization

Figure 1. Relationships between language, achievement, and cognitive processes.

that provide the basis for early seriation and math, or they play with pots and pans and discover notions about size relationships. In addition, as part of daily routines, adults frequently sing the alphabet song, count fingers and toes, draw pictures, and read stories that are forms of representation. Thus, the rudiments of written language are formed very early in life. Indeed, Vygotsky (1978) suggested that writing begins with the first gesture, a kind of visual symbol that is followed by drawings, symbolic play, and then writing.

New studies on early literacy (McLane and McNamee 1990) emphasize that learning to read and write begins long before formal instruction in school. All types of symbolic behavior such as play, drawing, story telling, reading nursery rhymes, labels, or signs with significant adults in the environment, contribute to literacy. Read (1986) says that young children have a natural interest in writing and that they enjoy playing with various types of representation. But, Read says, adults must show a genuine interest in the child's writing attempts as a means of expression. An enabling environment is essential. This includes responses to the child's questions (Bissex 1980) and awareness that the first scribbles, marks, and drawings have significance.

While there are many relationships between oral and written language, writing is not simply talk written down, albeit what one says can be transcribed. According to Vygotsky (1962), one of the major differences in the two forms of language is that writing involves an absent audience whereas in oral communication, a speaker can obtain immediate feedback when a message is not clear. Thus, one can clarify a point to meet the audience's needs. In recent years investigators have studied conversational repair among normals, and found that even relatively young children make adjustments for the listener. However, an investigation of children with language disorders (Woolf 1983) indicated they were less adept than normals in modifying their original message, perhaps because of limited vocabulary and/or the ability to see another person's point of view.

Written language also needs to be more complete and explicit than oral language. One must create a legible text, use vocabulary and syntax that is appropriate for the reader, and "imagine" what the reader needs to know. If the context is familiar to the reader, however, the writer may not need to be so explicit.

Levels of formality also need to be considered in both oral and written language. Clinical observations of adults with learning disabilities (Johnson 1987) indicated that some wrote letters that were too formal for the situation and others wrote too colloquially. In certain instances the levels of formality changed within a single text.

Finally, writing tends to be more difficult than oral language because one must work in isolation. Whereas some writers enjoy the isolation, many find it difficult to work alone. They find collaborative learning more satisfying and productive. Nevertheless, in the end, as Lopate (1975) said, the writer must "go underground" and work alone. According to Litowitz (1981) the writer must manage the subject matter, the text, and the reader. Because of the complexity of these processes, breakdowns can occur at any level.

RULE LEARNING

Any study of language development also requires an investigation of rule learning (both acquisition and application) because all language is rule governed. In oral language we investigate phonologic, syntactic, morphologic, semantic, and pragmatic rules. In written language we study orthographic, syntactic, morphographemic, spelling, and discourse rules. Without an emphasis on rules, instruction may focus on isolated skills or memorization. This is not to suggest that children must memorize explicit rules. Rather, most rules are acquired implicitly over time with repeated experiences. In the case of exceptional learners, we are interested in knowing whether they are acquiring rules normally, at a slower rate, or in a different manner.

Studies of rule acquisition among normal children provide developmental data that can be used to compare various populations and to plan intervention. However, many rule-based studies are conducted by analyzing only what the child says or writes; the assumption is that the child's utterances or written products reflect what he or she knows. While expressive language in any form is revealing, one must be cautious when studying handicapped or exceptional learners because of various output, retrieval, revisualization, or access problems. Therefore, we recommend a comprehensive study of both receptive and expressive processes to determine whether the individual has problems with some aspect of rule acquisition, application, or automaticity (Johnson 1988). In addition, multiple rule usage should be studied because all language systems require the integration and use of multiple rules. Such studies are particularly crucial when planning intervention. We need to know whether instruction should be designed to help the child acquire various rules or to use them across contexts. For example, some children can adhere to certain spelling conventions on dictated tests but not when writing on their own. Similarly children may be able to write sentences on highly structured tasks but make numerous errors in context. In addition, there is evidence to suggest that many children and adults with learning disabilities have knowledge they do not use spontaneously or that they cannot use automatically because of information overload.

Language also can be studied by examining forms, content, and usage (Bloom and Lahey 1978). In their analyses of oral language forms Bloom and Lahey include phonology, morphology, and syntax. Content includes semantics and the subcategories of object knowledge, object relations, and event relations. Language usage includes function and contexts. Using their three broad categories for the study of written language, we can analyze *forms* including rules for handwriting, spelling, and syntax. In the area of *content* we can study vocabulary (including type-token ratios), semantic relations, and level of abstraction. When studying *usage* we can investigate the functions of writing, sense of audience, and the ability to adjust language for various contexts. Whichever approach is used, it is necessary to investigate relationships between auditory receptive and expressive language, reading, and writing. If one looks only at a written product, the intervention may be inappropriate. For example, a sixth-grade student who is reading at a third-grade level cannot be expected to memorize spelling words that he cannot read. Similarly the adult who writes, "I want to speaker and read better" tells us that at least part of her difficulty is in oral language. On the other hand, the youngster with a severe oral apraxia or motor planning disorder may be able to convey ideas with a typewriter or computer.

The remainder of this chapter is devoted to specific areas of written language. However, whenever problems are observed we examine possible co-occurring deficits in cognition, oral language, reading, and other forms of symbolic behavior.

HANDWRITING

While handwriting may not be the most important aspect of written language, many individuals with learning disabilities have problems with handwriting long after such skills should be acquired. In these instances, the "vehicle" for writing is not sufficiently developed to express ideas they want to convey. Often these people have high verbal, low performance intelligence scores and particularly low scores on tests such as Block Design, Coding, and Mazes (Johnson 1987). Others have problems learning new motor patterns, though they have no paralysis.

There are several excellent reviews of the literature regarding handwriting among normal individuals. For example, de Ajuriaguerra and Auzias (1975) summarize the preconditions for the development of writing and state that writing is language plus praxis (i.e., motor learning). In other words, one needs both linguistic and perceptual motor competence. Skills required for writing include prehension of a writing instrument, speed of writing, tonic regulation, and spatial skills, any one of which may be impaired among individuals with learning disabilities. Thomassen and Teulings' (1983) review of the major theories of handwriting illustrates the complexity of the skill. Writing involves many coordinated movements that require visual guidance and visual monitoring as well as motor skills. The closed-loop theory states that an intended movement is selected from long-term motor memory. Presumably a stored motor trace determines the start of the movement and the performance depends upon previous memories.

The open-loop theory, according to Thomassen and Teulings (1983), hypothesizes that skilled performance is under the control of central motor programs that are autonomously responsible for sequencing and timing movement patterns. The motor program contains the information necessary for the correct performance and is built up with practice. In this theory feedback is less necessary than in the closed-loop theory.

Schmidt, in Thomassen and Teulings (1983), proposed a schema theory that assumes that movements are organized according to some generalized motor plan that develops with experience. Thus, a schema is a generalized, abstract motor program for a class of movements that develops with experience (p. 184). In writing, the class may be a letter, a high-frequency group of letters, a signature, or a high-frequency word. The authors quote Merton who adheres to this theory and says it can be verified to a certain extent by the fact that one's handwriting looks roughly the same on paper or on a blackboard even though very different sets of muscles may be involved.

Developmental data regarding children's copying of geometric designs and complex figures can be found in Ilg and Ames (1965), Thomassen and Teulings (1983), and books on child development. In general, one expects children to copy a circle at age three, a square at four, triangle at five, and a diamond at seven. Tests for more complex figure copying such as the Test of Visual Motor Integration (Beery and Buktenica 1989) can be used to determine whether there are problems.

In school, children generally learn to copy and write manuscript before cursive letters, although the theories about which to introduce first will vary. Some educators feel that cursive is better for children who have visual spatial problems and reversals. On the other hand, if teachers use cursive writing, they should make certain that children can read it. Severe dyslexics may even be unable to read upper and lower case manuscript. Hence, an evaluation of their ability to deal with various type fonts and forms of the code is needed.

For those who say that in today's world we need not worry about handwriting, one should interview adults with serious problems in order to understand the consequences of not being able to write a signature the same way twice or cash a traveler's check. This is not to say that all dyslexics, or people with learning disabilities, have handwriting problems. Rather, those with faulty graphomotor coordination may need special education, occupational therapy, or alternative modes of communication such as typewriters, word processors, and computers in order to demonstrate what they know. When planning intervention strategies such as verbal mediation, the use of visual cues and stencils should be considered. In remediation, we work toward as much automaticity as possible so that writing can be used for daily activities. However, we emphasize the quality of these students' ideas, not their faulty visual-motor skills.

Often there is a lack of synchrony between an individual's cognitive and sensory-motor skills. Some people have good ideas but poor perceptual-motor skills. Others have superior handwriting but faulty language or ideas. Even among normal children one may see an imbalance for a short time when the child seems to know more than he or she can convey. Gifted preschoolers who have learned to read often are frustrated by their perceptual-motor limitations. They have no disability but their motor skills are not at the level of their cognition. In these cases primary typewriters and computers are advantageous.

Finally, one only needs to read the book, *My Left Foot*, by Christy Brown (1954) to see how an output or performance deficit can interfere with the ability to convey ideas. In many instances it is necessary to investigate spelling, syntax, and other linguistic skills by using modes of response other than handwriting.

SPELLING

The last fifteen to twenty years have produced an abundance of literature on development and disorders of spelling (Bryant and Bradley 1980; Read 1986; Temple et al. 1988; Frith 1980). While it is impossible to provide a comprehensive review, I highlight work that has significance for studying both normal and atypical learners.

Studies of early spelling reveal several developmental patterns (Read 1986; Temple et al. 1988; Beers and Henderson 1977). According to these investigators the first spelling attempts are often prephonemic because children have not yet learned how the writing system works. They simply write strings of letters. Most children at this level have not learned to read but they know how to make a few letters. The next stage, early phonemic spelling, is characterized by the child's attempts to write some sounds of words. According to Temple et al. (1988) children are discovering the phonetic principle and have some notions about how the system works, however, they might write only the first letter correctly and then omit others, or write a random list. For example, "the baby was at home" might be written "Bwh." At a later stage, according to many investigators, children use letter name spelling. That is, they use the name of the letter as a syllable. For example, the word "enter" might be written as "Ntr," "easy" might be written as "Ez," and many long vowels are represented by the letter name as in "mak." It appears that in today's world even adults use letter name spelling on their vanity license plates (e.g., "BB DOC," "EZ RIDR"). Somewhat later, children use transitional spelling. At this level, children include most sounds in words but do not use all of the correct graphic representations (e.g., *ay, ai, a-e*). They are aware of certain features including morphological rules and other patterns, but are not able to integrate them sufficiently to use standard spelling. Temple et al. (1988) say transitional spellers are readers who have learned about the orthography from seeing words in books and from memorizing spelling words. At the highest (or correct) level, writers have abstracted sufficient information from the orthography to be aware that there are many different graphic representations of the same sound and that combinations of letters can only be used in certain positions. For example, /f/ might be spelled with *f* or *ph* at the beginning of a word while *ff* or *gh* are used at the end. In addition, they have acquired rules for derivational morphology. In the end, Sloboda (1980) says, to be a good speller one must have acquired multiple rules and strategies, such as spelling by analogy, as well as good visual memory.

Most studies of dyslexics and other individuals with learning disabilities indicate they have deficient spelling. Even if they make good progress in reading, residuals of the problems are evident in their poor spelling. Many researchers have attempted to determine whether the spelling patterns of poor readers are similar to those of younger children. The investigations of Cook (1981), Gerber (1984), and Schwartz and Doehring (1977) indicate that they acquire the rules in a similar sequence. However, Bailet (1991) presents a case in which several errors deviated from the normal expected pattern. Johnson (1987) also said that if one analyzes the errors in both context and dictated spelling, some are atypical. Often these are the result of visual perceptual or sequencing disorders, (trian-train) transpositions, and faulty monitoring. Therefore, one must be cautious in drawing conclusions about patterns of delay and difference without examining performance in both single word spelling and context. The demands of multiple rule usage may overload the system so the individual produces atypical patterns when writing text. Thus, some individual components of writing may look similar to those of younger children; however, when one examines the entire text, it is not like that of a younger child because of the uneven patterns and scatter of abilities. In some instances, ideation is high while syntax is weak. In other cases spelling and syntax are adequate but cohesion is weak. Therefore, the intervention should be based on a comprehensive evaluation of all components of language in both structured and naturalistic settings.

SYNTAX

Studies of normal writers generally indicate that sentence length increases with age (Myklebust 1965). Hunt (1983) also reports an increase in the number of T-units (one main clause plus a subordinate clause or nonclausal structure that is attached to or embedded in it). While sentence length generally increases, some studies of normal writers (Johnson and Grant 1989) indicate that when children try to use more complex sentences they make errors. Thus, productivity as well as accuracy should be investigated.

When the syntax of learning disabled children is compared with normal children on the Picture Story Language Test, the results vary. Poteet (1980) found no difference on the overall syntax scale but reported that learning disabled students made more punctuation errors. In contrast, Johnson and Grant (1989) found significant differences between normal and learning disabled children who were reading at the same grade levels. Many mistakes were due to faulty subject-verb agreement, morphology, and pronoun usage. For example, the following are sentences written by learning disabled students who were reading at the first-grade level: "He is pilay wif people," "He is wrik them," "He likes to bilding," "A goy is palying wiht hims tos." These examples also provide evidence of numerous spelling errors. In this same study learning disabled students who were reading at the third grade level attempted to use complex sentences but made numerous errors. Examples include the following: "He did not had friend," "He had ben at a privet school adn very made friends," "They gave him some girl toy to see could tell the differts." In contrast, the normal children in this study made punctuation errors but no serious grammatical mistakes. The syntactic errors produced in spontaneous text resulted in faulty products that were not like those of younger children. This was due, in part, to the fact that the learning disabled poor readers were older and tried to express more complex ideas. Many errors were probably due to faulty monitoring and lack of time to revise the text. However, studies of poor readers' spoken language and reading miscues also are needed.

Researchers who used the T-unit to study syntax generally found no differences between the number used by learning disabled and normal students. Gregg (1982) for example, found no differences in number of T-units among learning disabled college students and normals, but the learning disabled students made more syntactic errors. In addition she found, on a sentence combining task, that the learning disabled college students made more errors that distorted meaning than either college freshman or basic writers.

Investigators who used a "deep" structure analysis found learning disabled college students differed from a comparison group in their use of compound, complex, and compound-complex sentences. Vogel (1986) found that learning disabled college writers differed in variables related to subordination and embeddedness.

In general, studies of syntax should include measures of length, complexity, and accuracy. In addition, information regarding both oral and written syntax is needed. We need to know if students have similar problems in both oral and written language. For example, on a measure of sentence building, Johnson and Blalock (1987) found that none of their ninety-three adult learning disabled subjects achieved a perfect score on the written tests and only seven achieved a perfect score on oral sentence building. Thus, many writing disorders reflect oral language problems and limited linguistic flexibility. Occasionally, students write better than they speak because of the opportunity for visual self monitoring (Johnson and Myklebust 1967).

CONTENT AND LEVEL OF ABSTRACTION

There are many ways of approaching the analysis of content. One can look at the vocabulary by investigating parts of speech used (Myklebust 1973) or by calculating type-token ratios, thematic maturity (TOWL-2, Hammill and Larsen 1988), or ideation.

The Picture Story Language Test (Myklebust 1965) includes an Abstract/Concrete Scale that was designed to evaluate meaning and the quality of ideas expressed by the writer. A major purpose of the scale was to study certain relationships between written language and thought processes. Building on theories from Goldstein (1948) and others, Myklebust hypothesized that young children and individuals with central nervous system disturbance would be more concrete than older individuals and those with no dysfunction. Written stories that were directly related to the stimulus (in this case a picture) were classified as concrete. Those that were detached from the stimulus were considered to be more abstract. The broad levels of the scale include (1) meaningless language, (2) concrete-descriptive, (3) concrete-imaginative, (4) abstract-descriptive, and (5) abstract-imaginative language. At the lower end of the scale, subjects tend to write only about the objects within the picture. At the highest level they may write allegories or stories with morals. When evaluating language on this dimension, any problems with syntax, spelling, and handwriting are ignored. Thus, a person could score high on the Abstract/Concrete (A/C) Scale but have deficient spelling or syntax. Conversely, some individuals may have perfect spelling and syntax with very limited ideation. In his original study, Myklebust (1965) found the mean A/C score increased with age for both males and females. In several studies of exceptional learners, Myklebust (1973) found that normal writers had higher A/C scores than those with dyslexia, mental retardation, and oral language disorders.

In a recent study of normal children in grades 1 through 3, Johnson and Grant (1989) found a similar increase in Abstract/Concrete scores with age. However, when the normal students were compared with learning disabled students who were reading at the same level as the normal students, some dyslexics scored above the normal students on the Abstract/Concrete Scale. It was hypothesized that because the poor readers were older than the normal students their ability to think abstractly was better. However, spelling, syntax, and handwriting were deficient.

COMPOSITION AND MODES OF WRITTEN EXPRESSION

Temple et al. (1988) define composition as "putting together the details of a message in a form that is understandable to an audience" (p. 118).

Using this definition, they think that children can compose before they write. When children dictate stories to adults orally, they have the rudiments of compositions. This issue highlights an important relationship between speech and writing. Children abstract the components of stories from listening and reading. According to Temple et al. (1988), these notions are evident from the fragments of real stories children include in their own compositions. While their stories may be generally new, they contain images or bits from "Peter Rabbit," "The Three Bears," and other stories they have heard.

Britton (1980) describes three types of writing used by young children. The first, which he calls Expressive Writing, is similar to oral language in that children use dialogue; according to Temple et al. (1988), this is somewhat like a monologue. Written journals, which are encouraged in many schools, are examples of expressive writing. The texts are loosely organized and are not intended to be read by a wider audience.

Transactional Writing, a second type of writing by young children (Britton 1970), is "designed to get things done." It includes exposition, description, and argumentation (Temple et al. 1988). Exposition includes simple directions and expository prose. Description, according to Temple et al. (1988), is a type of discourse that helps the reader visualize. For example, first grade children write descriptions of people or pets. The third type of transactional writing is argumentation. According to Phelps-Gunn and Phelps-Terasaki (1982), this is one of the most difficult forms of writing because it requires the writer to consider other points of view and to use logical thinking. Nevertheless, young children can be guided to use argument by giving them topics that are relevant to their own experiences (e.g., why children should obey their parents).

The third major mode of writing in Britton's schema is poetic and it includes narratives, poetry, and songs. Stories are considered to be in the poetic mode and can be analyzed in various ways. Applebee (1978) provides a developmental framework that incorporates theories from cognitive development. According to his schema, children begin telling or writing stories that can be classified as "heaps" with little organization. Eventually they maintain a theme and adhere to a topic.

Studies of individuals with learning disabilities indicate they have numerous problems writing stories. Often productivity is low, perhaps because of concerns about spelling, vocabulary, or grammar. Others include the essential nature of the story but do not provide sufficient detail. In a few instances, adults with learning disabilities do not always include a good clear beginning, middle, and end to the story

(Johnson 1987). Some of their stories resemble the unfocused chain described by Applebee (1978).

Educators should remember that narratives are but one form of writing. It is equally important to be able to take a telephone message, write a thank-you note, or a business letter. If one expects to see various forms of writing among children, then it is essential to make certain that they are exposed to many types of reading and are encouraged to write in different modes. One must make certain to assign topics that are of high interest to children (Lopate 1975) so they can write about what they know.

FUNCTIONS OF WRITING

In recent years, considerable emphasis has been given to pragmatics and the functions of both oral and written language. These studies were stimulated by the work of Halliday (1973) and others. For example, language can be used for instrumental purposes (to get things done), for regulatory purposes, or it can have interactional, personal, heuristic, imaginative, and representational functions. In addition, writing also serves an important mnemonic function when one uses writing to aid memory (Luria 1978).

When studying the functions of writing we are interested in knowing whether children understand why people write and whether they are aware of the forms one might use when writing to familiar and unfamiliar audiences across various contexts. Children should have an opportunity to write for many purposes rather than just to complete worksheets for handwriting, spelling, or grammar.

We are particularly interested in knowing whether and how they write for themselves. That is, do they make lists as an aid to memory? In some instances children are not aware of their own memory capacities. Kraker (1987) for example, found that when normal and learning disabled first graders were asked to remember the ingredients and procedures for making cookies, the learning disabled children were less aware of the use of writing to aid memory than the normal children. Even though neither group could spell all of the words needed for the task, the average achievers drew pictures, wrote first letters of words, and drew circles around their representations to indicate which ingredients should be mixed together. They knew that some written representation would help them remember.

Dyslexics are sometimes apprehensive about writing even for

themselves because of their spelling difficulties. Nevertheless, we encourage them to write as much and as phonetically as possible so they can relieve the burden on memory and improve their personal organizational skills.

SENSE OF AUDIENCE

One of the skills that all writers must master is a sense of audience. Temple et al. (1988) say it is a challenge for young writers to decide how much to tell the reader. Young children and many with language learning disabilities have a particularly difficult time because they cannot always take other perspectives. They cannot imagine what another person might need to know. Consequently, they do not always create a text that is meaningful to the reader. In young children this is known as egocentrism (Piaget 1974). In order to facilitate these skills, Temple et al. (1988) emphasize the importance of writing for real audiences in order to obtain feedback. Rather than simply doing spelling or grammar exercises or writing only for the teacher, children learn more about the functions of writing and gain a better sense of audience if they write for other real audiences. Students often take greater care with their handwriting, spelling, and grammar when writing for others. However, many learning disabled students are aware of their difficulties and are reluctant to write because they fear the reader may not be able to interpret the message. Kraker (1987) reported that one child with a learning disability in her study elected to draw the procedures for making cookies rather than trying to write because he thought the reader would not be able to read his writing.

Problems with sense of audience have been noted among adults with learning disabilities. Johnson (1987) reported that many omitted essential details such as the characters and the setting in a story. This same problem was observed on the telephone when they failed to give their names and other pertinent information. As a result, the listener needed to ask for clarification. While oral communication allows for immediate feedback, the writer with a poor sense of audience may not receive feedback until much later, if ever.

Britton et al. (1975) emphasize the importance of writing for self, familiar and unfamiliar audiences, or trusted and general audiences. The current emphasis on writing conferences and dialogue helps children acquire these skills early in life. Writing in teams at the word processor encourages children to collaborate on a text. Together they can ask each other questions and identify important missing information.

THE WRITING PROCESS

Analyses of written language should include a study of the writing *process* not just the product. If we are to understand strengths and weaknesses we need to look at what the writer does before, during, and after the writing process. Thus, one observes the search for materials, note taking, questions, and other activities of the writer. While the person writes we should note any external verbal mediation and utterances that might give clues to faulty spelling and syntax. We also should note the number of self corrections, rereading, and revisions. Some studies indicate that poor writers engage in less prewriting and revising than good writers.

For writers who say they cannot think of ideas or who have difficulty deciding on relevant points to include, Bereiter and his colleagues (1980) suggest "dialoguing" or brainstorming before writing to help generate ideas to be included in the text. This external questioning eventually should be internalized so the writer asks himself or herself questions that the reader might need to have answered. In many schools, writing conferences are held to help children generate ideas, express their intentions, select vocabulary, and to help with revisions (Temple et al. 1988; Graves 1983). Such conferences are particularly emphasized in classrooms where whole language instruction is used (Shanklin 1991; Harste, Woodward, and Burke 1984). Thus, in our overall study of writing it is necessary to look carefully at the environment and the ways in which reading and writing are taught.

During the composing process, from the earliest stages through adulthood, the writer juggles the interests of self, audience, topic, and purpose in writing (Temple et al. 1988). This "juggling of constraints" also is emphasized in the work of Gregg and Steinberg (1980) and Flowers and Hayes (1980).

In summary, the study of written language requires an understanding of the learner, including overall ability, linguistic skills, reading achievement, and motivation. While there have been many exciting studies of written language development during the past decade, few studies have included information about the intellectual levels, oral language development, reading, and written language on the same population. While a few investigations of spelling have been done on good and poor readers (Frith 1980), we may need many more comprehensive longitudinal studies in order to understand better the developmental patterns of good and poor writers.

REFERENCES

Applebee, A. 1978. *The Child's Concept of Story: Ages Two to Seventeen.* Chicago: The University of Chicago Press.

Bailet, L.L. 1991. Development and disorders of spelling in the beginning school years. In *Written Language Disorders. Theory into Practice,* eds. A.M. Bain, L.L. Bailet, and L.C. Moats. Austin, TX: Pro-Ed.

Beers, J., and Henderson, E. 1977. First grade children's developing orthographic concepts. *Research in the Teaching of English* 11(2):133–48.

Beery, K.E., and Buktenica, N.A. 1989. *Developmental Test of Visual-Motor Integration.* Cleveland: Modern Curriculum Press.

Bereiter, C. 1980. Toward a developmental theory of writing. In *Cognitive Processes in Writing,* eds. L. Gregg and R. Steinberg. Hillsdale, NJ: Lawrence Erlbaum Associates.

Bissex, G. 1980. *Gnys at Wrk.* Cambridge, MA: Harvard University Press.

Bloom, L., and Lahey, M. 1978. *Language Development and Language Disorders.* New York: John Wiley & Sons.

Britton, J. 1970. *Language and Learning.* Harmondsworth, England: Penguin Books.

Britton, J., Burgess, T., Martin, N., McLeod, A., and Rosen, H. 1975. *The Development of Writing Skills.* London: MacMillan Education.

Brown, C. 1954. *My Left Foot.* Chelsea, MI: Scarborough House.

Bryant, P., and Bradley, M. 1980. Why children sometimes write words which they do not read. In *Cognitive Processes in Spelling,* ed. U. Frith. New York: Academic Press.

Cook, L. 1981. Misspelling analysis in dyslexia: Observation of developmental strategy shifts. *Bulletin of The Orton Society* 31:123–34.

de Ajuriaguerra, J., and Auzias, M. 1975. Preconditions for the development of writing in the child. In *Foundations of Language Development. A Multidisciplinary Approach,* Vol. 2, eds. E.H. Lenneberg, and E. Lenneberg, New York: Academic Press.

Flowers, L., and Hayes, J. 1980. The dynamics of composing: Making plans and juggling constraints. In *Cognitive Processes in Writing,* eds. L. Gregg and E. Steinberg. Hillsdale, NJ: Lawrence Erlbaum Associates.

Frith, U. (Ed.) 1980. *Cognitive Processes in Spelling.* New York: Academic Press.

Gerber, M.M. 1984. Investigations of orthographic problem-solving ability in learning disabled and normally achieving students. *Learning Disability Quarterly* 1:157–64.

Goldstein, K. 1948. *Language and Language Disturbances.* New York: Grune & Stratton.

Graves, D. 1983. *Writing: Teachers and Children at Work.* Portsmouth, NH: Heinemann Educational Books.

Gregg, K. 1982. An investigation of the breakdown in certain aspects of the writing process with college age learning disabled, normal, and basic writers. Unpublished doctoral dissertation, Northwestern University, Evanston.

Gregg, L., and Steinberg, R. (Eds.) 1980. *Cognitive Processes in Writing*. Hillsdale, NJ: Lawrence Erlbaum Associates.

Halliday, M. 1973. *Explorations in the Functions of Language*. London: Edward Arnold.

Hammill, D.D., and Larsen, S.C. 1988. *Test of Written Language* (2nd ed.). Austin, TX: Pro-Ed.

Harste, J., Woodward, V., and Burke, C. 1984. *Language Stories and Literacy Lessons*. Portsmouth, NJ: Heinemann Educational Books.

Hunt, K. 1983. Sentence combining and the teaching of writing. In *The Psychology of Written Language*, ed. M. Martlew. Chichester, England: Wiley.

Ilg, F.L., and Ames, L.B. 1965. *School Readiness*. New York: Harper & Row, Publishers.

Johnson, D.J. 1968. The language continuum. *Bulletin of The Orton Society* 18:1–11.

Johnson, D.J. 1987. Disorders of written language. In *Adults with Learning Disabilities*, eds. D.J. Johnson and J.W. Blalock. Orlando: Grune & Stratton.

Johnson, D.J. 1988. Specific developmental disabilities of reading, writing, and mathematics. In *Learning Disabilities: Proceedings of the National Conference*, eds. J.F. Kavanagh and T.J. Truss. Parkton, MD: York Press.

Johnson, D.J., and Blalock, J.W. 1987. *Adults with Learning Disabilities*. Orlando: Grune & Stratton.

Johnson, D.J., and Grant, J.O. 1989. Written narratives of normal and learning disabled students. *Annals of Dyslexia* 39:140–58.

Johnson, D.J., and Myklebust, H.R. 1967. *Learning Disabilities: Educational Principles and Practices*. New York: Grune & Stratton.

Kraker, M. 1987. An investigation of normally achieving and learning disabled children's use of writing to facilitate task performance. An unpublished doctoral dissertation, Northwestern University, Evanston.

Litowitz, B. 1981. Developmental issues in written language. *Topics in Language Disorders* 1(2):73–89.

Lopate, P. 1975. *Being with Children*. New York: Doubleday & Company, Inc.

Luria, A.R. 1978. The development of writing in the child. In *Selected Writings of A.R. Luria*, ed. M. Cole. White Plains, NY: M.E. Sharpe.

McLane, J., and McNamee, G. 1990. *Early Literacy*. Cambridge, MA: Harvard University Press.

Myklebust, H.R. 1954. *Auditory Disorders in Children*. New York: Grune & Stratton.

Myklebust, H.R. 1965. *Development and Disorders of Written Language* (Vol. 1). New York: Grune & Stratton.

Myklebust, H.R. 1973. *Development and Disorders of Written Language* (Vol. 2). New York: Grune & Stratton.

Phelps-Gunn, T., and Phelps-Terasaki, D. 1982. *Written Language Instruction: Theory and Instruction*. Rockville, MD: Aspen.

Piaget, J. 1974. *The Language and Thought of the Child*. New York: New American Library.

Poteet, J. 1980. Informal assessment of written expression. *Learning Disability Quarterly* 3(4):88–98.

Read, C. 1986. *Children's Creative Spelling*. London: International Library of Psychology.

Schwartz, S., and Doehring, D.G. 1977. A developmental study of children's ability to acquire knowledge of spelling patterns. *Developmental Psychology* 13:419–20.

Shanklin, N. 1991. Whole language and writing process: One movement or two? *Topics in Language Disorders* 11(3):45–57.

Sloboda, J.A. 1980. Visual imagery and individual differences in spelling. In *Cognitive Processes in Spelling*, ed. U. Frith. New York: Academic Press.

Temple, C., Nathan, R., Burris, N., and Temple, F. 1988. *The Beginnings of Writing* (2nd ed.). Boston: Allyn and Bacon.

Thomassen, A., and Teulings, H-L.H. 1983. The development of handwriting. In *The Psychology of Written Language*, ed. M. Martlew. Chichester, England: Wiley.

Vogel, S. 1986. Syntactic complexity in written expression of college writers. *Annals of Dyslexia* 35:137–156.

Vygotsky, L. 1978. The prehistory of written language. In *Mind in Society: The Development of Higher Psychological Processes*, ed. S. Scribner et al. Cambridge, MA: Harvard University Press.

Vygotsky, L. 1962. *Thought and Language*. Cambridge, MA: MIT Press.

Woolf, C.L. 1983. Responses to requests for clarification in normal and language disordered children. Unpublished doctoral dissertation, Northwestern University, Evanston.

Chapter • 6

Teaching the Language– Handicapped Child

Regina Cicci

Language, with its content and form expressed along the language continuum, begins with the birth cry and extends until the last breath. From the babbling of the infant to a written poem, novel, or technical manual, the individual develops and uses the language of his or her linguistic community. The movement along this continuum may be straight or tangled. We have evidence from the previous authors of the richness and complexity of the language we all use, how it is acquired, and ways that barriers can prevent its easy acquisition.

Acquiring language and using it effectively is the birthright of every individual born into a culture. Many have been, and are, interested in studying how normally developing individuals in all the world's societies acquire language. The process by which this occurs remains unclear, but for most it is easy and is accomplished with little effort. It is often stated that spoken language is natural but that reading and writing must be taught and specifically learned. However, it is important when we regard language acquisition across the continuum to consider that for young language-impaired children, acquiring the oral code may be neither natural nor easy. Such children require different kinds of teaching depending on their individual needs.

Spoken language, the language we understand and use to express ourselves orally, forms the basis for learning later to read and write and to manage some kinds of math. A disorder in spoken language can affect the acquisition of reading and writing. Even a mild problem in spoken language may have a significant impact on later learning (My-klebust 1971).

Every teacher, from nursery to postgraduate school, is likely to have in his or her classroom a student or students with difficulty in one or the other of the language processes. Teaching students skills if they are not known, providing practice for those newly learned skills, and helping generalize the known to the unfamiliar are the aims of every teacher.

COMPONENTS OF THE LINGUISTIC SYSTEM

In teaching, whatever the age of the students, we must consider the language that is to be taught and the students to whom it is being taught. Rawson (1989) has referred to this as teaching the language as it is to the student as he or she is. For purposes of this discussion, we can assume that the language being taught is English. As a language, English, along with the other world languages, has rules pertaining to the use of phonology, morphology and syntax, semantics, and pragmatics, and many languages, although not all, have a printed representation referred to as its orthography.

Phonology refers to the sound system of the language with a phoneme being considered a speech sound for the purposes of this discussion. Newborn infants can perceive the difference between voiced and voiceless consonants in syllables such as "pah" and "bah" and, as first words emerge, very young children demonstrate that they are making discriminations from the stream of speech sounds they hear in order to understand and say words differently to represent different experiences. Normal preschool children have no problem in interpreting the difference in meanings of *cat, can, cab,* or *calf,* with the difference being on the final sound. All of us hear words such as *bag* or *bat* or *fat* as whole words; it is not really possible to divide the stream of speech into single sounds or phonemes. If we try to separate or segment words into sounds we introduce a distortion as "fuh—a—tuh," something that all of us have heard when children look at a word and are told to "sound it out." But in learning to read, most children somehow learn to map print onto the sounds of speech. They learn the way the letters stand for, or represent, speech sounds. Most do this easily with minimal teaching.

Another component of the linguistic system is *syntax. Syntax* refers to the grammar of the language, the way words are arranged in order to convey meaning. In English we put adjectives before nouns as *blue car* or *big car* and arrange the adjectives in order, as well, so that typically we do not say *blue big car* but rather *big blue car*. The *long red pole* (with the pole being *long* and *red*) means something different from the *red long pole* suggesting that all the poles are long but we are speaking of the red one. The ordering of words is important. The developing language user learns the importance of order and also learns that the order of the words must be changed to ask a question. We can say "It is a ball" but to ask about it we rearrange the order of the words to say "Is it a ball?"

Children learning language also learn that some words are all right in a certain position in sentences but others are not. It is all right to say "The horse looks terrifying," but it is not acceptable to say "The horse looks neighing." They learn that sometimes parts of sentences can be moved and the sentence will mean the same thing. "Mother makes a cake" and "A cake is made by mother" have similar meanings. They learn to make sense out of such statements as "He showed the boy the girl." They also begin to disambiguate such sentences as "Flying airplanes can be dangerous" or "Visiting relatives can be a nuisance."

In addition to order, the young language user learns that there must be agreement between what is talked about in a unit called a sentence and the action of that thing or subject—that one can say *a dog barks* but must say *dogs bark*.

Morphology as part of syntax deals with meaning units and is important for speech and later for reading and writing. Bound morphemes include prefixes and suffixes and markers for plurals and verb tense. Hearing and reading *ex-* or *intra-* or *-ness* and knowing their meanings help with oral vocabulary development as well as with later reading and spelling. *More than one* can be said with /s/, /z/, or /uz/ as in *cats, cars,* or *boxes*. Later there can be confusion for some children when the letter at the end of *cats* and *cars* is spelled with the letter *s* even if the words sound different.

Yet another component of language is *semantics*. *Semantics* refers to the meanings of the words that we use. In order to communicate, a linguistic community depends on the shared meanings of words. If there is no shared meaning there is no communication. Vocabulary continues to develop throughout our lives. We can always learn a new word or add new associations or concepts to words that have been part of our vocabularies from a young age. The variation in meanings of words and the richness of texture in speech or text provided by the choice of words with their shades of meaning are remarkable. We draw on relatively few words from the possible universe of words in our typical use of speech and writing.

Finally, there is a component of language referred to as *pragmatics*. This term refers to the use of language in a social context. *Social* is used as pertaining to at least two individuals and as opposed to *solitary*. Pragmatics includes the ways language use and behavior are modified depending on the situation. For example, greetings of "hello," "hi," or "good morning" are said differently to a family member, a friend, or the head of a school or company. Speech is different directed to a peer and an authority figure. Children must learn this and also when to keep the message short or to elaborate on it. They learn to question if unsure and speak with emphasis if they know their point of view is right. Little direct instruction is provided for most, and a lot of what is learned about using language in a social context comes from incidental learning, noticing how others behave. Excellent choice of vocabulary and good grammar mean little if the words and sentences are inappropriate for the situational context.

Language within all its components has rules. When teaching we must ask what the student knows about the language, and how well he or she knows and applies the rules. Seldom do we confront children *tabula rasa,* with minds totally free from impressions. Even babies at one year of age know a lot about their language, even if we are not able to determine fully what it is they know. The same is true of the illiterate adult. The individual may score poorly on reading and spelling tests but nearly always knows something about print representing speech. As far as possible we need to determine what the individual knows about the language before we design a teaching program. Developing children give us hints about their knowledge of language in their daily use and during the assessment process. Some examples of their difficulties follow.

EXAMPLES OF LANGUAGE PROBLEMS

An articulation problem or mispronunciation of speech sounds is an example of a problem with phonology. So is a difficulty with sequencing sounds within words as saying "aminel" for *animal* or "flutterby" for *butterfly* or that when a bear sleeps through the winter it is "nayborhiden" (hibernation) or that the sixteenth president was "hammerbuh-laken" (Abraham Lincoln). Such mispronunciations are of concern when they persist beyond the age when such errors are typical. Problems with rhyming, blending word parts into whole words, segmenting whole words into syllables and sounds, and hearing a word and deleting part of it as in "say supper without per" can also result from trouble with phonology. Liberman (1983), Blachman (1987 and this volume), Lundberg (1987), Liberman and Liberman (1990), and others have written widely about the relationship of phonology to reading. Some children easily learn the system of how print represents speech and some children have great difficulty in learning the system. By way of example, a ten-year-old boy with phonological problems affecting spoken, read, and written language showed imprecise articulation and difficulty sequencing sounds within words. He said "lectonik" for *electronic* and "harpiscord" for *harpsichord*. He read "expermt" for *experiment* and "kollasep" for *collapse*. Later when writing he spelled "prostice time" for *prehistoric time* and "enstanked" for *extinct*. This example illustrates the interrelationships among speech, reading, and spelling and provides a beginning point to design a program to teach this youngster how he can improve his reading and spelling.

Another example is a seven-year-old second grader who did well with phonological skills presented to him orally. He could rhyme, segment words into parts, and blend parts into whole words. His speech was clear and free from articulation problems. His difficulty was with reading at the level of integrating or associating the sound of the letter with its printed equivalent. He knew short *a* as /a/, similar to the broad *a* used by the British. Because this was the only vowel he knew at all he was presented with a task where the consonants on either side of the vowel were changed. The *a* was so strong for him as an inflexible pattern pronounced in only one way, he could not allow for its variation depending on the context of the two consonants. This resulted in *ham*, *fat*, and *rag* pronounced much as "hum," "fut," and "rug," which he did not know were: to put in a sandwich, obese, or a thing used for cleaning. This ability to adapt to pronouncing the vowel differentially depending on the consonants around it comes easily to able readers, is difficult for some reading disabled children, and is painfully slow for others.

Problems with phonology also affect spelling and can be seen with individuals who do not show good representations in their writing of the way the word sounds. Examples include writing *hesting* for *hesitating*, *coster* for *customer*, *blanching* for *balancing*. In these instances the writer wrote the initial part of the word correctly and had some other appropriate letters, but the words do not show good grapheme-phoneme correspondences. This is in contrast to a child who writes *costamer* for *customer* and *ballenses* for *balances*.

Children may also show problems with syntax as when they say "you both eat them" for *you eat them both*, or "I going home" for *I am going home*. More subtle problems such as saying "between him and I," "the set of toys are broke," "he don't know," or the older student writing "When an adolescent grows up they . . ." or the "person that knows" for *who* knows, or "there's two reasons why. . . ." Poorly developed spoken syntax does not allow for easy prediction of a word that might occur next in reading a printed sentence. Deviant syntax in oral language is often reflected in students' written work or may prevent easy formulation of written sentences. Sometimes these early spoken syntactic problems may be reflected in later written formulations even when spoken syntax has improved to the point of showing few errors.

Problems with semantics mean that individuals have difficulty with understanding the meaning of language. Such students provide a challenge to the teacher in nursery school or graduate school. Meaning changes with context. It is hard to teach the flexibility of words and how they change depending on the situational context. It can be confusing for some young children to grasp the notion of words that can be used as nouns or verbs. Words such as *circle* or *match* may cause trouble. Relational words can be difficult for the young child. The experience or event for the word *behind* varies with the context. Seeing a person *behind* a tree, placing one's body to stand *behind* Johnny, putting one's hands *behind* oneself, being *behind* in one's reading may differ spatially, but the word *behind* is said and written in the same way. The child, who stops in the middle of solving a word problem in math, to reflect on how interesting it is that *tablet* as a pad of paper and *tablet* as medicine are two such different experiences represented by the same word, might have an interesting linguistic mind but may also get behind in his math lesson.

Some children and adolescents have problems with using language in a social context. These are the individuals we all know who are constantly putting the proverbial "foot in their mouth." Young children who have difficulty with the part of language referred to as pragmatics may have trouble with understanding and using the language of instruction, of discipline, and of social interaction. They may not have the words to say such things as "I don't know." "Help me," "Say it again," "I'm afraid," "I'm tired," "I'm hungry," "I'm sad," or "I'm disappointed." Older children may not know how to ask questions to gain information they need, to request clarification, to expand a point, or to direct anger appropriately using words. Using a demanding tone rather than a requesting one as when a young child wants a new toy or an adult calls for a professional appointment, or calling older persons by their first names upon just being introduced, are examples of problems with pragmatics or using language in its social context. Such individuals may have trouble getting into the mind of the writer for reading comprehension and may have difficulty in feeling the sense of the reading audience while writing. All of these components of language have a place as we consider the effective use of language in the classroom—language that is understood and is used expressively.

We need to know what knowledge about language the student brings to the learning situation. Some children are identified early as having spoken language disorders and thus have weak bases on which to build skills of reading and written expression. Other students may be second language users and as such are learning English in its spoken and written forms at the same time.

Then, there is a large group of children in this country, particularly in our cities, who are speakers of a dialect that differs from standard English used in formal situations and in printed text. They do not have the same syntactic base on which to read sentences and predict words that may come next in print. When they enter school, they do not have the same system of spoken language as that used in books. The language of the text does not in any way represent "talk written down" for them. They are also at a disadvantage when asked to write. They may be graded on how they write, using standard English for a model, when their spoken speech does not have the same rules. For example, a ten-year-old girl with a mild reading problem, but a greater problem with writing that affected homework and tests, was quite willing to write at length. She wrote, "Long ago men was attack by lots a elephants. They attack some of the cave men and some were killed and stamp on." She shows some awareness of past tense markers with the -ed on *killed* but not for *attacked* and *stamped*. Perhaps we might think the voiced *-ed* was easier to recall and represent in writing than the voiceless pronunciation of the ending for *attacked*. But later in the same passage she wrote "some fathers had die." and the ending would have been voiced. When she read this back she read it in the same way that she wrote it. When it was read to her using standard form she did not detect the difference from my speech to her text. This is another example of the interrelationships among speech, reading, and written expression.

SOME LANGUAGE PROCESSES

So far we have regarded language from the perspective of analysis of phonology, syntax, semantics, and pragmatics. Another helpful way for teachers to consider language is using the hierarchy of language development according to certain processes. A way of considering processes important in acquiring and using language as adapted from Johnson and Myklebust (1967) and Johnson and Blalock (1987) includes:

- Attention
- Nonverbal cognition
- Sensation or reception
- Perception or interpretation
- Memory or storage
- Retrieval
- Organization
- Expression

No one can learn unless attention can be focused on the task and sustained. To be a successful learner one must learn to attend selectively, to put things in the foreground or background as the case may be. So much depends on taking in the information from whatever worlds we inhabit. The superb cook has become so by studying and observing. The scholar is stimulated by attention to books, what is written, and what is between the lines. The artist views the world in unique ways with his or her own vision and is able to create something new. The difference between the outstanding clinician, whether in medicine, psychology, or education, and the merely adequate one is often the attention that is paid to what is present and also to what is only suggested. Individuals who are successful in negotiating their ways through daily living must be in some state of constant attention. When individuals display attention problems it is important to discover if the inattention results from attention deficit disorder or from anxiety. Often there are components of each. A depressed child or an anxious child also may be inattentive. And there is a group of children who meet the former criteria of attention deficit disorder without hyperactivity (DSMIII 1980). There does not have to be hyperactivity to have an attentional disorder and we must recognize that not all individuals with attentional difficulties have trouble learning (Clemmens, Kaiser, and Kenny 1983).

Some tasks are particularly sensitive to attentional difficulty. Tasks of short-term memory have long been regarded as clues to inattention. Furthermore many individuals with attentional difficulties do not seem to have an alternative plan when they do not immediately know an answer. They become impatient with themselves. Responding to analogies seems to cause children with attentional difficulties some problems. If they must supply the second word in the second of two pairs of words quickly, they are satisfied. But if the word does not occur at once, they do not have the persistence to try an alternative approach. We cannot begin to speculate what must happen with silent reading for children with attentional problems. Everyone has faced the situation of reading to the bottom of a page and realizing not one word has really been read. As sophisticated readers we notice this and re-read the page. Many poor, or inattentive, readers are not aware of this phenomenon and just continue reading. They have little sense of monitoring.

Nonverbal cognition (Johnson this volume) refers to what Myklebust (1954) called inner language. This includes the sensorimotor exploration of the environment in the early months and years of life in addition to all the experiencing we do throughout our lives. Discussing a movie only after having heard and read reviews may fool the listener, but a speaker who actually saw the film would use a different inner language or nonverbal cognition. Describing a child with Attention Deficit Hyperactivity Disorder (ADHD) from characteristics listed in DSMIII-R (1987) may be correct but the words represent a different experience when one has known hundreds of children with such disorder.

Reception means that the signal reaches the brain. Partially sighted or hearing-impaired persons have signals that are distorted, unclear, or absent for seeing and hearing.

Interpretation or perception involves assigning meaning to what is received—a sound such as the telephone, doorbell, or fire engine; a word that is heard; a picture or a word in print. This can also include comprehension of everyday language as well as figurative language. A colleague walked by an open door of a kindergarten room in a school and heard a teacher say, "We'll eat lunch at our desks." A child walked up to the teacher and queried, "Did you say we were to eat *at* our desks or *on* our desks?" An adult with advanced postgraduate degrees was studying for a multiple-choice standardized exam (such as licensing exams in speech pathology and psychology, board exams for physicians, and the bar exam for attorneys). He called to ask about interpretation of questions. What became evident was that he did not really understand the meanings of the conjunctions *and, or,* and *but.* Other adults with difficulty in written expression and in their oral expression have similar difficulties. The coordinating component of *and,* the balanced sense of choice when the word *or* is used in the phrase *one or the other,* and the subordinating nature of *but* are learned intuitively by most, but can cause confusion for language-impaired persons. Another example is provided by a teenager who was confused when she was asked to comment on the *social climate of the times* on a test. Because climate refers to weather, she attempted to visualize in her head some kind of social weather.

It is possible to find naturally occurring examples of the devastating effects of reading words without understanding what is being read. Children with such a problem have been variously described as idiot savant, pervasive developmentally disabled, severe receptive language disordered, or hyperlexic (Healy and Aram 1986; de Hirsch 1971). They can read words far in advance of their age but with no, or little, understanding of the words. They can decode almost anything in print but it does them little good. Words that are read must have underpinnings of meaning or the act of pronouncing them from print is nearly worthless.

Storage refers to memory. A problem with storage is a memory problem. A memory problem can be short or long term. A short-term memory problem would be one in which something is heard or read and immediately forgotten. A long-term memory problem is one where information is stored for a short while but does not become a part of long-term memory. Examples of such problems might be with holding on to the correct spelling of words only until the day of a test, or remembering math facts, or the multiplication tables.

At times information is held in a kind of memory but the trouble is with retrieving it from storage. Retrieval is recalling information when it is needed. When people have such a problem, sometimes called a word-finding problem or dysnomia, they have the words in their heads but cannot quickly recall them for use. A word retrieval problem can cause difficulty in conversation, with questions to be answered orally, and with fill-in-the-blank tests. Sometimes the person gives an associated response such as saying "lock" for *hinge,* or provides a related within class response such as saying "chipmunk" for *squirrel,* or combines word parts as labeling an igloo an "eskiloo" (a combination of eskimo and igloo), or confusing words with similar sound patterns as "period" for *pyramid.* One second grader could not recall the awful thing she had to do. It was that hated thing that she called "teacher work" for *homework.*

After information is recalled it must be organized before it can be expressed. Early problems with oral formulation can appear later as problems in written formulation. Being asked to tell the difference between *dialogue* and *narrative,* a child responded, "Dialogue is someone using words an' somebody is telling a story. A narrator—someone is telling about it. Oh! they use words. Dialogue they use words—someone SAYS it an' a narrator tells a story." What must it be like for this youngster to formulate an answer to an essay question even when the answer is known?

SPOKEN LANGUAGE PROBLEMS AND OTHER LEARNING

Language disorders can result when there is a breakdown in any of the language systems or with any of the language processes. Speech is an expression of spoken language whereas writing is the expression of printed language. Language facility is acquired over time. Disorders of language can have a different effect on the individual depending on the age. A reading disabled child with oral language problems is a different individual from one who has excellent spoken language skills.

We must not neglect spoken language in all its parts. Phonology is important for decoding and spelling. But semantics, grammar, and pragmatics as well as phonology are essential for effectively learning to read with understanding and to express oneself with clarity and a sense of audience. Early spoken language problems are likely to persist; they do not go away. They may look different but they may continue to have an effect. The child who at three said, "What for iss?" instead of, *What is this for?* and could not retrieve the word *train* was frustrated at age nine when he could not recall the name of the story character Robin Hood. As he approached the target name he said, "Don't tell me. Why do I forget? Christopher Robin, not Christopher Robin, not Robin, yes Robin, Robin Hood!" At age 11 he said, "I timed it," when asked to tell how he had tried to solve a multiplication problem.

A young woman who had significant oral language disorders at age six, had minimal help with her underlying language disorder but much tutoring to get through courses. At age 18 as a high school senior, she showed scores in oral language and reading comprehension in the 80s, but scores in reading single words, spelling, and math computation in the superior range of 120 and above.

Intervention can only be successful with verbal learning disabilities if there are cooperative efforts among classroom teachers, parents, special teachers and/or speech-language pathologists, and other members of the school team who can include the nurse, psychologist, counselor, social worker, and principal. To help individual children best it is also important that the information and skills of community consultants be used. Increasingly, with budget cuts and for other reasons, when students are tested within school systems they are being considered for eligibility for help rather than to determine the specific nature of any problem and what can be done about it instructionally. This leads to children and adolescents living with the notion that if they only knew how to try harder they would be successful. Denying they have language learning disabilities that are responsive to treatment can destroy children's and adolescents' trust in adults and prevent them from using their cognitive abilities and their talents to the maximum.

SOME PRINCIPLES FOR TEACHING

For teaching in the classroom, in remediation, or at home when parents help with homework there are some principles that may be useful for the teacher teaching and for the learner learning across the language continuum. The suggestions are based on the notion that learning disabled persons, including those with verbal learning disabilities, may learn differently from other people. They may not acquire knowledge in the same manner, may not absorb information in an incidental way, and may have difficulty relating what is new to what is already known.

Provide An Experientially Rich Environment With Age Appropriate Stimulation

The environment and individual's action upon it develops the inner language or nonverbal cognition as a base for nonverbal problem solving and for language learning.

- Toys for preschool children should be objects that can be manipulated in numerous ways, being stacked, pulled, rolled, bounced, pounded, and torn, for example, and that have different textures and can produce different sounds.
- Objects should be provided that can be used in multiple ways to increase experiences about how things work, how to predict consequences, and how to solve problems.
- Pretend play should be fostered.
  —Replicas of furniture, housekeeping equipment, and ride-in toys such as bicycles and wagons can help children imitate actions of adults.
  —Toy tools and utensils can be manipulated.
  —Common objects such as paper towel tubes, blocks, and boxes can be used in multiple ways to represent objects in the environment.
  —Role playing not only fosters "as-if" thinking but also provides a way for children to act out frightening experiences, such as going

to the doctor or the hospital, or getting a haircut. Through such play, children can conquer fears and feel a sense of control.
• Art supplies should be provided early in a setting where messes can be made. Such materials provide pleasure, allow the creation of something unique from raw materials, can show how one is feeling without words, and can help with mastery of impulses that are little understood. Activities can include:
—shaping clay;
—using paints, crayons, markers, and pencils on different textures of paper and other materials; and
—tearing different kinds of paper including construction and tissue paper to be pasted onto paper, plastic, or wood.
• As the child shows interest in drawing with crayons or pencil, correct grasp should be taught. Grasp becomes a habit quickly, so learning a correct grip on the crayon or pencil from the beginning is essential.
• Exploration of materials is important but new skills need to be taught.
—Clay can be pounded but also rolled.
—Paper can be torn, folded, rumpled, and rolled.
• Trips to zoos, factories, museums, flea markets, and fairs broaden awareness.
• Rides on buses, subways, and trains provide exposure to ways people go from place to place.
• Attending children's symphony programs and theatre can develop talents that may surprise and interests that may last for life. Exposure to various kinds of music from an early age should be promoted and musical toys should be provided for exploration.
• Families can play games to enrich experiences. They do not need to be educational games. Board games and card games help children develop rule learning, and help in learning to wait, to take turns, to make predictions, to develop strategies, to accept losing, to manage winning, and to develop mastery generally.

Children with language learning difficulties might need help to learn mastery in areas of art, nonverbal experimentation, and problem solving—or they might excel. Different management is required based on differing needs.

Provide a Verbally Rich
Environment Structured to Meet Individual Needs

Preschool. Immersing the developing child in language allows him or her to understand its power and serves as a model for its use.

For the young language-impaired child the input may need to be controlled and reduced so that it can be understood. The words used must be timed to occur at the same time as the experience or event (Zigmond and Cicci 1968; Johnson and Myklebust 1967).

- Names of common household objects are taught by the adult repeatedly associating the word said orally with the experience. The adult says the word while the experience is occurring.
  - —The child can be asked to point to body parts (elbow, neck, and knee) and common objects (toys, furniture, eating utensils), and parts of objects (shirt sleeve, shoelaces, coat button, cup handle).
  - —Verbs can be taught associated with actions.

    Many repetitions are provided as an action is happening.

    Appropriate verbs are presented around the activities of eating, bathing, and playtime (eat, drink, chew; swallow, cough, sneeze; splash, spill; roll, jump, hop). The correct verb form should be used to talk about something that *will* happen, and after it is over, that it happen*ed*.
- Words for feelings should be taught at appropriate times (*happy, sad,* but also *angry* or *mad, disappointed, scared,* etc.). Sometimes young language-impaired children are regarded as having difficulty expressing feelings when their specific problem is lack of words to express what they feel. With basic words available to inform parents and teachers of hunger, needing help, hurting, being tired or scared, frustration can be reduced a bit.
- Adjectives (as *hot-cold, big-little,* etc.) can be introduced. Sensory adjectives can be associated with experience as *soft* (pillow, toy, face) to be contrasted with *hard* (table, finger) and, later, *loud* (noise, voice).
- Objects around the house could be repetitively counted (socks, shoes, spoons, books, cups, shirts, etc.) beginning with two, then three, and increasing as the number is mastered. Phrases such as *let's count* and *how many?* should be used appropriately.
- Real objects that can be manipulated should be used first with children. Then photographed objects should be used before line drawings. It is essential to assure that the child understands the visual representation on the two-dimensional plane before being asked to incorporate the picture in language use.

    Because it is generally accepted that facility with reading and spelling requires phonological awareness, or an awareness of how speech is represented by print, children should have practice in the preschool years in playing with speech sounds just as they play with

toys. The goal is to help the play and pleasure with language and the sounds of speech before children confront print. Activities should involve:
—auditory discrimination;
—rhyming;
—sequencing sounds in words;
—blending word parts of compound words, two and three syllable words, and sounds into whole words;
—segmenting words in parts of syllables and sounds; and
—deleting sounds.
• These activities should be carried out as games, and if there is resistance, they should be stopped and resumed in a week or two. Combining the play with speech sounds and rhythmical movements helps reluctant children begin to enjoy the activities.
• Reading rhyming stories and making up rhymes spoken in an exaggerated way can facilitate interest.

These activities using phonology need to occur before the child is expected to read or deal with phonics (or at the same time but in a different part of the lesson). For such play with sounds it is important that children learn a sense of temporal order and what *first* and *last* mean and the spatial order of printed letters before they are to manipulate first and last sounds or first and last printed letters in words.
• Private time spent with the child by the parents such as bathing, eating, dressing, and saying goodnight and later while sharing food at home or in a restaurant, helping with chores, and riding to appointments in the car or bus, all serve as opportunities for language development with the young and the older child. These are opportunities for learning to use the give and take of conversation for sharing ideas, requesting information, asking for clarification, and elaborating verbalizations. Parents must not feel that learning occurs only with a sit-down and listen-and-do activity. A great amount of what we all learn occurs through incidental learning, scanning the background of our lives while attending to the immediate or the foreground.

School Age. As children grow and enter school, those with spoken language problems may continue to have difficulty and may need structured teaching in the understanding and use of spoken language. At this age the relationship between the language that we speak and the language that we read and write needs to be emphasized with children (Johnson and Myklebust 1967; Cicci 1978, 1979). The following are some teaching suggestions:

- For vocabulary development in school age children words can be drawn from social studies, science, and math materials, as well as from common words that are expected to be known by this age.
- Words that express comparative relationships, temporal and spatial words, passive verbs, and words to be described by similarities and differences, and words for categorization and classification can be used.
- Some work with using pronoun referents (*it, he, she,* etc.) will be helpful. Children with formulation difficulties often have difficulty in both clarity of expression and comprehension of 'who did what to whom' in such structures as *The girl gave the boy the book* or *The cat is chased by the dog.*
- Situations should be constructed to include such sentences as, "Ask Tom to tell Bill _____." Who will be doing the talking? What would he say? "Tell Bill to ask Tom _____." Who would be doing the talking? What would he say?
- Practice with fantasy in oral language and writing can be helpful and can include such questions as: What would happen if _____?, How would _____ feel if _____ happened?, What do you predict will happen when _____?, What happened to cause _____ to occur?
- Teaching the use of figurative language is important. Figures of speech ("out on a limb," "raining cats and dogs," "in a pretty pickle," "that's it in a nutshell") and proverbs ("a stitch in time saves nine") may need to be taught.
- Words that have multiple word meanings (*bank, coach, run*) may need to be taught directly and the child helped to understand that it is possible for words to have more than one meaning. Some will capture the idea and then generalize on their own; others need more direct instruction.
- Words that can be used as both nouns and verbs may need to be taught (*circle, train*).
- Practice in telling how to make or do something such as preparing a sandwich, or making a paper plane, or playing a game can help the child or adolescent understand the importance of order to convey information. Stress is on step-by-step instructions that can be carried out by the clinician on the child's instructions. This can make the need for clarity of oral formulation dramatic.
- Playing a game where there is a barrier (piece of cardboard or easel) blocking the view of the table directly between the child and clinician is helpful. An object or picture is placed in front of each. It must be described by one person giving clues. The other person must guess what is being described.

- The same set up as the previous example can be used but with questions being asked, worded in such a way as to guess what the object or picture is. Later an imagined object or person can be a target as questions are worded for guessing.
- Syntactic development may need to include both receptive and expressive skills. Included should be activities to develop the student's skill in:
  —answering specific questions;
  —matching answers with the kind of questions asked;
  —formulating questions to get information;
  —manipulating morphological endings in an explicit way to indicate awareness that *-ed* indicates past tense, *-s* plural or possessive, *-er* a person who does something or to make comparison, etc.;
  —oral formulation by developing;
  > sentences for single words,
  > sentences for pictures,
  > and sequencing sentences to form paragraphs.
- Work with humor can be helpful. Verbal jokes, plays on words, nonverbal humor in cartoons, understanding patterns of prosodic features (pauses, intonation, melody of speech) for exaggeration and emphasis can all be of value for comprehension of spoken language and reading.
- Concepts of time, including understanding and remembering days of the week and months of the year, holidays and months in which they occur, need review and if not mastered should be taught.
- Meanings of prefixes and suffixes should be taught. The words used for oral vocabulary development should be presented in print, as well as orally, as a way of integrating the meaning and the reading of the word (Henry 1990; Stoner, Cross, and Anderson 1990).

Spelling

Remediation with spelling may need to include work with words that are spelled the way they sound (have a close phoneme-grapheme correspondence), those that follow rules of English spelling (such as "i before e except after c," and those that need to be retained by sight (*enough, does*).

- Practice should be provided to develop improved phonological skills of spelling words the way they sound. Polysyllabic words can be used. The words can be presented visually divided into syllables, heard in syllables, said in syllables, the whole word can be seen, heard, said, and then practiced by reading lists of such words and spelling them. This approach will improve decoding for longer words as well as teach spelling (Cicci 1980, 1983).

- Spelling "demons," words that are frequently misspelled, need to be practiced using a fading approach where the word is spelled aloud as it is written with copy present. The word should then be covered and written while being spelled aloud.

- Practice in spelling and writing of homonyms (*there-their*) and frequently confused words such as *where, were, we're* is important because these are frequently used incorrectly in spontaneous writing.

- Practice with structural analysis of words helps with attention paid to regular and irregular verbs with attention to changes in endings.

- Work with underlying relationships between words such as *sign, significance, significant, signify* can be useful for both reading and spelling and for improving understanding or word meaning (Chomsky 1970).

- As the students are composing, if they are not sure of a spelling of a word, they should write the word and underline or circle it. They can then go back and try to recall the correct spelling or look up the word. In this way the flow of thinking is not interfered with by the burden of trying to recall the correct spelling during the process of formulation. Alternatively, students may think of words they may need for the writing project and request the teacher to give them a list with correctly spelled words. For some additional information about spelling see Frith (1980, 1983).

Written Expressive Language

For students with difficulty in written expressive language, principles of correct writing need to be taught explicitly. Just receiving comments about what is wrong such as "run-on sentences," "choppy sentences," "wrong word," etc., is not helpful to students who are having difficulty with writing. They often have no idea of what is adequate and what is not. A student must be conscious of what good writing is before he or she can execute it.

It is of value to spend a considerable amount of time in formulating a single sentence. Students with formulation difficulty may find new worlds opening to them when they can see what they are able to do to modify a sentence.

- Sentences can be expanded using modifiers of single words and phrases.

- Different kinds of sentences should be written
  - —to include declarative, interrogative, exclamatory sentences;
  - —with parts of sentences moved to show how sentences can be flexible;
  - —to describe, explain, inform, convince, request; and
  - —to make explicit subject-verb agreement.
- Beginning at the level of the sentence and continuing through paragraphs and longer units, practice should be given in identifying and writing fact versus opinion.
- Sentence combining should be practiced, learning various ways several sentences can be rewritten into one compound or complex sentence.
- Sentences, and later paragraphs, can first be written for pictures and then for structured ideas presented by the teacher. Later less structured writing can be done.
- Specific instruction must be given about what a paragraph is and how it is developed.
- When good paragraphs can be written, the student can be shown how a paragraph can be expanded into an essay by writing a topic paragraph, two or three supporting paragraphs, and a concluding one.
- Instruction should be provided about the difference between creative writing and report writing. Practice should be provided for each.
  - —For report writing the required format for various subjects should be taught.
  - —For creative writing students need to experience the freedom of writing to the limits of their imaginations. Obviously some will be more creative than others but all children should experience this kind of free expression.
- Students should keep a list that must be checked off for every writing assignment to include such items as
  - —Are complete sentences used?
  - —Are capital letters present and used correctly?
  - —Is punctuation present and used correctly?
  - —Is the beginning of the paragraph indented?
  - —After indenting the beginning of the paragraph do the rest of the lines written go to the margin?
  - —Has the passage been read aloud for errors?
  - —Are subjects and verbs in agreement?
  - —Are pronoun referents clear?
  - —Is there a topic sentence?
  - —Are supporting sentences used?

—Is there a concluding sentence?

—If what is written is longer than a paragraph, are correct transitions made and transition words used between paragraphs and ideas?

For suggestions about teaching writing to children who are learning with few problems see King (1985); Vail (1981); Hennings and Grant (1981), and for children with learning disabilities see Cicci (1980, 1983); Phelps-Gunn and Phelps-Terasaki (1982); Johnson and Myklebust (1967).

Be Sure of Clarity in the Signal

When children have trouble with learning it is important that the signal is clear. They may not be perceiving information in the same way as the adult would or as the adult intends. For example, if we are on a train and hear the distorted sounds of the conductor's voice informing us of the next stop, what we hear or perceive him saying depends on whether or not we know what the possible communities or stops could be. In the same way until a child is sure of the stops along the way, or until knowledge is flexible enough to fill in what is not there, material presented must be consistent, precise, and distinct.

- Visual materials must be easily interpreted. Drawings of objects or letters to be matched must be exactly alike.
- Pale purple dittos or light gray photocopies cannot be filled in or guessed at by the learning child as they can be by an adult.
- Until children can read cursive writing easily, materials for them should be typed or neatly printed. Many do not have the sophistication to realize that multiple kinds of script all represent the same experience, word, or even letter.
- Oral directions, commands, questions, and explanations of instructional materials and disciplinary rules need to be unambiguous at home and school.

Focus on Interaction, Expecting a Response

Language by its nature is social, involving exchanges of ideas and information. One speaks to another. One reads to capture meaning expressed by another. One writes for an audience of one or of great numbers. We might even question if verbal thought could exist if we had no intention of sharing language with another. Babies in the arms of their caregivers demand a response. The adult, unless experiencing some psychopathology, must smile and coo at an infant and by their vocalizations expect the baby to respond. If a baby does not give immediate feedback to the parent, there is a tendency to discontinue providing stimulation. Parents with their babies, with their children as they grow, and teachers with their students must encourage active responses. Learning is active. Little is learned by passivity. Facile readers read all the time. Street signs, notices on bulletin boards, signs on buses, newspaper headlines in boxes on the street are read. Who among us can resist reading the tabloid headlines in the supermarket checkout lines? Poor readers do not get this kind of practice, pleasure, and ways to prevent boredom while waiting.

Individuals can respond in any number of ways. They may carry out a gross motor activity such as running. They may point, mark something by circling or underlining, make a bodily gesture such as a cry, nod, shrug, or smile, or they may speak or write.

Children with language disorders may tune out because of attention problems or difficulty with receptive language; or they may not attend because it is not expected that they are involved and should respond. Children who learn from television are likely to be ones who are already active learners and responsive to events. They then engage in an active way with what is on the television screen.

Teachers of children with language disorders need to arrange questions so that children can respond by nodding or pointing or respond to a multiple choice format while others in the same group give long responses. One nine-year-old said "It is not fun if you don't get called on." Questions need to be worded so that children can get practice in using language. They also need help in learning how to question so they can gain new information or request clarification.

We must consider the kind of response in relationship to the input or the question. Some language impaired children are quite willing to answer the question—they just answer the wrong question.

Teach Self-appraisal

Many children and adolescents I see have no sense of whether they have completed an item or a task well or poorly. There are a few who have an inflated sense of themselves so they expect to do well and are always surprised if, for example, they fail a test. But the greater number are very hard on themselves. They do not evaluate their performance in a realistic way. They say things such as "I don't need no help. I just gotta get motivated" or "I could do it if I wanted to. I'm just lazy." They are often unaware of their strengths or think that their strengths are unimportant, things that no one cares about.

Teachers need to help children evaluate their positive qualities from the beginning of school. Rather than give false praise, try helping the child to be accurate in judging success.

• Children can judge their drawings, the way they make a circle, and the way they form a single letter.
• When reading at the sentence level they need to reflect on whether or not what they have read makes sense.
• As they read longer units they should be helped to read actively, to think about meaning.
• They can be helped to think about how another would feel if an event occurred and to think in the same way about characters in stories.
• In writing they need to be helped to detect errors.
• They need to find errors in typed copy before they are expected to find errors in their own writing.
• Much error detection of single sentences should be done before proofreading of longer units is required.
• The students should be encouraged to read aloud, pointing to each word as it is read to pick up word omissions.
• The students should read the sentence for:
  —sense of meaning conveyed;
  —beginning capital letter;
  —correct punctuation;
  —correct word endings.
• After they are skilled with proofreading single sentences they can move on to longer units.
• For a while there should be a separate reading-through of the work for each type of error (word usage, misspelling, run-on sentences, flow, use of transitions).

Do Not Assume Readiness

There is no predetermined time when all individuals are expected to have a skill or to be ready for new learning. This notion is even more important for the child with language disabilities. Most babies use two word combinations by their second birthdays, but not all of them do. Not all children are ready for nursery school at the same time, nor are they ready to learn letter names and sounds, to use a pencil, or to learn to read. They are not ready at the same time to complete homework without supervision, to remember to take books and assignments home, or to take necessary materials to school. It is important to achieve a balance of giving help that is necessary while gradually teaching skills for independence.

- School-age children should be helped with learning to judge time and what can be accomplished in a certain amount of time. Students in middle and secondary school and in college may also need help to be realistic about what can be accomplished in a given amount of time.
- If a number of projects must be completed, students need help to decide the order in which they are to be done.
- Children need to be respected for what they know and for their opinions.
  —They should be included in the planning of what is to be learned.
  —They should be asked what their problems are. They most often are superb diagnosticians about themselves.
  —They need to be comfortable in giving opinions about their tutors, teachers, and those who see them for testing. They may misinterpret but they also have a right to let adults know their perceptions.

Balance Teaching the Code With Teaching Meaning

Meaning is essential in all learning. Children who have difficulty understanding oral language of vocabulary, word endings, multiple word meanings, sentence grammar, ambiguous sentences, and all the other aspects of spoken language will be likely to reflect this same difficulty in reading comprehension. Children referred for reading comprehension problems may have trouble with oral formulation of answers or with writing them. It is essential to determine if the problem is with reading comprehension or could be with formulation of responses.

- Students may require specific teaching to learn to comprehend single words, sentences, and paragraphs that they hear and read.
- Comprehension needs to be taught from the time the child reads single sentences.
- Readers need to understand differences between speech and text (Carlisle this volume).
- Comprehension of formal oral language such as polite address, language of lectures, and figurative language may need to be taught before the child is able to comprehend language in print.
- Students need help to learn various ways that text can be read.
  —Skimming to answer a specific question is different from reading poetry or kinds of literature.
  —Reading technical material is different from reading a short story or a novel.

For instructional suggestions for reading comprehension see Maria (1990).

Encourage Students to Visualize Absent Objects and Events

Certain visual memory skills are necessary for recognition of visual information and remembering having seen a letter or word or event before. Visual memory is essential in learning to spell. Some words can be learned only by holding on to visual images in contrast to those words that are spelled the way they sound or those that must be learned according to rules of English orthography (Johnson this volume; Jansky 1981).

Visualizing a situation can aid in solving math problems. For example, if there are 30 seats in the classroom and six seats in a row and the child is asked how many rows of seats there are, many would be helped by visualizing the room in order to solve the problem. Picturing how a character in a story looks, how a room is furnished, or what the countryside is like in a story adds richness to the reading experience. Visualizing historical figures in the dress of their time may help some to remember the individual, while retrieving the pictures of war equipment might help others retain facts they need to know. Those who grew up in the age of radio may have pictured in their mind's eyes the characters and settings of programs, a skill that may be absent cognitively in children growing up with television. Today's children may need more encouragement to make pictures in their minds as they read text.

Teach Principles of Organizing

A basic requisite of learning and of retaining what is learned is to relate new material to what is already known and to learn how to classify bits of knowledge into concepts or larger chunks of meaning. Some children learn to do this easily. Many language-impaired children need help with principles of organizing and planning. Some combine extreme disorganization of their person and their lives with disorganized speaking and writing. Others may have difficulty in one area but not in another. Such children need help with organizing their lives and with learning to organize material to be learned. Practice is necessary to acquire organizational skills.

• From early on, teaching clean-up with appropriate containers, shelves, or drawers to hold objects helps to develop early categorization.

- Using consistent schedules allows children to begin to learn the meaning and value of organizing time.
- Helping to sort laundry (big socks-little socks, Daddy's shirts, Michael's shirts) and groceries (to shelf, refrigerator, or freezer) can start the development of concepts about classification and categorization.
- Over-scheduling children should be avoided. If they are allowed free time and helped to plan its use wisely they begin to sense what can be done in a particular amount of time.
- Teaching various classification systems of how things are described can be of value. Perceptual attributes of size, shape, color, texture; function or use; and category can be taught.
  —These attributes can then be used to tell how things are different and alike.
  —Work with analogies can be done using words and concepts that are similar.
  —After proficiency is developed in describing concrete objects and experiences, then the same procedures can be used to *compare, contrast, discuss,* or *list* ideas rather than objects.

Some students have difficulty with organizing what they want to write and require help to understand that organizing schemes such as outlines are meant to be helpful, not punitive.

- As topic headings are written for a linear outline, several lines should be left so that ideas can be filled in as they occur. Forcing oneself to think of all ideas that belong under A before starting with B can be counter-productive.
- Not all individuals think in linear outlines. Thoughts come to them in scattered ways. They can take advantage of this thinking by writing the topic in the middle of a page and then writing words and ideas as they occur any place on a page. They can then look at what they have written and circle in blue those ideas that belong together and in red other ideas that can be appropriately grouped. Each set of color-marked words can then form the basis for a paragraph or a section of the written work. They may then make a linear outline or begin writing directly.

Begin Teaching Where the Individual is in His or Her Knowledge of Language

It is essential that we consider what the child understands about spoken language, how the language is expressed, what is known about the alphabet with its phoneme-grapheme relationships, and how his or her written expressive language is developed in handwriting, spelling, and formulation.

What a child knows must be determined before teaching begins. Standardized tests give one kind of information, but to begin to provide a remediation program for language-impaired children, the teacher must know what those children know about the language. If they already know the meaning of a word, the meaning does not have to be taught. If they can read words, those words do not need to be taught. If they know the sounds of the consonants by looking at the letter and saying the sound, hearing the sound and pointing to the letter, and hearing the sound and writing the letter, they do not need work on single consonant sounds except as review. Children do not need to learn what they already know. This becomes particularly important in special education classrooms where each September some children are working on the same units or materials that they experienced the previous September.

If the child does not learn the first time the material is presented and practiced, some modification of teaching procedure may be necessary.

Teach for Mastery

Teachers from preschool to graduate school expect, when they present a concept or a unit, that it will be learned. Often this is not the case. With the language learning disabled individual we must teach for mastery. What we teach must be practiced until it becomes part of the person. The understanding of a novel, preparing a chapter for study, or learning a new concept, word, or letter sound must be learned as a skill, practiced repetitively in a structured way, and finally generalized to novel or unfamiliar instances.

Respect the Students' Intelligence and Their Awareness of Themselves

Many language impaired children are quite bright and become fascinated with studying about language in general, its roots, how languages differ around the world, and how communication has developed from the time of cave paintings to the time of FAX machines. When they see their learning to talk, read, and write as part of this communication process they can become excited about the tasks they face.

They need to know the reasons for tasks presented. They have to be helped to understand how the, perhaps tedious, individual tasks they face relate to the larger structure of the language system. Language-impaired students need to share in the decision making about their lives, their schools, their tutors, and their learning. They must be helped to know that their ideas and feelings will be respected. They often tell us about themselves, their problems, and their strengths better than any professional could if we would only listen.

Aldous Huxley (1962) wrote "Words do have a magical effect. . . . Words are magical in the way they affect the minds of those who use them. . . . Words have power to mold men's thinking, to canalize their feelings, to direct their willing and acting" (p. 1). It is for this magic that we must consider the full language continuum in helping those we seek to serve.

REFERENCES

The American Psychiatric Association: Diagnostic and Statistical Manual of Mental Disorders, Third Edition, Revised, 1980. Washington, DC

The American Psychiatric Association: Diagnostic and Statistical Manual of Mental Disorders, Third Edition, Revised, 1987. Washington, DC

Blachman, B. A. 1987. An alternative classroom reading program for learning disabled and other low-achieving children. In *Intimacy with Language,* ed. R. Bowler. Baltimore, MD: The Orton Dyslexia Society.

Chomsky, C. 1970. Reading, writing, and phonology. *Harvard Educational Review* 40:287–309.

Cicci, R. 1978. Evaluation of oral language disorders in children. *Bulletin of The Orton Society* 28:194–207.

Cicci, R. 1979. Evaluation and treatment of oral language disorders. *Communicative Disorders: An Audio Journal for Continuing Education* 3.

Cicci, R. 1980. Written language disorders. *Bulletin of The Orton Society* 30:240–251.

Cicci, R. 1983. Disorders of written language. In *Progress in Learning Disabilities,* Vol. V., ed. H.R. Myklebust. New York: Grune & Stratton.

Clemmens, R.L., Kaiser, T.H., and Kenny, T.J. June 1983. Attention deficit disorder and childhood hyperactivity: Changing scene. *Maryland State Medical Journal.*

de Hirsch, K. 1971. Are hyperlexics dyslexics? *Journal of Special Education* 5:243–46.

Frith, U. (Ed.) 1980. *Cognitive Processes in Spelling.* London: Academic Press.

Frith, U. 1983. The similarities and differences between reading and spelling problems. In *Developmental Neuropsychiatry,* ed. M. Rutter. New York: The Guilford Press.

Healy, J.M., and Aram, D.M. 1986. *Annals of Dyslexia* 36:237–52.

Hennings, D.G. and Grant, B.M. 1981. *Written Expression in the Language Arts: Ideas and Skills,* (2nd edition). New York: Teachers College Press.

Henry, M.K. 1990. *Words.* Los Gatos, CA: Lex Press.

Huxley, A. 1962. Words and their meaning. In *The Importance of Language,* ed. M. Black. Englewood Cliffs, NJ: Prentice Hall.

Jansky, J.J. 1981. Developmental reading disorders (alexia and dyslexia). In *Comprehensive Textbook of Psychiatry*, vol. III, (3rd Edition), eds. H. Kaplan, A. Freedman, and B. Sadock. Baltimore: Williams and Wilkins.

Johnson, D.J., and Blalock, J.W. (Eds). 1987. *Adults with Learning Disabilities: Clinical Studies*. Orlando: Grune and Stratton.

Johnson, D.J., and Myklebust, H.R. 1967. *Learning Disabilities: Educational Principles and Practices*. New York: Grune and Stratton.

King, D.H. 1985. *Writing Skills for the Adolescent*. Cambridge, MA: Educators Publishing Service.

Liberman, I.Y. 1983. A language-oriented view of reading and its disabilities. In *Progress in Learning Disabilities*, vol. V, ed. H.R. Myklebust. New York: Grune and Stratton.

Liberman, I.Y., and Liberman, A.M. 1990. Whole language vs. code emphasis: Underlying assumptions and their implications for reading instruction. *Annals of Dyslexia* 40:51–76.

Lundberg, I. 1987. Phonological awareness facilitates reading and spelling acquisition. In *Intimacy with Language*. Baltimore: The Orton Dyslexia Society.

Maria, K. 1990. *Reading Comprehension Instruction: Issues and Strategies*. Parkton, MD: York Press.

Myklebust, H.R. 1954. *Auditory Disorders in Children: A Manual for Diagnosis*. New York: Grune and Stratton.

Myklebust, H.R. 1971. Childhood aphasia: An evolving concept. In *Handbook of Speech Pathology and Audiology*, ed. L. Travis. New York: Appleton-Century-Crofts.

Phelps-Gunn, R., and Phelps-Terasaki, D. 1982. *Written Language Instruction*. Rockville, MD: Aspen.

Rawson, M.B. 1989. *The Many Faces of Dyslexia*. Baltimore: The Orton Dyslexia Society.

Stoner, J., Cross, E., and Anderson, W. 1990. *Essential Roots*. Cambridge, MA: Educators Publishing Service.

Vail, P.L. 1981. *Clear and Lively Writing: Language Games and Activities for Everyone*. New York: Walker and Co.

Zigmond, N., and Cicci, R. 1968. *Auditory Learning*. San Rafael, CA: Dimensions in Early Learning.

Index

(Page numbers in italics indicate material in tables.)

Abstraction, 158
Adams, M.J., 43
Attention, 174
Audience, sense of, 161–62

Ball, E.W., 51–54, 55–56
Bally, T., 23
Basal reader programs, 65
Becoming a Nation of Readers, 42–43, 45
Beginning to Read (Adams), 43–44
Blachman, B.A., 51–55, 55–56
Book reading, preschool children and, 18–19
Books in the home, 44. *See also* Environments
Bottom-up and top-down processes, 70–71
Bradley, L., 50–51, 52
Britton, J., 159
Brown, Christy, 154
Bryant, P., 50–51, 52

Chomsky, N., 10
Clarity in teaching, 186
Classrooms: money for adequate, 110; questions and responses in, 186–87
Cloze procedure tests, 140
Code emphasis reading lesson, 56
Cognition, nonverbal, 175
College students, syntax of learning disabled, 157
Commission on Reading, report of, 42–43
Composition and modes of written expression, 158–60
Comprehension: different types of problems with, 140; of passages (assessing), 133; sentence and text, 118–21; text structure effect on recall and, 121–23. *See also* Language comprehension; Reading comprehension; Sentence comprehension; Text comprehension
Content, analysis of, 157–58
Conversation: adult-child, 11–14, 16, 26; car talk, 17; family structure and, 16–17; interactions with objects (toys, foods, etc.) and, 17; meal times, 17–18; peer, 26; topics of, 29
Cooperation among teachers, parents, and other educational professionals, 177
Copying designs, figures, and letters, 153
Cunningham, A.E., 46, 48

Dialects, 173
Dickenson, D.K., 18, 19, 22, 23, 26, 27
Disabled readers. *See* Dyslexics; Poor readers
Dyslexics: apprehensions about writing, 160–61; discourse-level deficits of, 22–23; spelling and, 155–56
Dysnomia, 176

Englert, C.S., 125
Environments, 178–79; children from enriched verbal, 63–64; enabling, 150; verbally rich, 179–84
Error detection by children, 188

First-grade reading lesson, 56–57
Flesch, R., 65
Fordham University, 87
Formality, levels of, 150
Free recall, 129–30
Frost, J., 48

Goodman, K.S., 65, 67
Grapheme-phoneme processing, 70
Graphic processing, 72

Head Start, 26
Horowitz, R., 125, 129

Inner language, 147
Instruction, learning to read without, 64
Instructional procedures, problems with translating reading-process models into, 67
Integrated Skills Method (ISM), 68, 69; application and results of, 98–106; classroom management and, 87; classroom learning centers and, 87; essential features of, 110; *Linguistic Pattern Series* and, 78, 79, 80, 81–86; one-day training for teachers in the, 110; in practice, 86–87, 88; regular classroom applications of, 106–109; small group lessons and, 87; teaching the linguistic code for reading by, 87–98
Interactive information processing model, 67
Interdependent Learning Model, 87
Interpretation of stimuli, 175–76

Language acquisition: book reading and, 18–19; commands and, 16; optimal inputs for, 20–21; parental corrections and, 15–16; parental imitation and, 14; parental questions and, 14–15; preschool programs and, 24–25; processes important for language use and, 174–77; television and, 19–20; theoretical accounts of, 10–26
Language comprehension: elements

of, 116; at microstructural levels, 117–18; published tests of, 118
Language development, 1–2; discourse development and, 5–6, 7, 8; emergent literacy and, 8–9; phonological development and, 2–3; reciprocal pattern of, 148; semantic development and, 3–4; social influences on, 10–11, 11–14; syntactic and morphological development and, 4–5; typical five-year-olds', 9–10
Language-learning problems, permanence of preschool, 126
Language problems, examples of, 172–73
Language processes, 173–77
Learning-disabled students, syntax of, 156–57
Learning to read: language-literacy relationships in, 21; linguistic representations and, 23–24; phonemic awareness and, 22; preschool programs and, 24–25; without instruction, 64
Liberman, I.Y., 45
Linguistic approaches to teaching reading, 65
Linguistic system, components of, 168–72
Listening: assessing, 127–29; model for relationship between reading and, 126–27
Listening comprehension: comparison of reading comprehension and, 139–40; as a function of thematic importance, 135, 136
Literacy, early, 150
Lundberg, I, 48–50

Mastery, teaching for, 192
Matthew effect, 123
Meaning, teaching the code balanced with teaching, 189–90
Meaning expectancy, 71, 72; and word recognition, 76–77
Memory: problems with, 176; writing and graphics to aid, 160
Metacognitive skills needed to recognize text structures, 125

Meyer, B.J.F., 121, 132–35
Models: interactive information processing, 67; problems with translating into instructional procedures, 67; psycholinguistic guessing game, 67 ; reading process, 66–68, 74–77; for relationship between listening and reading, 126–27; serial, 67
Morphology, 170–71
Morris, R., 23
Multiple rules, overloading due to demands of, 157
Mykelbust, H.R., 147, 148
My Left Foot (Brown), 154

Nelson, K., 14, 15, 16, 17, 26
Nursery rhymes, 22

Olofsson, A., 48
Oral language: levels of formality in, 150; rules in, 151
Organization of information, 176–77
Organizing, teaching the principles of, 190–91

Parents: language acquisition and, 14–16; use of ISM by, 110
Past tense markers, awareness of, 173
Perception, 175–76; variations in, 186
Peterson, O., 48
Phonemic processing, 72
Phonological awareness, providing for individual differences in, 58
Phonological awareness instruction: study showing impact of combining learning to connect sound segments to letters and, 51–54; with explicit connections between sound segments and letters, 50; without making explicit connections between sound segments and letters, 48–50; providing for individual differences in, 58–59; steps in, 54–55
Phonological segments in words, awareness of, 46
Phonology, 168–69

Picture Story Language Test (Mykelbust), 156, 158
Pinker, S., 10
Poor comprehenders, the problems of different types of, 140
Poor readers, phonemic processing and, 74
Pragmatics, 170, 171
Preschool literacy experiences, 43–45
Preschool programs, 26–27; language growth and, 24–25
Preschool years, chronicity of language learning problems of children in, 126
Pretending, 26
Primary Phonics (Educators Publishing Service), 57
Proficient readers, 74
Proofreading by children, 188
Psycholinguistic guessing game model, 67

Questions in the classroom, 186–87

Read, C., 150
Readiness, language teaching and, 188–89
Reading: assessing, 127–29; consensus about, 41–42; emphasis on language and, 41–43; model for relationship between listening and, 126–27; relationship between phonological awareness and spelling and, 50–51
Reading aloud to children, 42–43, 44
Reading comprehension, comparison of listening comprehension and, 139–40
Reading failure, a history of, 64–66
Reading problems, two types of, 126–27
Reading process models, 66–68; applied to instruction, 74–77
Reception, 175
Reciprocal processes between cognition, language comprehension, and production, 148
Respect for students, 192

Response and interaction in teaching, 186–87
Retrieval, 176. *See also* Memory Revising, 162

Samuels, S.J., 125, 129
Self-appraisal, teaching of, 187–88
Semantics, 169, 171
Sentence comprehension as a function of text structure, 132–37
Sentences: age and length of, 156; logical and linguistic cues that link, 122
Serial models, 67
Sesame Street, 20
Shankweiler, D., 42, 45
Sight-word approach, 64, 70
Snow, C.E., 11, 12, 13, 15, 23
Social context, using language in, 169
Social interactionism, 10–11
Sound categorization, 50–51
Speech: relationship between writing and, 159; understanding how alphabetic transcription represents, 46
Spelling, 154–56; causal relationship between phonological awareness and reading and, 50–51; invented, 148; teaching, 183–84
Spoken language problems, 177–78
Stories: first-grade reading of, 57; language development and, 18–19; problems with writing, 159–60; social predictability and, 30
Student progress, monitoring of, 111
Syntax, 156–57, 169, 170

Teacher education, 110–111
Teaching the language-handicapped child: components of linguistic system and, 168–72; examples of language problems, 172–73; language processes and, 173–77; principles for, 178–93; spoken language problems, 177–78
Teaching reading: basal reader programs, 65; characteristics of reading process model useful for, 67–68; controversy over beginning reading and, 45–47, 73; emphasis on letter sounds and phonics, 64; graphic and phonemic processes in, 73; linguistic approaches to, 65; meaning expectancy in, 72–73; money and, 110; phonological awareness and, 47–56; reasons for failure in, 65–66; recommendations for, 27–29; sight-word approaches to, 64, 70; student monitoring and, 111; teacher education and, 110–111; top-down processes in, 73; whole language approaches to, 65. *See also* Instructional procedures; Integrated Skills Method (ISM)
Television, 19–20; children who learn from, 187
Temple, C., 155, 162
Teuling, H.-L.H., 153
Textbooks, readable, 132
Text comprehension, 137–38; metacognition and, 122, 125; tasks and, 139–40
Text comprehension tests, 126
Text presentation, texts, tasks, and modality of, 127–37
Text(s): how children learn about, 121–22; meaning of, 115; poor comprehenders' understanding of, 123–27; tasks and characteristics of, 129–32
Text structure(s), 118; effect on comprehension and recall, 121–23; methods to assess awareness and use of, 129–30; sentence comprehension as a function of, 132–37; student's age and sensitivity to, 122; students' sensitivity to, 122–23
Thinking, 70
Thomas, C.C., 125
Thomassen, A., 153
Tizard, B., 25
Tomasello, M., 15, 16

Understanding, reading words without, 176
Urban dialects, 173

Visualizing absent objects and events, 190
Visual reception, 68–70

Whole language approaches, 65
Why Johnny Can't Read (Flesch), 65
Wolf, M., 23
Word-finding problem (dysnomia), 176
Word recognition skills, control for possible group differences in, 125
Words, order of, 170; processed as part of integrated flow of information, 71
Writing: functions of, 160–61; non-narrative, 160; for real audiences, 161; in teams, 161–62;

three types of young children's, 159
Writing conferences for children, 162
Written dictation, 57
Written expressive language, teaching of, 184–86
Written language, 147–48, 150–51; composition and modes of written expression, 158–60; content and level of abstraction of, 157–58; forms and content of, 152; functions of, 160–61; handwriting, 152–54; rule learning, 151–53; sense of audience and, 161–62; spelling and, 154–56; syntax and, 156–57; usage and, 152; the writing process and, 162–63